History of the Cholas

History of the Cholas

Kings, Temples and the Making of an Empire

M RAJAMANIKKANAR

Translated by
Peer Mohamed Azees and
Srivarshini V

Vitasta

Published by
Renu Kaul Verma
Vitasta Publishing Pvt Ltd
4348/4C, Ansari Road, Daryaganj
New Delhi-110 002
info@vitastapublishing.com

ISBN 978-93-47098-05-5
First published in Tamil

First Edition 2025
MRP ₹1195

Editor: Kanagam King
Cover Design by Shubhpreet Kaur
Typesetting by Smriti Maheshwari
Printed by Vikas Computer and Printers, New Delhi

Mission Statement

This is an initiative of the Tamil Nadu Textbook and Educational Services Corporation (TNTB & ESC) under the aegis of one of the announcements for the year 2023-24, by Honourable Minister for School Education Thiru. Anbil Mahesh Poyyamozhi titled the Translation of Rare and Nationalised Literary Tamil Works into English. These ventures are to be undertaken as either independent or joint publications with collaborating English language publishers.

Members, Academic Advisory Committee (Translation)

1. Dr. R. Balakrishnan, IAS, Researcher and Writer
2. Thiru. S. Ramakrishnan, Writer
3. Thiru. S. Madasamy, Educationist

Project Execution Team

1. Thiru. Dindigul I. Leoni, Chairperson, TNTB & ESC
2. Dr. M. Aarthi. IAS, Managing Director, TNTB & ESC
3. Dr. C. Usha Rani, Member Secretary, TNTB & ESC
4. Dr. T. S. Saravanan, Honorary Advisor (Translations), TNTB & ESC
5. Tmt. S. Theynmozhi, Deputy Director (Publications), TNTB & ESC
6. Dr. P. Saravanan, Assistant Director (Publications), TNTB & ESC
7. Thiru. M. Appanasamy, Consultant, TNTB & ESC
8. Tmt. Mini Krishnan, Co-ordinating Editor, TNTB & ESC

Contents

Foreword

The Tamil civilisation reached newer heights thanks to the phenomenal work of the Chola kings. The whole of South India was under the Chola spell for 300 years. Peace prevailed. Stone temples of small and big sizes were constructed. Beautiful stone sculptures were made. Cholas made brilliant sculptures in bronze too. They helped create amazing paintings. Businesses and artisanship proliferated. Great poets such as Sekkizhar, Kambar, and Ottakoothar nourished the Tamil language with their epic works. Not just India, but the whole of Asia celebrated the Chola kings.

It is a good thing that Vidwan (the English equivalent is scholar) M Rajamanikkam chose to write about these glorious centuries in Tamil. Though it is a well-researched scholarly work, he made it accessible to all by using simple language. He is well-versed in the research on that subject. He has also independently researched the topic. Some of his conclusions may not have consensus. He understands that very well. We will continue to have a difference of opinion on our shared past and history.

Books like this one will serve as tools to communicate learned decisions on the subject. I am confident that many readers will find this book very useful.

K A Neelakanta Sastri
University of Madras
14 March 1937

PART I

ONE

Sources of Chola History

Sangam Age

The understanding of the Cholas of the Sangam Age requires knowledge of the Sangam books such as *Ettuthogai, Pathuppattu, Pathinenkeelkanakku*, and epics such as *Cilappatikaram* and *Manimekalai*. Among the *Pathinenkeelkanakku* books, a few including Tiruvalluvar's *Tirukkural* and *Kalavazhi* belong to the Sangam Age. Other works belong to the later Sangam Age (aka Jaina Sangam). *Iniyavai Narpathu* (Sweet Forty) of *Pathinenkeelkanakku* belongs to a period later than Sangam. *Purananuru, Akananuru, Natrinai, Pathupattu, Cilappatikaram*, and *Manimekalai* help us decode the story of the Cholas of the Sangam period. We will go into the details of this in the second chapter. The travel accounts of Pliny and Ptolemy are useful in the research.

The Middle Age

Sangam Age ended in the third century CE. Aditya Chola defeated the Pallavas and established the Chola Empire in the ninth century CE. The interlude of 500 years between the end of Sangam and the rise of the Chola Empire can be deciphered best from 1) Pallava inscriptions 2) Pali–Sanskrit–Tamil books of that period 3) Pandya inscriptions 4) Inscriptions of Chalukyas, Kangars (Rulers of Mysore), and Rashtrakoodars. The texts of *Tevaram* are useful as well. Sekkizhar wrote *Periya Puranam*, a lyrical history of the sixty-three Shaivite Saints or *Nayanmars*, with further support from epigraphical evidence. The Vaishnavite holy text of *Nalayira Divya Prabandham* and *Divyasuri Charitam* are also helpful resources.

Later Chola Inscriptions

Thousands of inscriptions and copper plates help us understand the period from Vijayalaya Chola to the thirteenth century CE. The best among these are the inscriptions and copper plates from the period of Rajaraja Chola. These sources document the military expeditions of the king first and mention the year of the action later. The last portion of these inscriptions and plates states the purpose of the documentation. We understand the military expeditions, family status, political information, charity work, religious work of a king, and the names of the officials involved with the king through these sources. The inscriptions assumed religious significance from the time of the Pallavas. They have information on the temple, the *mutt* (religious authority), and the donations made in favour of the people who recited the scriptures. They have information on the construction of new temples, renovation of old temples, and the consecration of temples. The first part of the inscription provides information about the king, the rulers he defeated, and the years of his military victories. It is very useful in understanding history. Some inscriptions have greater significance in terms of governance. They narrate stories of taxation, land tax, professional tax, decisions of village panchayats, trade and political administration. Several inscriptions in the temples document the sale and purchase of land by the people of the place. Some temple walls carry *Tevaram* songs by Sambandar that are not seen in the book of *Tevaram*. The inscriptions help with the understanding of history in many ways. They also help us comprehend the transformation of Sanskrit and Tamil over the years. *Vattezhuthu* (Old Tamil script), Pallava script, and the Chola script are prevalent in the inscriptions.

Temples

The temples are the best source available to understand the history of the Cholas. The Cholas built amazing stone temples across Tamil Nadu. They took inspiration from the Pallavas. Pallavas created magnificent places of worship such as the Temple of Lord Shiva in Kooram. Parameswara Varman, a Pallava King, built it. Kailasanathar temple in Kancheepuram is another magical piece of temple architecture from the Pallavas. On the walls and the pillars of the temples were inscriptions. Whenever there was a renovation of the temple, the Cholas copied the inscriptions and installed them in the new structure. The sculptures in the temple tell us a lot about the skill sets prevalent during the Chola regimes. The murals and paintings on the walls of temples help us decipher the artistic capacities of the people during the Chola regime. The works of art also reflect the lifestyle of the people from that era. A closer look at the temple architecture of the Cholas shows that it is evolutionary. Indeed, the Cholas did take forward the inspiration of the Pallavas. They converted temples of significance into stone structures. The change in architecture made the temples more popular. However, there is no comprehensive study of the temple architecture of the Cholas. Temples remain a great source of knowledge about the Cholas.

Chola Coins

The Cholas, like the Pallavas, released coins in gold, silver, and copper. Every coin had the Chola insignia of the tiger. Next to the tiger were the fish of the Pandyas and the bow of the Cheras. The name of the king who released the coin was also etched on it. Another coin found is the 'Eezha Coin' (Ceylon Coin). One side depicts a strong man standing, while the reverse shows the same figure seated. This coin was in circulation from the period of King Rajaraja Chola to that of Kulothungan I. We can infer that the Cholas released this coin when they ruled over the island of Sri Lanka.

Literature

Our literature is deeply buried in religious texts. Some prominent historians have warned us against building history on the foundation of literature. There is evidence to say that the epics such as *Ramayana* and *Mahabharatha* have undergone significant changes over time. When we use Tamil literary and religious texts such as *Thiruvilaiyadal, Parani, Ula,* and *Periya Puranam*, it is important to identify and choose historically relevant information.

Literature flourished in South India during the time of later Cholas. Nambiandar Nambi compiled Shaivite hymns in this period. *Thiruthondar Puranam*, the last and twelfth of the Shaivite holy books, was compiled at this time. Poet Sekkizhar who authored *Periya Puranam* recorded history with maximum accuracy. As one who researched inscriptions, I can find an astonishing level of accuracy in *Periya Puranam*. Sekkizhar belonged to the twelfth century. When he wrote about the Nayanmars, the sixty-three prominent Shaivite saints, he travelled back in time and captured their lives accurately. Sekkizhar was a unique poet; the first minister of the Chola Empire; a great Shaivite; he had an amazing knowledge of Tamil Nadu. He studied the inscriptions of the Cholas and the Pallavas extensively. Sekkizhar painstakingly gathered credible information about the period referred to as the dark period in the history of Tamil Nadu. As Sekkizhar records only evidence-based history, his writings can be treated as authentic.

Kamba Ramayanam, the Tamil epic written by twelfth century poet Kambar based on Valmiki's Ramayana, is another great resource for our journey into the history of the Cholas. *Moovar Ula, Kulothungan Pillai Tamil*, and *Thakkayaha Parani* authored by Ottakoothar, a prolific poet of the twelfth century, are about three Chola Kings. *Kalingathu Parani* authored by Jayamkondar is of greater historical significance. This text helps us decode the invasion by the Kalinga rulers. The collection also helps us understand the Chola dynasty, the role of Kulothungan, and that of Karunakara Tondaiman. The Chola Age saw the birth of Vaishnavite literature such as *Divyasuri Charitam* and *Guru Parampara*. These texts help us understand Ramanujar, the Vaishnavite reformer, better. The *pasurams* of Alwars found commentaries during this period. Buddha Mitrar wrote *Veerachozhiyam* in the Chola regime. Literature such as *Yaapparumkala Karigai* and *Vriddhi* came out at this time. Shaivite religious literature also witnessed a boom.

Evidence from Outside the Chola Raj

Documentary evidence from the kingdoms that surrounded the Chola Empire is useful in compiling this work. The inscriptions and copper plates of the Western Chalukyas, Eastern Chalukyas, Rashtrakoodars, and Kangars are helpful. The documents from the small kingdoms under the Cholas also hold a key to the history of the Chola Raj.

The diaries of some Chinese travellers, Arab merchants, and the notes of Marco Polo, and Mahavamsam have references explaining the many aspects of the Chola kingdom.

Chola History Books

Professor KA Neelakanta Sastri wrote a detailed history of the Cholas and found lasting fame for the work. Before him, scholar NM Venkatasamy Nattar wrote about the history of the Cholas. Scholar Ulaganatha Pillai wrote the biographies of Karikalan and Rajaraja Chola, two popular kings of the Chola Empire. PN Subramanian authored the history of Rajendra Chola, a prominent ruler of the Chola dynasty. Sathasiva Pandarathar and L Srinivasan wrote the history of Kulothungan I, another popular ruler of the Chola Empire. Historian Ramachandra Dikshitar wrote the story of Kulothungan III. I have written an account of Kulothungan II.

Kottar Shivaraja Pillai authored the story of the ancient Tamils in the English language. JM Somasundaram Pillai researched and wrote about the temples built by the Cholas and the Big Temple in Thanjavur.

Research is infinite; it evolves. There are new books that have not been listed above. My goal is to do justice to both history and the Tamil language, and I find that my intent is well served by the approach I have adopted in compiling this work.

TWO

The Sangam Age

Several historians have concluded that the final phase of the last Sangam Age may have been in the third century CE. Historian Rao Sahib M Raghava Iyengar established with evidence that the period started in the fourth century BCE. As we research Sangam literature rigorously, some of them go back as early as 1000 BCE. Narayana Iyengar, who edited the magazine *Senthamizh*, in a research article, said that Valmiki wrote a poem in *Purananuru*, a Sangam-age compilation of poetry about public life. Valmiki lived in the eighth century BCE according to many scholars. A song in *Purananuru* directly addresses Dharmar, the seniormost of the Pandavas. A Chera King is praised in a *Purananuru* song for feeding both sides of the Mahabharata war. *'Perunchotru Uthiyan Cheralathan'* is the title given to the King. Some of the events in Ramayana are mentioned in *Akananuru* and *Purananuru*. This literary evidence suggests the period of Tamil writers could be as old as 1000 BCE. The Pallava Kings started ruling Tondai Mandalam with Kancheepuram as their capital in 300 CE. During 400–450 CE, the Chola Kingdom came under the control of Achutavikandar, a Kalapira ruler. This was documented by Buddhadutta, a Buddhist monk. Kalapiras conquered the Pandya Kingdom after the rule of Palyagasalai Muthukudumi Peruvazhuthi. At the end of the sixth century CE, Kadungon, a Pandya King, defeated Kalapiras and wrested the Pandya Kingdom. Velvikudi deed, a set of records, has documented this event. The Sangam Age literature does not mention Pallavas or Kalapiras. That is why the last Sangam Age is estimated to be around 300 CE.

The Period of Tolkappiyar

Tolkappiyam, the most ancient Tamil grammar text, does not mention either Buddhist or Jain references. Hence the text could have originated before the fourth century BCE. Historian Vincent Arthur Smith mentions that the Sanskrit-speaking North Indians entered Tamil Nadu in 1000 BCE. The Sanskrit speakers might have completely merged with the Tamil speakers. Sanskrit words had found a place in the Tamil country over the years. That is how the Sanskrit language found its way into Tolkappiyam, a treatise on Tamil grammar.

The two rules mentioned in Tolkappiyam for joining Sanskrit words with Tamil words are not merely the prerogative of Tolkappiyar, the author. It is the outcome of two languages interacting for 300 to 400 years.

Tolkappiyar is said to have had expertise in *Aynthiram*, an old Tamil grammar text. *Paniniyam*, the Sanskrit grammar book, came much later. Panini wrote this book in the seventh century BCE. Tolkappiyar does not mention *Paniniyam* in his text. The period of Panini is definitely after the period of Tolkappiyar.

Iraiyanar Kalaviyal Commentary, a treatise on the love life of Tamils, says that Kapadapuram was devoured by the sea during the time of Tolkappiyar. The devouring of land by the sea occurred across the coast of Sri Lanka and the Tamil country at the same time. *Mahavamsam* and *Rasavazhi*, the texts dealing with the history of Sri Lanka, talk about the sea devouring land in 2387 BCE, 504 BCE, and 306 BCE. The second occurrence in the fifth century BCE is when Kapadapuram on the Tamil coast was devoured by the sea. It is during the same period that Tolkappiyar lived and promoted the Tamil language.

Books Before Tolkappiyam

In 16 percent of the formulas in *Tolkappiyam*, Tolkappiyar mentions scholars who preceded him. Statements such as, 'Those who knew poetry will say it is poetry' and '...six poets...' indicate that numerous poets and scholars existed before his time. If there were multiple grammar texts, it meant that great literature was made in the land. This is evidence to prove that the Tamil language had amazing literary and grammatical texts in 1500 BCE. It is important for both linguistic and historical research.

Conclusion

Tamil literature had a wide-ranging timescale as evidenced by the multiple records mentioned above. The literature of love life and public life—*Akam* and *Puram*—in Tamil is classified by some scholars as belonging to the last Sangam period. *Kalaviyal* commentary, a treatise on the love life of Tamils, classifies ancient Tamil literature as belonging to three different Sangam periods—first, middle, and last.

As the Sangam period has a vast timescale, I think it is proper to call them Sangam literature. As concurred by several researchers, the third century CE is the last phase of the Sangam Age. Let us look at the notes on Cholas in this vast timescale.

Our Challenge

We can list the names of the kings from the Chola dynasty as they appear in Sangam poetry. However, it is a huge challenge to organise them in a chronological order. NM Venkatasamy Nattar and KA Neelakanta Sastri have carefully organised the stories of the Chola kings from the vast and rich body of literary evidence. Their works are commendable. The methods adopted by these two scholars may can be regarded as the best until further evidences emerge to tell their stories more elaborately.

Our Duty

The key character of the Sangam Age Cholas is Karikalan. The period of his existence can be determined using available evidence. Sangam literature, some later Chola literature, and some inscriptions provide information on him. Some scholars disregard evidence from later Chola literature and inscriptions arguing that they cannot be corroborated by Sangam literature. We have lost a considerable amount of Sangam literature. What we have got is only a portion of the Sangam literature compiled in the later period. Poets such as Jayamkondar (twelfth century CE) recorded information about the Chola dynasty, taking into account the literature that may have been lost over time. The later Cholas created deeds and records to preserve history. Though these records belong to the later period, it is crucial to factor them in. TG Aravamudhan's work to determine the time of Karikalan is commendable as he has been open to eclectic resources of history.

THREE

The Times of Karikala Chola

If you read Sangam poetry closely, you will see that Karikala Chola is not just one person. There were other kings named Karikala Chola both before and after the Karikala Chola, who conquered the Himalayas. If we can figure out the times of the Karikala Chola who reigned supreme, it is easy to understand the periods of the other two kings who have the same name. Let us dive deep into the story here.

Sangam literature does not refer to Karikala Chola as one who ruled over Sri Lanka. However, *Kalingathu Parani*, a twelfth century war poem in Tamil, mentions it. His travel to the Himalayas is mentioned in *Cilappatikaram*, one of the five epics of the Tamil language. Ilango Adigal, who authored *Cilappatikaram*, is the son of a Chera King. He does not have to praise a Chola King with a piece of unverified information. He mentions it as a proud moment for the whole Tamil country. The determination of the times of Karikala Chola's expedition to Sri Lanka and the Himalayas is crucial for our understanding of Chola history.

Scholar Aravamudhan, who wrote a book on Karikala Chola,

has discussed the timeline in detail. 'Chandragupta Maurya, Bindusara, and Ashoka were dominant from 327 BCE to 232 BCE. No ruler from the south ventured into the north at this time,' he explains in his book. Pushyamitra Shunga ruled from 184 BCE to 149 BCE. The north of India had a dominant Satavahana dynasty in the first two centuries of the Common Era (CE). According to Aravamudhan's account, the possible window for Karikala Chola's expedition to the north narrows down to just three options:

1. The period after King Ashoka (BCE 232 to BCE 184),
2. The time after Pushyamitra Shunga (BCE 148 to BCE 27), and
3. After the weakening of the Satavahana rulers in early third century CE.

After the reigns of Gautamiputra Satakarni and Vasishthiputra Pulumavi, the Satavahana dynasty began to weaken from 163 CE onwards. The window of opportunity began to open well before the period mentioned by Aravamudhan. Hence the possible windows are BCE 232–184, BCE 148–27 and CE 163–300. Cheran Senguttuvan went on an expedition to the north during the third period mentioned here. That was the time Gajabahu ruled Sri Lanka. That was also when Satavahana reigned supreme in India. It should be CE 166–193. The second century CE was also the time Ilango Adigal wrote *Cilappatikaram*. Hence the time of Karikala Chola's expedition was restricted to the first two options.

According to the history of Sri Lanka, Tamil Kings ruled over it from BCE 170 to 100 and BCE 44 to 17. The Tamil expeditions to Sri Lanka recorded later in history are during CE

660, 1065, 1200–1266. Karikala Chola's invasion of Sri Lanka should be during one of the first two periods before the common era. In the first period, they witnessed an expedition by Elaran, another Tamil ruler. So, BCE 44–17 is the time of the invasion of Sri Lanka by Karikala Chola. It aligns well with the Northern invasion period of BCE 148–27. The period of BCE 60–10 fits best as the time of Karikala Chola after factoring in all the developments of that era.

Data from maritime trade also aid in this conclusion. *Porunar Aatrupadai* and *Pattinappalai*, both belonging to the Sangam period of Tamil literature, sing praises of Karikala Chola. In both these poetry texts, the greatness of maritime trade and Poompuharpattinam is celebrated. Although the trade relations between the Tamils and the Romans began before the time of Karikala Chola, the trade ties reached their peak during the first century BCE. This has been documented by the Romans. Roman Emperor Augustus was in power from 39 BCE to 14 CE. A Pandya king sent him emissaries in BCE 20. This serves as proof of the flourishing maritime trade between the Tamils and the Romans.

Expedition to the Himalayas

The period of Karikala Chola, derived from multiple authentic sources, falls between 60 and 10 BCE. The power of the Magadha empire transitioned from the Shunga dynasty to the Kanva dynasty. Vasudeva Kanva assumed the throne of Magadha in 73 BCE. Three more rulers from the Kanva dynasty ruled until 28 CE. They were not perceived as strong rulers. The Vatsa Kingdom, with its capital at Kosambi, and the Avanti Kingdom, with its capital at Ujjain, may have become autonomous at this time. *Cilappatikaram* mentions that Karikala Chola received a warm welcome in the Magadha Empire, Vatsa Kingdom, and Avanti Kingdom on his way back from the Himalayan expedition. These kingdoms had been subjugated by Chandragupta Maurya and were later ruled by Harsha. We have no evidence of Karikala Chola's expedition to the Himalayas apart from references in Tamil literature.

Two Karikala Cholas

Research scholar Sivarasapillai infers that there were two Karikala Cholas in history with appropriate evidence—Paranar, who sang about two Chola kings before Karikala Chola, mentions one Karikala Chola. Paranar did not live during the reign of Karikala Chola. He based his account on oral histories. I researched all the poetry mentioning Karikala Chola. I realised that the poets who sang about the different Karikala Cholas were also different. Kalathalaiyar and Vennikuyathiyar are the two poets who spoke of the first Karikala Chola. Kabilar, who is of the same age as Paranar, says that Kalathalaiyar was from a previous generation. Kalathalaiyar and Vennikuyathiyar recorded the defeat of Peruncheralathan or Perunthol Adhan at the hands of Karikala Chola. Peruncheralathan sacrificed his life, unable to bear the shame of defeat. Kalathalaiyar sang of Peruncheralathan. Vennikuyathiyar sang about Karikala Chola.

Porunar Aatrupadai, a Sangam poetry text, sings about another Venni war. Mudathama Kanniyar is the author of this war poem. It is a war between Karikala Chola and Cheran–Pandyan duo. Karikala Chola killed the enemies and won the war. *Porunar Aatrupadai* sings the praise of Karikala Chola. It does not mention the name of the Chera king or the Pandya king killed in the war. If it were the same war narrated by Kalathalaiyar, he would have mentioned the Pandya king. Vennikuyathiyar also does not mention anything about the Pandya king. Mudathama Kanniyar does not talk about the Chera king killing himself after the defeat.

Paranar wrote of Karikala Chola defeating a king and eleven noblemen on the Vennivayil battlefield. He also speaks of Karikala Chola defeating nine kings at a place called Vagai. These wars are not part of the stories of the later Karikala Chola, who was praised in *Porunar Aatrupadai* and *Pattinappalai*. The instances of battle with a king and eleven noblemen and nine kings belong to an earlier period when Cholas did not consolidate their power enough. The later (second) Karikala Chola fought with Pothuvar, Aruvalar, and Pandyan, according to *Porunar Aatrupadai*. Eleven noblemen and nine kings are important mentions from the text of Paranar. Uranthai, Vallam, Kudanthai, Paruvur, and Perundurai are places where the Cholas reigned supreme. Before the time of the second Karikala Chola, the Chola Kingdom seemed to have been scattered across the land. It was a time of intense battles for control over the land, according to existing Tamil literature. The first Karikala Chola should have been the one who ruled from Azhunthur and belonged to the Chenni tradition.

The second Karikala Chola is the one who went on an expedition to the Himalayas. Vennikuyathiyar sang about the first Karikala Chola. The first Karikala Chola belonged to an earlier generation, and according to available evidences, his time was BCE 120–90.

Chronology of the Cholas of the Sangam Period

The chronology of Chola kings can be determined roughly from the existing evidence. Sangam compilations, *Cilappatikaram*, and *Manimekalai*, mention several older kings of the Chola dynasty. Sibi, Musukunthan, Kanthan, Thoongeyi erintha

Thodithol Chembiyan, and Manuneethi Chola are the oldest kings mentioned in the literature. A Chola king ruled over Sri Lanka in the middle of the second century BCE. Manuneethi Chola's story of killing his son under the wheels of a chariot for wrongdoing finds a mention along with the one who conquered Sri Lanka. Manuneethi Chola should belong to the second century BCE going by that record. Others mentioned here are older, according to Sangam literature.

Cheruppazhi erintha Elanchet Chenni, who stood up against the invasion of Maurya-Bindusaran (the story comes later in the book), belonged to BCE 298–272. The first Karikala Chola belonged to BCE 120–90. The second Karikala Chola lived during BCE 60–10. Kochengad Chola thrived in fifth century CE. Before him, during the *Cilappatikaram* period (150–200 CE), Nedumudi Killi was the Chola King. Nalankilli and Killivalavan ruled after the second Karikala Chola and before Nedumudi Killi. We have a chronology of Chola kings here. It is an approximation based on the evidence available to us.

1. Chola kings before the third century BCE
   - Sibi
   - Musukunthan
   - Kaanthan
   - Thoongeyi erintha Thodithol Chembiyan

2. Chola king of the third century BCE
   - Cheruppazhi erintha Elanchet Chenni

3. Chola kings of the second century BCE
   - Manuneethi Chola
   - Karikala Chola I

4. Chola king of the first century BCE
    - Karikala Chola II (who went on an expedition to the Himalayas)

5. Chola kings who ruled from 1 to 150 CE
    - Nalankilli, Nedunkilli, Mavalathan
    - Killivalavan
    - Perunarkilli
    - Kopperun Cholan
    - More Kings from the dynasty

6. Chola kings who ruled from 150 to 300 CE
    - Nedumudi Killi
    - Ilankilli and others

FOUR

Chola Kings Before the Third Century BCE

Sibi

In references to the early Cholas, both Sangam poets and later poets mention Sibi. He finds a mention in the epics of *Ramayana* and *Mahabharata*. Sibi gave away a piece of his flesh to protect a pigeon that had sought his refuge, fearing a vulture.

Tamil books mentioning Sibi: *Purananuru, Cilappatikaram, Kalingathu Parani, Moovarula,* and *Periya Puranam.*

> You are a descendant of the Chembiyan King (Sibi) who sacrificed his flesh to protect a pigeon.
>
> —Purananuru

> A slow-walking pigeon has entered his house to protect itself from a vulture. King Sibi gave away a piece of flesh from his body to the vulture to safeguard the pigeon. That is the tradition of our rulers. You belong to such a lineage.
>
> —Purananuru

For the protection of the pigeon, he has sacrificed his flesh. Such is the pride of our King.

—Cilappatikaram

Unafraid of sacrificing his life, he has helped save the life of a pigeon; he earned eternal glory by this selfless act.

—Kalingathu Parani

He is a pure soul and the only King in the whole world to sacrifice his flesh for a little pigeon.

—Vikrama Chola Ula

Chola Land has sacrificed human flesh worth the weight of a pigeon to protect it.

—Periya Puranam

Musukunthan

Musukunthan, a Chola King, ruled over the land with Karur as his capital. He helped Indra, an emperor, win a war and earned his goodwill.

In the service of Lord Shiva

He was a great devotee of Lord Shiva. He received seven lingams, including the one worshipped by Lord Indra. He installed them in Tiruvarur, Tirunagai Karonam, Tirukarayil, Tirukolili, Tirumaraikadu, Tirunallar, and Tiruvaimoor. These shrines are called Saptavidanga Thalam.

Phantom in a Marketplace

Indra sent Musukunthan a phantom as his bodyguard. The phantom came to Poompuhar city and worked from a marketplace between Maruvoorpakkam and Pattinapakkam. People in the era of *Manimekalai* epic believed that if Poompuhar city did not celebrate the Indra Festival, the phantom would bring about a catastrophe.

Tamil Books Mentioning Musukunthan

Cilappatikaram, *Manimekalai*, *Kalingathu Parani*, *Kanthapuranam*, and *Oruthuraikovai* mention Musukunthan. Kaveripoompattinam (Poompuhar) was prospering under Musukunthan as per the narratives in these books. The literature also vouches that South India had a legacy of flourishing maritime trade with the West since the sixth and seventh centuries BCE.

Kaanthan

This Chola King ruled from Kaveripoompattinam (Poompuhar). He was very fond of the sage-poet Agasthyar. The epic *Manimekalai* says that he got Kaveri to flow into his country with the blessings of Agasthyar. Kaanthan ruled during the time of Parasurama. Parasurama had the habit of killing rulers.

When Parasurama travelled to South India, Kaanthan sought the advice of Agasthyar. Heeding the advice of the sage-poet, he anointed Kaanthan, a son born out of wedlock, as the ruler, and went into hiding. After Parasuraman left South India, he came back to rule the Chola country.

The Story of Kaveri

Manimekalai, the Tamil epic of the second century CE, says that the Kaveri river originated from the pitcher of sage-poet Agasthyar. Kaanthan is said to have taken advice from Agasthyar and diverted the Kaveri river through his country. The poetic text *Veera Chola Ula* records this as follows:

From the Western Coorg, Kaveri flows
As Ponni river into the Eastern land.

Kaveran was a Chola King. He meditated in the forests adjacent to Poompuhar. The river got the name Kaveri from him. *Manimekalai* records that Kaanthan brought Kaveri to the Chola country and mentions this.

Kakanthi Forests

According to *Manimekalai,* when Kaanthan handed over the reign of Poompuhar to Kaanthan, he told him, 'Name this city as Kakanthi to reflect you and protect it'. Kakanthi is one of the several names given to Poompuhar city since then.

Reddypalayam (Gudur Taluk) in Nellore division was called Pavithri during Sangam Age. The region around this was known as Kakanthi, according to inscriptions. This land was under the sea for quite some time. 'Sea-devoured Kakanthi' is another name for this area. The similarity in names is worth researching.

Thoongeyil Erintha Chembiyan

This Chola King is known to have destroyed the fortresses of enemies with his valour. The title *Thoongeyil Erintha Thodithol Chembiyan* is a reward for his courage. According to *Cilappatikaram*, he destroyed three fortresses of enemies.

Sangam Age poets described Chembiyan as an example of courage. Poets have invoked the name of Chembiyan to instil confidence and courage in other kings. Sangam poet Marokkathu Nappasalayar singing of Kulamutrathu Thunjiya Killivalavan says:

> ...if you think of Thoongeyil Erintha Chembiyan, you will find courage and your glory will rise.

Indra Festival

King Chembiyan was the first ruler to celebrate the Indra Festival in Kaveripoompattinam on the orders of the sage-poet Agasthyar. He prayed to Indra to stay in the city for twenty-eight days and Indra heeded the request, says *Manimekalai.*

Books Mentioning Chembiyan

Purananuru, Cilappatikaram, Manimekalai, Sirupanatrupadai, Pazhamozhi, Kalingathu Parani, and *Moovar Ula* mention Chembiyan's courageous acts.

> The Great Chembiyan has strong and broad shoulders that destroyed mighty fortresses.
>
> —Sirupanatrupadai

> Three mighty fortresses destroyed by the Great Chola King Chembiyan.
>
> —Cilappatikaram

> Strong-shouldered Chembiyan's fury destroys mighty fortresses.
>
> —Pazhamozhi

> Chembiyan can destroy fortresses
>
> —Kalingathu Parani

> Chola who destroyed the fortresses of his enemies.
>
> —Moovar Ula

FIVE

Chola King of the Third Century BCE

Cheruppaazhi Erintha Elanchet Chenni (BCE 290–270)

Several songs mention that the Maurya invasion of Tamil country occurred during his reign. Ancient Tamil country had good relations with the land of Magadha which had Pataliputra as its capital. Nandhar who ruled this land before Mauryas maintained diplomatic ties with the Tamil kings, according to many poems.

Chanakya, one of the senior ministers in the Chandragupta Maurya Kingdom, mentions Tamil country in his book *Artha*.

> Gems from Tamil country, cat's eye from Chera country, black shawls from Pandya country, and thin fabric from Madurai reached the warehouse of Chandragupta Maurya.

It proves the trade ties between Magadha and the Tamil land. Tamils had known the Pataliputra of Nandhar and Mauryas. Tamil poets distinguished between various kings in the north. They used the name Vadugar to refer to those who were in the north and below Vindhyas. They called the people of Magadha land Northern Vadugar. Mamoolanar, a poet, exhibited phenomenal historical sensibility. He spoke of the Nandhar and Maurya invasion in the same poem.

It is with the support of the armed Vadugar
That the Maurya could invade the
Southern Land.

It is because our people
Refused to bow down
That the Maurya fought us.

The Mighty Maurya
Took on the Cholas
With local support.

The Empire of Mauryas
Invaded the South
And expanded further.

The Vadugars and Kosars supported the Maurya invasion of the South, as evident from the poems of that period. The literature further mentions that the Mauryas sent both these armies as an advance deployment in preparation for their subsequent invasion. The use of the troops of the colonies for war is a tradition that continues until today. The Mauryas adopted the same technique by using Vadugars and Kosars, who had already been colonised by them, in the war against the South Indian rulers.

Who are Vadugars and Kosars?

They come from beyond Venkata Mountains
(Tirupati Mountain/Tirumala Hills),

And speak in a different tongue.
Vadugars speak a different language.
Vadugars' tongue is different from Tamil.

These lines go on to say that the Vadugars were people who spoke Telugu and Kannada. Kosars were also called Northern Vadugars, as mentioned in *Purananuru* song 378. Scholar Krishnaswamy Iyengar says that the Kosars were people from the East Bengal region. The *Akananuru* songs 15, 113, and 196 describe Kosars as very obedient people. Tamil kings appreciated the skills of Kosars and kept some of them in their service. KA Neelakanta Sastri, a historian, says that the Kosars were the 'Sakthi Puthirar' mentioned in the inscriptions of Emperor Ashoka.

The Mauryan Invasion

The Mauryas maintained their own army in addition to those of the Vadugars and Kosars. The Maurya army had chariots. The army of Kosars reached the South first. The Kosars came through the north-western side of Tamil Country and reached the Tulu country. They drove Nannan, the Tulu King, into hiding in the forests. The Kosars killed the royal elephant of Nannan. They took complete control of the Tulu country. The Vadugar army which came later stayed in Paazhi of the Tulu region. They took charge of the security of the region.

The Kosars who conquered Nannan's Tulu country went into the Chera kingdom and attacked Pittam Kotran, the king, and his armies. We do not have information about the outcome of this battle. Ezhini Athan, a king who ruled over Vattaru and Sellur, came under the attack of the Kosars. The battlefield was to the east of Sellur. The Kosars killed Ezhini in the battle. The Kosars reached the Chola Kingdom and fought with Azhunthur

Velan Thithiyan. Thithiyan hit back so strongly that the Kosars had to retreat. The Kosars then attacked Mohur. Mohur did not surrender. The Vadugars came as a forward troop of the Mauryas. The Mauryas also attacked Mohur. We do not know the outcome of this battle. The Mauryas created pathways across mountains and valleys along their expedition route. Mohur could have come under attack as it was close to the strategic Athur pass in the South Arcot region. The Chola king, Elanchet Chenni, defeated the northern Vadugars who reached South Arcot region. He wanted complete victory over the enemy. So, Elanchet Chenni followed the retreating army up to Paazhi city and decimated them. He got the title 'Cheruppaazhi Erintha Elanchet Chenni' for defeating the enemy in their high-security environment.

The Mauryan invasion came to an end because of the valiant resistance of Elanchet Chenni. Had Chenni not resisted enough, Tamil Nadu would have come under the rule of the Mauryas. The Mauryas did not know the military strength and the geographical advantage of Tamil Nadu. They conquered the Tulu country and went into the Chera kingdom. After visiting Vattaru, they entered the Chola kingdom. Thithiyan defeated them. They wandered a bit and came back into Chola territory only to be defeated summarily.

The Mauryan invasion of the Tamil country failed. Tamil country maintained its independence during Emperor Ashoka's rule as well. The defeat of the Mauryas at the hands of Elanchet Chenni is sung by poets in detail. The poets did not mention Cheras and Pandyas in these poems. Karavelan, in the second century BCE, claimed that he destroyed the 113-year-old Tamil alliance. Going by this statement, the unity of Tamils against the northerners existed even after the Mauryan invasion.

Later Aryans, Kosars, Vadugars

A deeper research of Tamil classical poetry referencing Kosars, Vadugars, and Mauryas has led us to several observations in this chapter. It appears that the later Aryans, Kosars, and Vadugars had no connection with the invasion of the Mauryas. Emperor Ashoka died in 232 BCE. Satavahana rulers who followed Ashoka had an empire that extended from the banks of the Ganges to the Tirumala Hills (Venkata Mountains). A Vadugar Border Security Force was positioned at the northern frontier of the Tamil country. Kosars of the Maurya dynasty could have persisted in the region. The Aryans who lived in Vadugar country, Vadugars, and Kosars could have been the target of attacks by Malayaman and Aryapadai Kadantha Nedunchezhiyan (Nedunchezhiyan who conquered the Aryan army). Nedunchezhiyan lived in the *Cilappatikaram* period. That was 150–200 CE. The time of the Mauryan invasion was 298–272 BCE. This was the period of Bindusara, the father of Ashoka. We have referred to the Aryans, Kosars, and Vadugars of two distinct periods in the course of history. Historian Krishnaswamy Iyengar also makes this distinction in his narrative.

SIX

Chola Kings of the Second Century BCE

The King Who Killed His Son for Justice

History

This king ruled over the Chola kingdom from Tiruvarur, a town in the delta districts of Tamil Nadu. He was a great devotee of Lord Shiva. Veethividangan was his only son.

One day, as Veethividangan rode to the temple in a chariot, a calf came under its wheel and was killed. The mother cow brought the grievance to the king by ringing the bell that people used to alert the king of their demands. The king delivered justice to the cow by crushing his son under the chariot. God appreciated the king's sense of justice and resurrected both the calf and the prince. *Periya Puranam*, a Tamil epic authored by Sekkizhar in the twelfth century CE, narrates this story.

The Account of the History of Sri Lanka

Mahavamsam, the history of Sri Lanka, records the following incident:

In the middle of the second century BCE, a highly cultured Chola king came to Eezham (Sri Lanka). At the time, Sri Lanka was ruled by a king called Ashoka. The Chola king won the battle and then ruled over Sri Lanka for forty-five years. He was known as Ellala. He possessed a strong sense of justice and dispensed it impartially to both friends and enemies. He punished his son with death for killing a calf. He was not a Buddhist. He showered love on the Buddhist monks. He led a people-friendly regime. He ruled over the northern part of Sri Lanka. Later, Sri Lankan King Dutthagamani fought and defeated Ellala. Dutthagamani chased Ellala up to Anuradhapuram and fought with him. Ellala died in the battle. Dutthagamani fought and defeated Ellala primarily to preserve the Buddhist faith and curb the spread of Tamil religious traditions. Dutthagamani did the last rites for Ellala and constructed a memorial for him at the site of the battle. All the later rulers worshipped Ellala at this site.

What Is the Name of the King?

Tamil epics *Cilappatikaram* and *Manimekalai* appreciate the work of this king but stop short of mentioning his name. Jayamkondar, Ottakoothar, and Sekkizhar—poets who lived in the eleventh and twelfth centuries CE—called him Manu Neethi Chola. Sangam literature does not mention Manu, Manu Neethi, or Manu Nool. So, this particular name might be a later invention. *Cilappatikaram* calls him *Arum Perar Puthalvanai Aazhiyin Madithon*—the one who sacrificed his dearest son under the wheels of a chariot. *Manimekalai* calls him *Mahanai Murai Seitha Mannavan*—a King who sacrificed his son for justice. Both the epics do not record his name. Other literature of the Sangam Age does not have his name.

What Do We Know?

The *Cilappatikaram* refers only to the justice he delivered through the sacrifice of his own son.

Periya Puranam mentions the devotion he had for Lord Shiva and other virtues. The same virtues are seen in the Tamil king mentioned by *Mahavamsam*. The name Ellala is different. It may have been a nickname. Jayamkondar, Ottakoothar, and Sekkizhar invented a name for him. *Mahavamsam* may have also invented a name for him. Where did the sacrifice of the son happen? *Mahavamsam* does not say that it happened in Eezham (Sri Lanka). *Cilappatikaram* and *Manimekalai* do not mention the place of the event. Sekkizhar says that the event took place in Tiruvarur. The stone chariot referred to is located next to the temple at Tiruvarur. The Chola king may have ruled over Sri Lanka after this incident.

Did He Invade Sri Lanka?

According to *Mahavamsam*, 'A Tamil king ruled over Sri Lanka for forty-five years in the middle of the second century BCE.' Did the Chola kingdom have the navy to subdue Sri Lanka at that time? Is there any evidence available for that?

The Cholas engaged in maritime trade with Western countries as early as the sixth and seventh centuries BCE. Management of maritime trade required the navy. The British, the Japanese, and the Americans used their navy for better management of their maritime trade. The Chola dynasty always wanted to rule over foreign lands. The first Karikala Chola lived between 120 and 90 BCE. Vennikuyathiyar, a woman poet of the Sangam Age, sang about him. The following is the section of the poem that says Karikala Chola of the second century BCE had an ancestor who went across the ocean to win a war:

In the ocean filled with water, he went to war in a big ship. The wind was not there. He prayed to God for the wind. The wind blew and helped the ship sail. He won the war. You have come from the tradition of such kings.

What is the Country That Was Conquered?

Sri Lanka is an island close to Tamil Nadu. Other islands are at a distance. Rajendra Chola of the eleventh century CE won over this island. The previous expeditions to Sri Lanka were not recorded. Sri Lanka had documents to say that the island came under foreign rule in the second century BCE.

Mahavamsam confirms that the Cholas invaded Sri Lanka in the second century BCE. The period of conquest should be between 160 and 140 BCE—the period of the grandfather and father of the first Karikala Chola. This requires further study.

Karikala Chola I (BCE 120–BCE 90)

Chenni-Killi Traditions

Karikala Chola I belonged to the Chenni tradition. They ruled a part of the Chola kingdom with Azhunthur as their capital. The Killi tradition ruled the other part of the kingdom from Uraiyur.

Capital Cities

The first Karikala Chola ruled from Azhunthur first. Then he moved the capital to Kudavasal.

The Wars

He won the battle against eleven rulers and other kings (Chera, Pandya) at Vennivayil. He defeated nine kings at Vagai Paranthalai. Thithiyan was his Commander-in-Chief. The army chief had some well-trained soldiers called Kosars from the

Northern side of India. The Kosars blinded the father of Anni Gnamili, a woman. She came and complained to Thithiyan at Azhunthur. At Venni Paranthalai, Karikala Chola I fought with Peruncheralathan, a Chera king. The arrow sent by Karikala entered Peruncheralathan's chest and came out through his back. Peruncheralathan fasted unto death because getting an injury in the back was considered a humiliation. The tradition among kings was to treat such a situation as dishonour and end their lives. Sangam poet Kazhathalaiyar sang about the sacrifice of Peruncheralathan in defence of his honour. The victory of Karikala Chola I was extolled in a song composed by Vennikuyathiyar, a woman poet of the Sangam Age.

> In the ocean vast and full, he went to war in a great ship. When the wind failed, he prayed to the god, and the wind arose, filling the sails and driving the vessel onward. Thus he won his war. From the tradition of such kings you have descended, O Karikala Valava! You, with mighty elephants in your army, advance into battle and emerge victorious, your strong shoulders bearing the weight of valour. The village of Venni, rich in revenue, has now become a famed battlefield. Peruncheralathan, struck by a wound in the back, chose to end his life in fasting; yet that does not make him a greater warrior than you.

SEVEN

The Chola of the First Century BCE

Karikala Chola II

He has got other names such as Thirumavalavan and Karikal Peruvalathan. *Cilappatikaram*, *Porunar Aatrupadai*, *Pattinappalai* help us understand him better. Some poems from *Ettuthogai*, *Kalingathu Parani*, and *Periya Puranam* lend us insights. Every Chola king wanted to claim the legacy of Karikala Chola. The Telugu Cholas ruled Pothappi, Nellore, and Chittoor during the fourteenth century CE. They claim to be Karikala's descendants. The Renandu Cholas ruled Kuddappa and neighbouring areas. They prided themselves on being part of the Karikala Chola tradition. Inscriptions tell us that many kings in the Kannada country claimed the same legacy. King Vijayalan of the later Cholas mentions his association with Karikala Chola in copper plates and inscriptions. Karikala Chola's extraordinary talents and courageous acts made him a hero forever. He lives on in literature, inscriptions, and copper plates.

His Youth and Governance

He was the son of Elanchet Chenni. Chenni was the younger

brother of the king. He could never become the king. He married the daughter of Azhunthur Vel. She gave birth to Karikala Chola at a highly auspicious time. Karikalan learned several art forms and excelled in warfare. The king died. His father died. Karikalan did not try to crown himself. He left the capital city of Uraiyur and wandered across various places. Meanwhile, chaos erupted throughout the land. The scholars after discussing the challenge, following ancient custom, sent the royal elephant to bring back the rightful heir to the throne. The elephant wandered a long distance and finally found Karikalan in Karur. It brought him to Uraiyur. The people of Chola kingdom felt happy about his return. They made him the king of the Chola Empire.

His rivals later imprisoned him out of jealousy over his rising popularity. They burned down the prison. The courageous Karikala Chola escaped the attempt on his life. Irumbidar Thalaiyar, his uncle, helped him defeat the conspirators. He came back to power.

Some old poems say that 'Karikalan' (Black-legged Person) was an acquired name. His limbs had darkened as he escaped the burning prison. The authenticity of this account is still unverified.

The Wars He Fought

Porunar Aatrupadai, a Sangam-age war poetry, documents the wars he fought. *Cilappatikaram*, a Tamil epic, describes the successful war expeditions led by him.

1. He fought with the Cheras and Pandyas to take complete control of the Tamil country. The battlefield was in Venni. Karikalan, hailed as 'the embodiment of Murugan's wrath', defeated them. Mudathama Kanniyar, the author of *Porunar Aatrupadai*, describes the victory in a poem.

With a leaf of the palm tree on one side, and
a bouquet made of beautiful neem flowers on the other side,
the fearsome and courageous Karikal Valavan, wearing Athi garland,
at a place called Venni, defeated the powerful kings of the Cheras and Pandyas.

(Lines: 143-148)

2. Karikalan went to the Pandri country. Nagapattinam was its capital. It was north of the Pandya land. Eyinar is a dominant community in the Pandri country. Nagars are a subset of the Eyinar clan. Oliyar are a part of the Nagar community. Oliyar ruled over the land. Karikalan conquered them. He then went towards the Pandya country.

3. He crossed the Pandya country and reached the western parts. He conquered Karka (Palakkad) and Venad (Travancore). Kuttam (Kochi), Kudam (Southern Malayalam), and Poozhi (Northern Malayalam) also came under him.

4. He went to the Middle Land and brought Pothuvar community (Kings of the Middle Land) under his control. He brought leaders of Vellalas such as Irungovel under his kingdom.

5. He then went to the Aruva land (Tondai Country) in the northern part of Tamil land. He brought Kurumbars under his control. He conquered the Aruvas. He controlled twenty-four divisions of the Tondai land. He settled Vellalas in all these divisions.

6. He then reached the country of Malayaman. It was on the banks of the Pennai river. Tirukovilur was its capital. Malayaman came under the Chola dominance.

7. He moved on to the northern parts of the Indian sub-continent with a huge army. Many small Vaduga rulers came under his rule.

8. Karikalan went to the Himalayas. Magadha land then transferred power from Sungvar to Kanvar. In 73 BCE, Vasudeva Kanvar ruled over the Magadha Kingdom. After him three Kanvar rulers reigned until 28 BCE. Andhra rulers then took over the Magadha land. It was during the rule of Kanvars that Karikalan went on this expedition. Vachra land with Kosambi as its capital was independent. Avanti land with Ujjain as its capital enjoyed autonomy then. The King of Magadha lauded Karikalan in his court. The King of Vachra land honoured him with a special crown; the King of Avanti welcomed him with an arch in his honour. *Cilappatikaram* has documented these events. The Kings of Vachra and Avanti lost their autonomy during Chandragupta Maurya's reign. And the condition persisted even under King Harsha.

The Conquest of Sri Lanka

Karikalan focused on Sri Lanka and mobilised his navy. This after his return from the Himalayas. He conquered the island of Sri Lanka. He appointed one of his deputies as its king and came back to the Chola country. He brought 12000 people from Sri Lanka when he returned home. *Kalingathu Parani*, a twelfth century war poetry by Jayamkondar, has documented it.

The Chola Empire

The Kakatiya country comprises of Gudur and surrounding regions according to inscriptions. *Manimekalai*, a Tamil epic written in the second century CE, mentions the Kakatiya country. Renandu rulers claim that they belong to the tradition of Karikala Chola. Karikala Chola renovated the city of Kancheepuram. He deforested Tondai Mandalam and made it liveable. *Kalingathu Parani* and *Periya Puranam* record this information. The Chola Empire under Karikala spread from the Northern Pennaiyar to Kanyakumari.

The Politics

Tondai Country:

During the Sangam age, Tondai land and Chola land prospered under the rule of Karikala Chola. He changed the landscape of Tondai country. He deforested the land and created several tiny liveable villages with cultivable lands. He created twenty-four divisions in the country for ease of administration. 1. Ambur 2. Ilangadu 3. Ekkadu 4. Manavil 5. Ootrukadu 6. Eyil 7. Kadigai 8. Kaliyur 9. Kalathur 10. Kundravattanam 11. Sethur 12. Sengadu 13. Senthirukai 14. Sembur 15. Thamal 16. Paduvur 17. Palkundram 18. Puzhal 19. Puliyur 20. Paiyur 21. Venkuntram 22. Vengadam 23. Manavur 24. Vellore

Kancheepuram was the capital of Tondai land. Karikala Chola built a huge wall around the city. He settled a lot of people there. He appointed Ilanthirayan as the king of that land.

Chola Country

He ensured that the Chola country had food security. He took steps to stem the devastation caused by the flooding of the Kaveri river. He wrote to all the kings along the path of the Kaveri to build bunds. He sent them money and labour to build the bunds. The fifty thousand workers he brought from Sri Lanka helped strengthen the banks of the river. He built many canals and irrigation tanks to enable agriculture in the nooks and corners of the Chola country. The Chola land prospered, and the saying 'Chola land always has food' became a well-known proverb. He got the name *Karikal Peruvalathan* (The Prosperous Karikalan). The Kaveri river is called Ponni. The King is Valavar (One who presides over Prosperity).

He did not stop with streamlining the Kaveri (Ponni) river. He built tanks and temples in the villages. He built forts across the country. *Pattinappalai*, a poem of the Sangam Age, narrates this.

Peace Prevailed

The Chola country's capital Kaveripoompattinam saw the coming of foreign traders—the Romans, Chinese, Arabs, and other foreign merchants. The merchants had lodging facilities in the city. The merchants and common people of the Chola country interacted with the foreigners. People practiced Buddhism, Jainism, and Vedic religion. It was the governance model of Karikala Chola that enabled such a peaceful atmosphere.

Delivery of Justice

Two elderly men visited Karikala Chola to resolve a case. Seeing that he was very young, they doubted his ability. He made them wait for a while and came back disguised as an old man. He heard the case and sorted it out. Then he revealed his identity. The elderly men felt ashamed for doubting his judgment. Several books, including the book of Tamil proverbs (*Pazhamozhi*), mention this story.

Maritime Trade

Maritime trade prospered under his rule. He was the one who made Kaveripoompattinam rich. Providing lodging facilities for foreign merchants was among the many measures he undertook to facilitate business. Kaveripoompattinam was where the Kaveri river met the ocean. It was a deep and wide harbour where ships and boats could move about with ease. The port had a light house. Custom houses situated at the port received the goods, stamped them with the Tiger logo of the Chola Kingdom and sent them to warehouses and godowns. The port infrastructure featured well-built docks and piers. Detailed accounts of the goods imported are found in *Pattinappalai* and *Cilappatikaram,* as well as in *Oor Kaan Kathai Urai*. The Roman coins and the Satavahana coins found in Kilakarai should also be taken into account. The port was a hub of maritime trade activity, facilitating commerce both within the sub-continent and with regions beyond. Karikal Peruvalathan's rule was regarded as the 'Golden Age' of ancient Tamil Nadu.

The Development of the Tamil Language

The Tamil language flourished under the leadership of Karikala Chola. His uncle Irumbidar Thalaiyar was a renowned Tamil poet. The poet was also the king's guardian. Karikala got his language training from him. Poet Uruthiran Kannanar says that the king gave him 1600000 gold coins. It is in *Pattinappalai*. *Porunar Aatrupadi,* authored by Mudathama Kanniyar, sings praises of the king. His skills in warfare, his compassion, and his victories are in this book. A poet from Kaveripoompattinam—Kari Kannanar—sang of the phenomenal qualities of the king. When Karikala was with Pandya Velli Ambalathu Thunjiya Peruvazhuthi, this poet met them and wrote several poems about

Karikala Chola. Maruthuvan Damodaranar is another poet who sang songs about Karikala Chola.

> Your country has both the ocean and the hills. You are a king capable of great things.

The poet goes on:

> Your drum beats success. Your sword sways to the side of justice. Your crown resembles a full moon. I sing about you and get the prizes showered by you.

Konattu Erichalur Madalan Madurai Kumaranar is another poet who praised Karikala Chola. When he visited the king, Karikala Chola delayed giving him the prize for reasons unknown. At that time, the poet, feeling disappointed, composed a song. Within that composition, his description of Karikalan's greatness in general terms is noteworthy:

> The horses of Karikalan's chariots race with the wind. He has a navy that can dominate the ocean. His elephants can fight the hills and win. Even thunder cannot beat better than his drums. He is always a winner in the wars.

Many poets who came after Karikalan's time also sang his praises. Paranar, Nakkeerar, Ilango Adigal, Jayamkondar, and Sekkizhar wrote about his feats. Sangam literature is proof that he nurtured the Tamil language. He organised debates for enhancing the knowledge of poets. He put together the best teachers and created universities. He welcomed poets into the Royal court and offered them prizes. He saw them off, walking with them seven feet. He ruled over a land stretching from Northern Pennaiyar to Kanyakumari. He never let power go to his head. His gesture of walking with the poets seven feet to see them off reflects the value he placed on the Tamil language. His patronage of Tamil inspired others, leading to generations of continued support for the language. He was a trendsetter.

Arts

The prosperity during the period of Karikala Chola led to the growth of music, theatre, and dance. The Sangam age literature serves as proof of the flourishing patronage for the arts during the reign of Karikala Chola. When Madhavi acted in theatre in the second century CE, the tools and techniques were of remarkably high quality. That was a continuation of the work done by Karikala Chola.

Religion

Several faiths co-existed during the time of Karikala Chola. In the third century BCE, the kings of Tamil Nadu honoured Emperor Ashoka's request and allowed the peaceful propagation of Buddhism. Buddhist schools and temples proliferated in the kingdoms of Cheras, Cholas, and Pandyas. Indra Vihar was there in Kaveripoompattinam during the time of Karikala Chola. Jain places of worship also existed at that time. The followers of Vedic religion practiced their Vedic beliefs during the period. Foreign merchants who landed in the Chola country practiced different faiths. The followers of many faiths worked together under the leadership of Karikala Chola. The king respected all the faiths and treated all with dignity. Karikala believed in Shaivism. He renovated the Ekambaranathar temple in Kancheepuram and worshipped there. Shaivite saint Thirugnana Sambandar of the seventh century CE has praised Karikala in his *Tevaram* hymns:

The gods above chant the Vedas and sacred hymns;
devotees with loving eyes walk to the Lord's feet;
Karikalan too sought Him.
This is the glorious sight of Ekambaranathar in the beautiful city of Kanchi,
where the Lord dances adorned in divine ornaments.

A statue of Karikalan can be seen in the Ekambaranathar Temple. He also performed Vedic rituals and sacrifices.

Karikala Chola's capital Kaveripoompattinam had temples for several Gods and Goddesses, including those for Lord Shiva and Lord Buddha.

His Contemporary Kings

Pandya Velli Ambalathu Thunjiya Peruvazhuthi and Cheraman Kudako Cheral Irumporai were his contemporaries. Enathi-Thirukkilli (A king of a tiny land) lived during his time. Irnthurkizhan Thoyan Maran and Chozhiya Enathi Thirukkuttuvan were also the contemporaries of Karikala Chola. Karikala Chola defeated a king called Irungovel.

His Family

Elanchet Chenni was his father. His mother was the daughter of Azhunthur Vel. He married the daughter of Nangur Vel from Sirkazhi division. Some accounts say that he had more than one wife. His daughter's name was Hathi Manthiyar. More research is needed in this area.

His Death

In the century before Christ, Karikala Peruvallathan, who established the Chola Empire and ruled it under one umbrella of authority, is believed to have spent his final days at a place called Kurappalli. It is believed that Kurappalli refers to a sacred Shaivite temple site (*Thiruvidai Sivathalam*), where the Kura tree serves as the temple's holy tree (*sthala vriksha*).

EIGHT

Chola Nalankilli

His Time

Karikalan's period was from 60 BCE to 10 BCE; and according to *Cilappatikaram,* the period of Senguttuvan was from 150 to 200 CE. *Manimekalai* talks about Nedumudi Killi who lived during this time. Kochengad Chola came after him. Many researchers claim that the Sangam period ended with Nedumudi Killi. Sangam Tamil anthologies talk about Chola rulers from 10 BCE to 150 CE.

According to Sangam literature, Chola Nalankilli was the son of Karikal Peruvalathan. He ruled over a large kingdom with immense power. He had a huge military power. *Purananuru* has ten poems on him. He appreciated poets such as Uraiyur Muthukannan Sathanar, Kovur Kizhar, and Alathur Kizhar. These poets have documented his story.

Wars

Nedunkilli

As Nalankilli assumed the throne, rivalry erupted between the relatives. Nedunkilli was in charge of Aavoor and belonged to the Chola ruling dynasty. Nalankilli took over the Chola dynasty's top job at a ceremony in Kaveripoompattinam. At the same time, Nedunkilli took control of Uraiyur. Nalankilli was upset. He vowed to avenge the treachery and waged a war against Nedunkilli. The following is the vow he took to avenge the treason:

> If someone reaches out to me with humility and asks me politely for my throne, I don't mind handing over my kingdom to him. I am ready to give my dear life. The one who blamed me without the realisation of the power of the King and Commander-in-Chief is like a blind man who accidentally stepped on a tiger. I will go and fight valiantly like an elephant. The elephant that eats bamboo for food. If I don't do that, let my garland fade in the company of harlots.

The Siege of Aavoor

The king laid siege to Nedunkilli's Aavoor fort. Nedunkilli locked himself up in the fort and did nothing to counter the incoming threat. The people around the fort suffered because of the siege. Poet Kovoor Kizhar realising the impact of the siege on the common people, addressed Nedunkilli in a song. The following is the message of the poet to Nedunkilli:

> The elephants of Nalankilli are damaging the villages. The elephants roar like thunder. Children are crying for milk. Women are tying their hair without flowers. Several women have become widows because of the death of soldiers. Many families are looking up to you in this moment of crisis. It is not right for you to remain in the fort while ignoring the suffering of the people. If you are a just leader, give up the fort

> and surrender. If you have courage, fight with the incoming army. It is a shame to hide yourself in the fort.

We don't have details of what transpired after the siege and the appeal by the poet. Nedunkilli escaped and hid himself in the Uraiyur fort.

The Siege of Uraiyur Fort

Poet Kovoor Kizhar was not happy that Nedunkilli was being adamant. He was also unhappy because Nalankilli was out to get Nedunkilli and had laid siege to the fort in Uraiyur. He appealed to both of them. The following is his message:

> Dearest Nedunkilli, the one who fights you is not the Chera King who wears a garland of palm flowers. He is not the Pandya King who wears neem flowers. You are wearing a garland of Athi flowers. The one who fights you also wears Athi flowers. Even if one of you loses the battle, it is the Chola dynasty that loses. Both of you cannot win this. It is not proper for you to engage in this fight. You may get some pleasure out of fighting. There is no good in it. It is best to avoid this conflict.

Ilam Thathan

Ilam Thathan was a poet who had received gifts from Nalankilli. He reached Uraiyur to meet Nedunkilli. Nedunkilli thought he was a spy of Nalankilli and wanted to murder him. Kovoor Kizhar heard of this development and rushed to meet Nedunkilli.

> My lord, he is but a simple poet who goes to patrons to get rewards for his poems. He has come to you to sing your praise for a reward. He does not understand the craft of spying. He

> walks with his head held high because of his learning. It would be cruel to kill him without understanding the purpose of his visit, said the poet.

The king, hearing these words, refrained from committing the deed.

Nalankilli succeeded in his siege of Uraiyur. He made Uraiyur his capital and ruled from there according to song 68 of *Purananuru*. Nedunkilli died in a battle at Kariyaru. 'Nedunkilli who died in Kariyaru' is an expression found in Sangam poetry.

Battle with the Pandyas

Nalankilli fought with the Pandyas. He took over the seven forts of Pandyas and planted the tiger insignia of Cholas as a mark of his victory.

The Great Warrior

He was a man who was always coming from the battlefield. He took immense delight in fighting wars that struck fear into his enemies. He rewarded bards and others at the battlefront. He had an efficient navy and cavalry and had the habit of riding in chariots. His infantry was organised into three divisions—the vanguard (*Thoosipadai)*, the central force (*Idaiyanipadai)*, and the rear guard (*Iruthiyanipadai)*. When marching to war, the first division would eat raw palm fruit (*nungu*). The second division would eat the ripe fruit of the palm tree. The third division would eat roasted palm roots.

This meant; the vanguard was always sent first and often completed the task on its own. Only if it failed, the second division would be sent. By the time the second division went, the raw palm fruit would have ripened. If the second division did not complete the work, the third division would go. The palm fruit would have become the palm root by this time. Nalankilli's strategy worked well. The staggered use of the armed forces paid off.

Emperor

Nalankilli had a powerful Navy. He would always be war-ready. He kept his enemies at bay through constant vigilance.

> Just as wealth and pleasure appear only after righteousness in proper order, so too the parasols of the Cheras and Pandyas appear only behind your royal umbrella. You desire to remain in the midst of your household, not in the midst of the city; yet your elephants, which do not submit, batter down the gates of enemy forts. At the very sound of the word 'war,' your warriors leap with joy; without battle they languish. Therefore, the northern kings long for the day when, in due course, the waves of the upper sea will beat against the hooves of your horses, even as the waves of the lower sea already do.

The above verse is poet Kovoor Kizhar's take on Nalankilli. These lines of Kovoor Kizhar demonstrate that Nalankilli was an emperor and the kings in the north feared him. The poet says this Chola king had the capacity to offer Madurai city to pretty dancers. Poet Thamappal Kannanar says that Nalankilli won over enemies and amassed wealth. Poet Alathur Kizhar sings that the armies of Nalankilli are capable of winning over the world.

Poet

The King had great understanding and knowledge of the Tamil language. His style, substance, and knowledge of metaphors were of great quality. His poem on revenge before subduing Nedunkilli is a good example of his poetic prowess.

Patron

He was a patron of eminent poets such as Kovoor Kizhar, Uraiyur Mudhukannan Sathanar, and Alathur Kizhar. He protected songsters, drama artistes, and danseuses and promoted the Tamil language through music, theatre, and other performing arts.

> He will offer the grand city of Vanchi so that artistes can have a satisfactory life. He will be ready to donate the beautiful Madurai city for the wonderful skills of our danseuses. So let us sing his praises and receive our rewards,

wrote poet Kovoor Kizhar. This song is sufficient to illustrate the king's generosity.

A Poet's Advice

Poet Mudhukannan Sathanar appreciated the military prowess of Nalankilli. He gave the king some good advice. A summary of it is here:

> My Lord, Chetchenni Nalankilli, many kings came to this world and went away. There are only a few kings who have the capacity for song and prose. The poets sing of the impermanence of life and educate people relentlessly. You have to support them as they keep the world sane. You are the king of a prosperous country. I wish you to have virtue, power, and pleasure. Your court should be filled with lots of poets. Your chest may be cared for by your women. The drum of your palace should shun the wicked and embrace the good people.

> 'Goodness will beget goodness. Bad actions will lead to bad outcomes,' should be the principle we should adhere to. You should always support the weak people who seek your help. The wealth you have earned will bring you glory.

Mudhukannan Sathanar's words melted Nalankilli's heart. Kovoor Kizhar strengthened Nalankill's morale when enemies laid siege to his palace. Nalankilli, known for his virtues, followed the advice of the poets.

> **Some More Information**
> The path of the sun, its motion, and the regions encircled by that motion; the vastness of the earth, the directions in which the wind blows, and even the sky, which stands without any visible support—these were measured and understood by learned men as if they had observed and studied them for countless years. Such scholars, who could say with precision, 'this much is its extent,' existed in that time.

This information in the *Purananuru* poem 30 tells us that there were astronomers and experts in celestial sciences in that era. It is also evident that there were great scholars who continually advanced their knowledge

> The sail has not changed. The ship is entering the riverfront. It brings prosperity to the fishing community and other people. The prosperity of maritime trade comes because of you, King!

reads a part of poem 30 of *Purananuru*. It tells us about the power of maritime trade during the reign of Nalankilli.

Poem 33 of *Purananuru* sings of the skilled persons who created beautiful paintings. The poem serves as evidence of the art of painting in the Chola Kingdom. Painting was one of the many art forms that thrived under the Cholas.

Poem 400 of *Purananuru* praises the king for taking care of the country, even with little sleep. It serves as a proof of Nalankilli's responsible governance.

Thambi Mavalathan

There is not much information about this king. He was the philanthropist who supported the poet Thamappal Kannanar. The king played discus throw with the poet. The poet played a bit of hide and seek during the sport. The king attacked the poet with the discus. Angered by this, the poet told the king that he was unworthy of belonging to the Chola dynasty. 'If you are part of the Chola dynasty, you would not have done it,' the poet told the king. The king understood his own pettiness and felt bad for it. The poet realising the impact of his retort, softened and consoled the king. The poet himself has recorded this event in *Purananuru,* poem 43.

NINE

Killivalavan

Killivalavan was regarded as the greatest ruler in the Chola tradition after Nalankilli and Nedunkilli. The poets who composed verses on them have sung about Killivalavan too. Uraiyur was his capital. Nine poets composed eighteen poems in his praise. Poet Nakkeeran mentions him in a poem of *Akananuru*, an anthology of 400 love poems of the Sangam Age. He was a great soldier, a great poet, and a patron of arts and literature. He was in the league of Karikalan and Nalankilli.

Wars Fought by Killivalavan

Many poems point to the wars led by Killivalavan. He demolished the fortresses of many enemies. Poem 40 of *Purananuru*—one of the 400 poems of courage from the Sangam Age—extols him for converting the golden crowns of many kings into his own anklet of victory. He subdued enemies on all sides of his kingdom. He excelled in the art of war. His forces could undermine the elephants of the enemy. His strong shoulders had the capacity to defeat even the well-equipped armies of some kings. In the blood-filled war fields, his infantry, horses and elephants ensured his victory.

Karuvur Siege

Karuvur siege was one of his many war expeditions. A king of the Chera dynasty spent his time merrily in the Karuvur fortress. He lacked courage. Poet Alandur Kizhar questioned whether it was even necessary for Killivalavan to fight such a man.

> Despite knowing the havoc wreaked by your forces, the Chera King remains in the fortress. He does not come to the battlefield. You will not score by fighting a coward. You can win. You can kill him. But it will not add to your glory.

Through these lines, Alandur Kizhar highlighted both the strength and valour of Killivalavan and the cowardice of the Chera king. Ultimately, Killivalavan defeated the Chera king and destroyed the Karuvur fortress.

In poem 39 of *Purananuru*, the poet Marokkathu Nappasalaiyar writing in praise of Killivalavan says,

> How can I ever find words to sing of your strength, O Killivalavan, whose might brought down the Chera king—he who guarded the hill country with a bow strung in vigilance, rode in chariots of exquisite craftsmanship, and ruled from impregnable Karuvur, only to see it reduced to ruins by your enduring power?

Fighting with Malayaman

Malayaman was a king who ruled over a hill country with Tirukovalur as its capital. His descendants continued to play a significant role in Tamil Nadu until the thirteenth century CE. He was a small king under the Chola Empire. For some reason, Killivalavan became angry with Malayaman. There are no records to indicate what happened between them. Killivalavan imprisoned the two sons of Malayaman. He wanted them to be trampled by elephants. Poet Kovoor Kizhar was upset when he heard about this. He went to the king and said:

> You come from a lineage where a king once sacrificed himself for a pigeon. The children were crying in fear until the elephants arrived. But, when the animals arrived, they stopped crying and gazed in wonder at the sight of the elephants. It is up to you to do the best in the situation.

We have no record of what happened afterwards.

The War with the Pandyas

Killivalavan fought with one of the Pandya kings. It was in Madurai. Pazhayan Maran was the name of the Pandya king. Though Killivalavan commanded the largest army, he was defeated in this war. The Pandya king confiscated Killivalavan's horses and elephants. Kokothai Marban, a Chera king, was delighted that the Pandya King won this war. In poem 346 of *Akananuru*, the 400 love poems of the Sangam Age, poet Nakkeeran mentions this incident. Had Killivalavan won this war, the nine poets who wrote eighteen poems on him would have written about it.

The absence of this war in the eighteen poems points to the defeat suffered by Killivalavan in this battle. Four poets wrote about Killivalavan after his death. They do not mention this battle with the Pandyas. Poets avoid the mention of such defeats. The Pandyas accepted the dominance of the Chola Empire during the rule of Karikala Chola. The defeat of Killivalavan at the hands of a Pandya king cheered the Chera king Kokothai Marban.

His War in the Chera Land

Killivalavan has a moniker *Kulamutrathu Thunjia Killivalavan* (Killivalavan who died in Kulamutram). Kulamutram is a town in the Chera kingdom. This expression shows that Killivalavan died in a war in the Chera kingdom.

The End of Killivalavan

He fought many wars. He attacked the Chera king who ruled from Karuvur. He angered King Malayaman. His attacks on small rulers indicate that they had started rebelling. The small kings who were subservient during the time of Karikala Chola started asserting themselves under the rule of Killivalavan. Their rise marked the end of Killivalavan.

A fair assessment of the situation at the time reveals that the Chola Empire, which had expanded under Karikala Chola, shrank under Killivalavan.

Emperor Killivalavan

In poem 35 of *Purananuru*, Vellaikudi Naganar praises Killivalavan's government as offering the best governance. 'If you want moon by the side of the sun or the sun to go to the moon, Killivalavan will get it done,'—this is how the poet Avoor Moonkizhar praises him in poem 38 of *Purananuru*. Iyur Mudavanar in poem 228 of *Purananuru* says: 'He has one of the largest armies. He has the praises of the finest scholars. He shines like the sun. He carries the legacy of Chembiyan. He is Killivalavan.'

Great Warrior

He fought many wars. We have read about them. Many poets have referred to him as a great warrior. In poem 397 of *Purananuru*,

Erukkattur Thayankannanar praises him for his ability to deal with the most challenging war situations.

Poet-friend

Killivalavan was also a poet as seen in the poem 173 of *Purananuru,* which is attributed to him. His friendship with Pannan is evident in this poem. Here is an interpretation of the poem:

> The birds gather and sing on a tree laden with fruits. The song of happiness reverberates in the home of Pannan as he feeds the poor. Like an army of ants carrying food to their hills before winter, people carry food from Pannan's home and walk back in clusters like the ants themselves. 'I am stricken with the disease of hunger. Where is the home of the doctor who cures hunger?' asks the poet. He then prays that Pannan be granted a long life—one that includes his own—so that the cure for the disease of hunger goes on uninterrupted for a long term.

This beautiful poem brings out the brilliance of Killivalavan's literary talent and the generosity of his friend Pannan. It captures the amazing relationship between him and Pannan as well.

Patron

Nine poets have sung about Killivalavan. They are Alathur Kizhar, Vellaikudi Naganar, Marokkathu Nappasalaiyar, Aavoor Moolankizhar, Kovoor Kizhar, Aduthirai Masathanar, Aiyur Mudavanar, Nal Iraiyanar, and Erukkuttur Thayankannanar. *Purananuru* records the poems of Aduthurai Masathanar and Erukkuttur Thayankannanar who wrote after the demise of Killivalavan. We don't have the poems they wrote when Killivalavan was the ruler. Killivalavan appreciated the literary skills of the nine poets. Pannan, a great philanthropist, had been his best friend for years. Killivalavan was a good philanthropist himself. Poets commended him for his generosity. Kovoor Kizhar, Marokkathu Nappasalaiyar, Aiyur Mudavanar, and Aduthurai Masathanar wrote poems on him after his death.

Humble Person

'O! Poet! You need not wait at Killivalavan's doorstep. You can go straight in,' writes Alathur Kizhar. This reveals the easy access scholars had to Killivalavan. 'Give us clothes and wealth to our satisfaction. I heard of your generosity and have come here. I will sing your praises,' writes Nal Iraiyanar. Word had spread about Killivalavan's generosity. His philanthropy was accessible to every poet in the land. Poet Erukkuttur Thayankannanar writes:

> He gave me meat fried in ghee and an exquisite drink.
> He also gave me an embroidered outfit.
> He showered me with wealth like a monsoon downpour, sweeping away my poverty!
> He presented me with many other goods as well.

(Part of *Purananuru* poem 397: The translation is based on a commentary by Puliyur Kesikan, a great scholar and commentator)

Poets Mourn His Demise

Killivalavan led many wars as a king; he supported many poets; he helped the poor; he promoted Tamil; the poets thought of his contributions and sang soulfully about them.

'Death could not have been successful with Killivalavan if it had fought him directly. It would have disguised itself as a poet seeking his life as alms,' writes Nappasalaiyar in poem 226 of *Purananuru*.

'O! Death! You are thankless! Killivalavan fed you on many battlefields. He is your equal. Yet your hunger is insatiable,' writes Aduthurai Masathanar in poem 227 of *Purananuru*. 'O potter, who makes the urn for the burial of Killivalavan! His fame has spread across the world. Can you confine him within a pot?' writes Aiyur Mudavanar in poem 228 of *Purananuru*.

In *Purananuru* poem 386, Kovoor Kizhar laments:

We are the warriors of the Chola land!
We are warriors, who do not fight.
Let the stars spread everywhere.
He understood what we wanted and provided it.
We never had to think of our needs.
Long live his glory.

What We Know from the Poems

Purananuru poem 397 describes how the Chola land had sacrificial ceremonies done by priests. Uraiyur was the capital of the Chola kingdom. A court in the capital dispensed justice. The fortress had a deep moat. The moat had crocodiles. The sentries of the town carried lamps and roamed the town in the middle of the night to ensure the safety of its citizens. Eating the meat of rabbit with millet rice cooked in milk was a common practice of those times. The bards played a fretless harp called *Yazh*. *Purananuru* poems 69 and 70 celebrate the honey-like music generated by the Yazh.

It was customary to bury kings and high-ranking individuals in urns. *Purananuru* poem 397 mentions that waking the king each morning was the duty of the bards. The same poem talks about the very fine fabric that was made in the Chola kingdom. They were as thin as snake sheds.

Purananuru poem 39 is about the Chera king, who lived before Killivalavan and famously planted the bow symbol in the Himalayas. This is a key information as the poet who is recording the story of Cholas is also registering a success story of one of the Chera kings.

Killivalavan had glorious Chola ancestors as well. The Chola King, who donated his flesh for a pigeon, was known for his generosity. Chembiyan, who destroyed three fortresses of enemies, was known for his valour.

NINE

Kopperumcholan

Introduction

Kopperumcholan ruled the Chola kingdom from Uraiyur, its capital. A man of great virtue, he was also an accomplished Tamil poet. He upheld the highest ethical standards. Pothiyar served as the official court poet. Several renowned poets, including Kannakanar, Pullattur Eyittiyanar, Karuvur Perunchathukathu Poothanar, and Pisiranthaiyar have celebrated him.

Friendship

Pisir was a town in the Pandya kingdom. Anthaiyar was a Tamil poet who lived there. He heard about the great virtues of the king and fell in love with him. He sent his appreciation for the king through others. The king in turn came to respect the poet after hearing of his talent from those around him.

Pisiranthaiyar, thinking of the king one day, sang to a swan. *Purananuru* poem 67 records it thus;

> Dear Swan, the moon shines bright this evening like the face of our successful king who won many wars for the country. I

regret my inability to go and meet my best friend, the king. When you travel from Kumari to the Himalaya, please stay in the Chola land with your partner. When you enter the palace and tell the king that you are a friend of Pisiranthaiyar, he will cover your companion in gold.

Fight with the children

Contrary to the virtuous nature of Kopperumcholan, his children displayed troubling behaviour. They ruled over different parts of the Chola kingdom. It is unclear whether they sought to unseat Kopperumcholan or were merely acting in disobedience. Kopperumcholan went to confront them with a big army.

Pullattur Eyittiyanar, a poet in his court, was worried about this situation. So he advised the king. His advice is recorded in *Purananuru* poem 213.

Oh! glorious king, ruler of the world!
Those who stand against you are not your enemies.
And when you reflect on it, you are not theirs.
Oh, leader! You have elephants that can destroy your enemies.
When you leave this world, it is your children who will inherit your kingdom.
You know that. Listen further.
If you kill your children in the war, who will inherit your kingdom?
If you get defeated, only shame will remain.
So, stop this war. Do what is right.
Come now, King! Long live your glory!

Fasting unto death!

Kopperumcholan was a virtuous man. Listening to the advice of his court poet, he ended the war. He handed over the kingdom to his children. However, he was filled with shame due to their wrongdoing and decided to fast unto death. This practice involved moving to an isolated place, facing north, giving up food, contemplating the Almighty and dying with the remembrance of God. During his fast, he left behind some advice, which was recorded in *Purananuru* poem 214.

> Those who are weak in mind, doubt their ability to do good and end up doing nothing. Those who confidently go on a hunt for elephants will be remarkably successful. Those who go hunting for quail will come back empty-handed. So be of those who have higher aims and noble character. If you really are blessed with the heavens, you will get it. If not, at the very least you will be freed from the cycle of several births. Or, if nothing else, your fame will endure forever. So, do good. Do only good.

Seeing the future

After giving advice, the king turned to his colleagues and said, Pisiranthaiyar, from the village Pisir of the Pandya kingdom will arrive here soon. His colleagues told him that Pisiranthaiyar would not come because of the long distance between the two kingdoms. The king reiterated,

> Oh, people of wisdom! Though my friend did not see me when I was rich, he will definitely come to see me when I am really poor. He is a person of great character. When people ask him his name, he tells them my name. Such is the bond between us. He will definitely come. Keep a space for him.

Pothiyar's Appreciation

Moments after the King's prophecy, Pisiranthaiyar arrived. He embraced the king and let tears of joy flow. Pothiyar witnessed this miracle and recorded it in *Purananuru* poem 217. The king's decision to fast unto death, despite having so much of wealth, is astonishing. A friend arriving from another country at such a moment is even more astounding. The king's prophecy that his friend would come is another miracle. He was a ruler of great virtues. The country has lost him. What will happen to this country?

Young Forever

The people around the Chola King asked Pisiranthaiyar, 'Your hair has not turned grey despite your advanced age. What is the reason?' Pisiranthaiyar replied, as recorded in *Purananuru* poem 191;

> Beloved people, my wife and children are wise. The workers obey me. My Pandya king protects his people. We have scholars rich in knowledge yet humble in spirit. That is why I look younger and happier.

Pisiranthaiyar fasts unto death

Pisiranthaiyar decided to sit by the side of Kopperumcholan and fast unto death. Poet Kannahanar recorded this moment in *Purananuru* poem 218.

> Gold, sapphire, pearls and rubies are born in different places. When a beautiful jewellery is made, all these precious stones come together.
> In the same way, people of great virtue are destined to meet and remain together.

Boothanar's Appreciation

Karuvur Perunchathukathu Boothanathanar's reflections on Kopperumcholan's fast unto death are recorded in poem 219 of *Purananuru*.

You are the hero who has subjected your body to suffering. Many wise people accompanied you and also fasted unto death. I came here much later. Does this trouble you?

Pothiyar Laments

It was a tradition for many poets to fast unto death along with the king. Pothiyar could not fast unto death as his wife was pregnant at the time. Kopperumcholan asked Pothiyar to join him after the birth of the child. When Pothiyar walked back, he saw Uraiyur. The sight of the city brought back memories of the King. His feelings are recorded in *Purananuru* poem 220.

> When a mahout loses his elephant, he weeps inconsolably.
> For years, the elephant fed him.
> Now as he gazes at the rod that once guided the elephant, memories overwhelm him and bring him to tears.
> In the same way, when I look at the Uraiyur council once presided over by you, my eyes brim with tears.

Looking at the hero stone erected in memory of Kopperumcholan, Pothiyar's memories come alive in *Purananuru* poem 221.

> You supported the poets who sang of your great deeds.
> You rewarded artists who came to see you.
> You never strayed from the path of justice.
> You were gentle with women.
> You were firm with your people.

You were a refuge for good people.
Alas! Your life has been taken away.
Oh! truthful poets! Let us curse the God of Death.
Our protector has become a hero stone.
Let us chide death!

After the birth of his son, he returned to the hero stone of the king and asked for a place where he too might fast unto death. He sat there and died from fasting.

Some Interesting Information

Kopperumcholan always listened attentively to poets and promoted all branches of the Tamil language. During his time, eating turtle meat with liquor was a common practice. Fish was also part of the staple diet. Eating millet rice with curd was common in the Pandya kingdom. The councils in Uraiyur were immensely popular with the people.

ELEVEN

Other Chola Kings

Purananuru poems sing the praises of many Chola kings. Some of them were emperors, while others were small kings.

Perunarkilli Who Did Rayasuyam

Introduction

His name suggests that he must have been an emperor. One who performs the Rayasuyam, must indeed be an emperor, who must have conquered and brought many lands under his control. *Purananuru* poem 16 praises his military prowess. The poem was composed by poet Pandarangannanar.

War Hero

He had a huge army. He had many military successes. His sword smelt of flesh. He plundered the food warehouses of enemies. His elephants instilled terror in the hearts of enemies. They followed his directions accurately.

War with a Chera King

Perunarkilli fought with Mantharancheral Irumporai, a Chera king. Malaiyaman who ruled over Tirukovilur supported

Perunarkilli in this expedition. In *Purananuru* poem 125, poet Vadamavanakkan Perumsathanar says,

> 'Without Malaiyaman, victory would have been impossible,'
> admits the Chola king, praising you.
> 'Without Malaiyaman, we would not have been defeated,' says even the Chera king, acknowledging your might.
> O noble one, famed for your generosity!
> Your valour is such that both friend and enemy sing your praises alike.

Friend of Cheras and Pandyas

Perunarkilli was close to the Chera and Pandya kings. Murryvenko, a Chera king and Kanapor thantha Ukkira Peruvazhuthi, a Pandya king, stayed with Perunarkilli for a few days. Avvaiyar praised the three kings.

> Even if the country is as good as Paradise, it will not go with us. It belongs only to those who meditate. When learned people approached you, you gave them gold and offered them several villages. You drank honey given by beautiful women. You gave jewellery to those who deserved it. Good deeds like this will help you live longer. I wish all three of you to have a longer life.

Generous King

Ulochanar, a poet, sang the praises of Perunarkilli. His generosity is celebrated in *Purananuru* poem 377.

Patron

Perunarkilli supported poets such as Avvaiyar, Pandarangannanar, and Ulochanar.

Porvai Kopperunarkilli
He was the son of Thithan.

Velpal Thadakkai Perunarkilli
He fought with Kudakko Nedun Cheralathan and died in the battle.

Mudithalai Kopperumnarkilli
He ruled over the Chola kingdom from Uraiyur. Not much is known about him except for a mention in poem 13 of *Purananuru*.

Thithan: He ruled from Uraiyur. Porvai Kopperumnarkilli was his son.

Chola Nal Uruthiran: Only one poem of *Akananuru* records him as a king of great values and virtues.

TWELVE

Nedumudi Killi (CE 150-200)

Claiming the Kingdom

Senguttuvan lived in the *Cilappatikaram* era of CE 150–200. He promoted Nedumudi Killi. Senguttuvan's mother Narchonai and Nedumudi Killi's father were siblings. Nedumudi Killi was the Chola cousin of Senguttuvan. Nine partners fought with Nedumudi Killi after his father died. Senguttuvan defeated all the rivals in Nerivayil and crowned his cousin.

Many Names

In the *Manimekalai* epic, he is known by many names such as Venver Killi, Maavan Killi, Vadivel Killi, Suzhar Killi and Killi.

Wife, Son, and Brother

He married a woman from a family of vagabond singers known as Banas (Bards). Her name was Seerthi. Her family ruled a part of North Arcot. Seerthi had one son. His name was Udayakumaran. Nedumudi Killi's younger brother was Ilankilli. He ruled over Kanchipuram that was the northern part of the Chola Empire.

Manimekalai and Udayakumaran

Udayakumaran fell in love with Manimekalai and did everything in his power to woo her. Since Manimekalai had chosen a life of celibacy as a Buddhist nun, she rejected his love. Udayakumaran met with a tragic end as he persisted in his desire for a woman who had chosen to become a nun.

THIRTEEN

Politics and Life of the People of the Sangam Age

Conditions During the Sangam Age

Tolkappiyam, an ancient treatise on Tamil language and life, records the strong presence of people from northern regions in Tamil Nadu. It talks about their customs and traditions. The Common Era third century was the last phase of the Sangam Age. Tamil poems talk about how the sacrificial fires and religious doctrines of the North influenced Tamil life. The influences were seen only in the urban people. People who lived away from cities were not influenced. However, the kings in Tamil Nadu started claiming that they belonged to the dynasty of the Sun or the Moon. This was certainly an influence of the Northerners. They started appreciating sacrificial fires. They had priests well versed in Vedas. The arrival and mingling of the Northern people changed the ancient Tamil marital customs, daily rituals, and religious practices. However, with careful observation and critical thinking, it is clear from the Sangam texts that the civilisation of the ancient Tamils had its own distinct identity. Only those unwilling or unable to discern will claim that it is impossible to distinguish between the two cultures.

Country

The Chola country had Thanjavur and Tiruchirappalli as an integral part of its geography. Vellar river flowed in the north and the south of the country. On the east was the ocean; on the west was the fortress. It was on the banks of the river. The riverbank was raised to build the fortress, which was in Kulithalai. The remains of the fortress can be seen even today. It was a plain with no mountains. The land was fertile thanks to the Kaveri river. The plains were high on the western side and low on the eastern side.

The Kaveri branches into many tributaries and joins the ocean. The alluvial soil brought by the Kaveri enriched the Chola land. It is a long plain where Kaveri and its tributaries join the ocean. It is a great scene. The paddy fields, mango trees, coconut trees, and fruit trees present a rich scenery. The Chola land does not have forests. In *Purananuru* poem 40, poet Avoor Mulankizhar says that in Chola land, even in a small plot where an elephant can lie down, rice that can feed seven households is cultivated. In *Porunar Aatrupadai*, the author mentions getting 64 tons of rice from about six acres of land.

Administrative Divisions

Kootram, Kottam, Nadu were common administrative divisions during the Sangam Age. Kurichi, Padi, Oor, Kudi, Pakkam, Pattinam, and Nagar were the names given to places. Pattinam and Nagar referred to big towns or places where rulers lived, with Pattinam referring to a coastal city.

Kaveri River

The river Kaveri was the main reason for the prosperity of the Chola land. Many stories are prevalent about the river. The epic

Manimekalai records these stories. Sivagnana, a monk, praises the Kaveri as a nurse tending to her people. As it showers gold on its people, it is also called Ponni. There are expansive groves on both sides, so it is called the Kaveri. Sekkizhar of the twelfth century common era refers to Kaveri as the flawless 'divine Ponni'. If a poet of a later time had such a great regard for it, it is no surprise that she is regarded as the nurse of the people of the Chola country. Every year, when new water flows into it, all the eighteen steps get immersed. People worship the river on that day. *Cilappatikaram* epic has many poems that describe Kaveri as a woman.

Towns

Kaveripoompattinam was a port city of the ancient Chola country. The ocean devoured the city during the time of *Manimekalai.* Now there is a village called Kaveripattinam in the same place. The village reminds us of the erstwhile city. The inscriptions found in the village prove that it was where the city of Kaveripoompattinam existed. Nagapattinam was also a port city. Uraiyur is a village now. It used to be a capital of the Cholas. Kumbakonam (Kudanthai) was one of the oldest cities of the Chola Empire.

Villages

The Chola Empire had many hamlets. Due to the richness of the Kaveri River, the hamlets were rice bowls. Lilies bloomed in the paddy fields. When they tried to boil sugarcane juice, the smoke dulled the flowers. Red rice variety grew so tall that buffaloes could hide inside the fields. Mango, plantain, jackfruit, coconut, and areca palms grew abundantly around villages. They gave amazing yields. Women wearing dazzling ornaments stood guard over the fields before the harvest. They chased away the birds that came to eat the paddy with their jewels. Children wearing anklets played games with toys. This description comes from *Pattinapalai*, an ancient Sangam poem about Kaveripoompattinam.

Chola Names

Many people have tried to find the meaning of Chola. *Neer Soozhntha Nadu*—meaning a country surrounded by water—may have been the origin of *Chola Nadu*. Just as *ulakkai* becomes *olakkai* in Tamil, *Soozha Nadu* may have changed to *Chola Nadu*.

Killi, Valavan, Chembiyan are the common names of Cholas. 'Killi' comes from a Tamil root word which means 'to till' and it refers to one who works on the land to bring prosperity. The name 'Valavan' represents someone belonging to a prosperous land. Chembiyan represents someone who has the legacy of Sibi Chakravarthy. Chenni is another name given to the Cholas. Chenni represents the best. The word was used to refer to the 'best kings' and rulers.

The Royal Emblem

The Cholas used the tiger emblem for the longest time. Their flags had the tiger on it. But the Chola land had no forests, where would the tiger have come from? It is possible that in ancient times, some old king of theirs may have hunted a tiger and used the emblem as a mark of honour. His successors may have retained the emblem in remembrance of his valour. The legacy of the emblem may have continued uninterrupted. Sangam books do not talk about the emblem. Cholas who ruled a part of the Telugu speaking country had the lion as their emblem during the medieval period.

Government

In ancient times, Chola Nadu existed as several independent kingdoms. Later during the reign of valiant kings like Karikala Chola, it got unified and the entire land came under a single ruler. The kingdom was handed down from father to son. If the son was weak, he was not allowed to ascend the throne.

Following the idea expressed in the *Tirukkural*, the unity between the people and the king was of paramount importance in the Chola Kingdom. For the government, land tax, customs duties, and the wealth of the countries conquered were the revenue sources. The government treasury was located in Kumbakonam. It had high security protection.

Advisory Council for the King

Two advisory councils supported the king. In one council, the minister, the priest, the commander, the ambassador, and the scout played key roles. It was called *Aymperunkuzhu* (the council of five people). The accountant, the lawyer, the wealth manager, the merchant, the city resident, the Commander-in-Chief, the elephant warrior, and the horse warrior formed the other council. It was called *Enperayam* or the council of eight people.

The village council played an active role in politics and got involved in the dispensation of justice. The *Akananuru* poem 46 talks about how the children of Malayaman were interrogated in the Uraiyur council. Poet Pothiyar is in tears as he looks at the Uraiyur Council, wherefrom Kopperumcholan presided over the kingdom. *Porunar Atruppadai* poems say that when scholars reached the council, public interest would be their sole focus. They would forget all their differences and only work for the common good at the Council. The kings governed by using this three-layered council. This consultative process is a legacy of the Chola dynasty.

Village Council

Sangam Tamils had village councils. The council discussed issues of public interest under the shade of a big tree. Along with discussions on village affairs, cultural performances were also held. Only during war times, the activities of these village assemblies were suspended. The Pallava inscriptions of the third century common era mention the governance of villages through these village councils. The elections to the village councils were also recorded.

Taxation

Taxes such as land tax, professional tax and customs duty were prevalent. The biggest chunk of revenue was from the land tax. Thiruvalluvar sang of the primacy of agriculture. Foreign trade thrived during the Sangam Age. The collection of custom duties was one of the preoccupations of the government staff during the Chola period. A vivid description of this can be found in *Pattinapalai*:

> In the broad road opposite the ocean, the staff of the king protect goods with utmost care. They collect custom duties daily. They work like horses without getting bored. Numerous goods reach the shore from the ocean daily. Goods get exported every day. On every package the tiger insignia is stamped before the goods reach the warehouses where they are securely stored.

This clearly shows that custom duties were an important part of the revenue system in the Chola kingdom.

The Prison

Manimekalai was imprisoned in Kaveripoompattinam. She converted the prison into a centre for education.

The Army

The Chola kings had a well-trained and disciplined army. It consisted of elephant corps, cavalry, chariot divisions and infantry. The army general was part of the *Enperayam* (council of eight commanders). The commander was part of the *Aymperunkuzhu* (council of five chiefs). The soldiers who proved their competence in combat were awarded a title called *Enathi* by the king. The awards included a golden garland and a ring. *Purananuru* poem 167 praises Enathi Thirukilli. *Purananuru* poem 394 recounts the work of Enathi Thirukuttuvan. Killi is the name of a Chola king.To have the name of the king was a tradition during the later Chola period. Enathi title was given by the Chola kings during the seventh, eighth and ninth centuries common era as attested in the *Periya Puranam.* For example, the verse in Sundarar's *Thiruthonda Thogai* from the ninth century; 'I am the devotee of those who serve Enathinathan, the great warrior.'

From the *Periya Puranam,* we also learn that providing military training was considered a noble profession as well. Inscriptions also indicate that the practice of giving the Enathi title persisted even during the later Chola rule.

When a Chola king set out for battle against an enemy kingdom, it was customary to dispatch three ceremonial symbols ahead of the army: the victorious sword (*vetri vaal*), the royal parasol (*kottra kudai*), and the war drum (*veera murasu*). These rituals were referred to as *Vaal Naadkol* (dispatch of the sword), *Kudai Naadkol* (dispatch of the parasol), and *Murasu Naadkol* (dispatch of the drum).

Before advancing on the enemy, the king, adorned with the *Vanchi* (a ceremonial garland), would distribute weapons and supplies to his soldiers and gifts to his retainers. After the campaign, he would host a grand feast for the army to celebrate their achievements.

Recognition

Just like the soldier was given the '*Enathi*' award, the minister, the accountant, and the farmer were awarded a title called '*Kavithi*'. The merchant was awarded a title called '*Etti*'. They were also given golden garlands as gifts.

Hero Stone

Laying a stone in memory of fallen soldiers was a tradition. It was a recognition of the sacrifices of the soldiers. It enthused the soldiers and inspired patriotism among the people. Many hero stones turned into temples over a period of time. *Tolkappiyam*, an ancient Tamil treatise on grammar, explains the practice of hero stones. It explains the selection, cleansing, marking, and the laying of the stone. *Cilappatikaram* details the process vividly. In *Vanji Kandam*, Senguttuvan lays a stone for a chaste woman. Laying a stone for a hero or a heroine was part of Tamil cultural tradition. Nine poems in *Purananuru* (221, 223, 232, 260, 264, 306, 314, 339, 335) sing of the hero stone tradition.

War

In ancient Tamil society, kings often personally took part in the battles. Before the start of the war, they would hold a grand feast for the soldiers. They would honour the soldiers and appreciate their work. On the battlefield, they encouraged the soldiers. If the king was hurt and down, the soldiers would end the war. The defeated king would fast unto death. For kings who died not on the battlefield but in other circumstances, their bodies were laid on kusha grass, and a ritual was performed where the body was symbolically slashed with a sword to mark them as having 'fallen in battle' before cremation. The belief was that by doing so, the king's spirit would attain the warrior's liberation (*veerar thurakkam*).

Women Poets

Sangam literature records about 700 poets and at least 44 of them are women. Avvaiyar, Aadhimandhiyar, Kakkai Padiniyar, Nachelliyar, Okkur Masathiyar, Velli Veethiyar, Vennikuyathiyar, Kuramagal Ilaveyini, Kuramagal Kuriyeyini, Kavarpendu, Kazharkeeran Eyitriyar, Kamakani Pasalaiyar, Nakkannaiyar, Nannakaiyar, Poongan Uthiraiyar, Ponmudiyar, Marokathu Nappasalaiyar, Ponthai Pasalaiyar, Allur Nanmullaiyar, Pari Magalir, Kannagi and the wife of Boothapandiyan are some of the significant women poets of the Sangam Age.

Marriage Customs

Sangam literature describes two types of marriages. One is an ancient system and the other one belongs to the *Cilappatikaram* period. In the earlier Tamil marriage tradition, the sequence included:

- Playing of musical instruments.
- Worship of deities.
- A ritual bath for the bride, performed by four women who were already mothers. Using water mixed with rice and flowers, they blessed the bride, saying, 'May you bear children like your mother before you.'
- On the same night, the couple would begin their married life.

- A wedding feast for all.

These ceremonies, described as having a beauty comparable to Lord Shiva's cosmic dance at Thiruvalangadu, are notable for their simplicity. In this marriage tradition:

- There was no ritual of tending a sacred fire (*erivalarttal*).
- There was no circumambulation of fire (*thee valam varuthal*).
- There was no priest (*purohita*) to officiate and receive dakshina.

Researcher PT Srinivasa Iyengar identifies this as the ancient Tamil marriage system.

Cilappatikaram was written in the second century common era. It describes the marriage between Kovalan and Kannagi in its first part. A unique feature in this account is that women rode on elephants to make a public announcement of the wedding in the city. This marriage also introduced some new elements:

- A Brahmin officiant (*mamutthu paarppaan*) guiding the rituals with Vedic chants.
- Circumambulation of a sacred fire.
- The setting up of a wedding pavilion (*palikai*).

After the wedding, the couple received blessings from the assembled guests. The gathering concluded with everyone offering their respects and blessings to the Chola king, as recorded in the *Cilappatikaram.*

Maritime Trade

Foreign trade thrived in Kaveripoompattinam. Foreign merchants lived in Poompuhar with their families. Gifts poured in. Pepper got exported. Gold, sandalwood and pearls were among the exported items. Food was imported from Sri Lanka and the Vijaya Empire (today's Indonesia).

The Chola Wisdom

The Chola Kings gave people of different faiths the opportunity to explain their religion in the presence of people. The *Manimekalai* epic records this in the Indra Festival section. People of several faiths coexisted peacefully in the Kanchipuram city under the Chola rule. In *Tirukkural*, Thiruvalluvar says that whatever you hear, no matter who says it, you should fact-check it. The Chola Empire lived up to the words of the sage-poet.

PART II

ONE

Dark Period of the Cholas

Pallavas-Kalapiras

At the end of the Sangam era, the land beyond Vengadam up to the River Ganges was ruled by the Andhra kings known as Satavahanas. The Pallavas governed the southern territories under their control. When the Satavahana Empire fell, the Pallavas took over the region extending from River Krishna to River Pennai and further attempted to annex the Aruva northern headland and Aruva regions to the south.

At that time, the Kalavas (Kalapiras), a rural group in Tamil Nadu with warrior-pastoralist ancestral traditions, lived in the forested areas of the Aruva northern headland up to Kadappa. The invading Pallavas oppressed the Kalavas. Unable to stay in their land, they left their country and entered the Aruva kingdom.

This confusion took place around CE 300. The Pallavas, who had driven out the Kalavas and conquered the Aruva northern headland, now drove them further down to the south of River Palar. Thus, around the early fourth century, the Pallavas ended up ruling the northern part of the Tondai Nadu (a historical region located in the northern part of Tamil Nadu and the southernmost part of Andhra Pradesh) with Kanchipuram as their capital.

The first Pallava emperor who ruled in this manner was Siva Skandavarman. (Refer Author's *Pallavar Varalaru* for more details)

Kalapiras-Cholas-Pandyas

Defeated by Siva Skandavarman, the Kalapiras, having no other choice, spread from the south of River Palar to River Kaveri; following which they invaded the interior part of the Chola Kingdom as well. Destabilised, the Chola government was taken over by the Kalapiras, who then went on to invade the Pandya Kingdom and made them flee.

Hence, it can be assumed that the Cholas and Pandyas lost their reign around CE 350–450. The Pandya Kingdom, which was thus defeated, regained stability in CE 590 under the Pandya king Kadungon. From then on, the mighty Pandya king grew powerful enough to oppose the Pallava emperor. Therefore, the Kalapiras, weakened in strength, became minor kings under the control of the Pandyas.

The Kalapiras ruled the Chola Kingdom until CE 575, after which they were completely defeated by a Pallava named Simha Vishnu. Having lost the Chola kingdom, they became minor kings in regions such as Tanjore, Vallam, Senthalai and Pudukkottai. They forged alliances with powerful forces and adapted to the changing times.

While the Pandyas were freed from the Kalapira rule by the sixth century, the Cholas had not yet been liberated. This was because the Pallavas, stronger than their contemporaries, had subdued the Kalapiras and occupied the kingdom. The Pallavas did not release their rule over the Chola kingdom until 875 CE. Therefore, it is important to note that the Cholas had to live without a crown and kingdom from approximately 350 CE onwards (Refer author's *History of the Pallavas* Chapter 4 for more information). Now, let us examine the available evidence and references about the Cholas during this dark period of their history.

Buddhadatta:

He was a Buddhist monk around 450 CE. He wrote the book *Abhidharmavatharam* while living in the Chola kingdom.

He writes,

> The city Poompuhar, by the river Kaveri, is full of rich merchants. Mansions filled; it has many pleasant meadows and palaces. I wrote this book in the Buddha Vihara (a Buddhist monastery wherein monks take shelter and practice religious learnings and meditation) built by Kandadasan at the request of my student Sumathi.

At the end of his work *Vinayavinichiyam* he states,

> This book was drawn up by Buddhist disciples. I wrote this while I was staying at the Venudasa Vihara at Buddhamangalam in the Chola kingdom. This Buddhamangalam is the Bodhi Mangai that's mentioned in the *Periya Puranam*; the place where Sambandar argued with Buddha and won. I wrote this book when Achutha Vikkandan, a Kalapira king, was ruling the world.

Kalapiras and Buddha

According to *Tamil Navalar Charithai*, the king of Kalapiras, Achuthan imprisoned the three Tamil crowned monarchs (*Muvendar*—Cheras, Cholas, Pandyas are collectively referred to as Muvendar). A tenth century CE Buddhist named Amitasagara has written a few songs about Achuthan. Since, Buddhadatta has written about him, its logical to assume that Achuthan may have been a Buddhist. As Buddhadatta says that he 'ruled the world', it can be assumed that Achuthan was the ruler of the Chola-Pandya kingdoms as well. Murthy Nayanar, the great legend mentioned in *Periya Puranam* belongs to his time. It seems likely that Achutha, being a Buddhist, was also a staunch adversary of Shaivism.

The *Velvikudi Pattayam* (the Velvikudi copper plates) states:

> The Kalapiras intervened... during that time, the emperors and Chakravartins (universal monarchs) disappeared... after which Kadungon drove away the Kalapiras and captured the Pandya kingdom.

The Kalapiras abolished the practice of *Brahmadeya* (tax-free land grants to Brahmins as a form of religious endowment). Kochadayan, a Pandya king, renewed this practice in the eighth century. Considering their actions, there can be no mistake in assuming that the Kalapiras were initially Buddhists and Jains.

During the *Manimekalai* period, Buddhamangalam in the Chola kingdom was regarded as a sacred place for Buddhists. But this place is also mentioned by Buddhadatta in the Kalapira period, indicating that Buddhists were present there around CE 660; note that they argued with Sambandar and lost. In CE 575, when the Pallavas, having oppressed the Kalapiras, ruled over the Chola kingdom, Buddhamangalam remained a Buddhist place well until Sambandar's time. Therefore, it is not wrong to assume that the Buddhamangala Vihara appeared during the Kalapira's time.

Kalapiras and the Jains:
In CE 470, the Digambara Jains met and established a Sangam in Madurai. According to the Jain text *Digambara Darisanam*, their leader at that time was Vachiranandhi. Kalapiras ruled the Pandya kingdom during this period. If the 'Digambara Sangam' was established in Madurai during their time and if these Digambara Jains influenced the Pandya king till the period of Sambandar (670 CE), does it not follow that the later Kalapira kings gave rise to it?

Therefore, it can be deduced that the early part of the Kalapira dynasty developed Buddhism and the latter part Jainism, and that during Sambandar's time, Buddhism existed in the Chola Kingdom and Jainism existed in the Pandya Kingdom.

Kalapiras:
References to Kalapiras are found in later Pallava charters such as those of Simha Vishnu, as well as in Western Chalukya inscriptions and others. Thus, it is clear that this new lineage once reigned over Tamil Nadu as emperors and minor kings.

Notes on the Cholas
The period between 300 CE and 875 CE was a dark period in the history of the Chola dynasty. Let us see what the inscriptions and literary sources spanning these six centuries reveal about the Cholas during this time.

400 CE TO 600 CE

Kochchenganan: Does he belong to the Sangam Period?
There are two reasons for believing that he belongs to the Sangam Period:

1. The footnote to the 74th verse of *Purappattu* states: 'Chera king Kanaikkal Irumporai, having fought a battle with Chola king Chenganan, was captured and imprisoned in the fort at Kudavayil. There, saying 'Give me water' and not receiving it, he turned over, took water himself with his hand, drank, spoke (a verse), and died. This is known as the *Thanneer Thaa* song.'
2. It is recorded at the end of the *Kalavazhi* palm-leaf manuscripts that Poigaiyar, by singing a Kalavazhi poem to the Chola king, secured the release of the imprisoned king.

Let us examine both these claims.

1. (1) The name Kochchenganan is not specified in the 74th verse. The footnote too was not written by the poet who composed it and this is understood from the phrase, 'the song of one who spoke and died without eating'. It is well known to scholars that the footnotes (written by poets from the later period) under the *Purananuru* verses are incorrect in many places. For example, in *Puram* verse 389, there occurs the phrase *ayudhangalai pola ni koduppayaka* (Give it like these are weapons), which was stated metaphorically.

   Without noticing this, the footnote says *adhanuṅganai padiya pattu* (This is a song sung by Aadhanungan) which is clearly a mistake. There are many such errors and incorrect footnotes; the one referring to Chenganan may be one such footnote.

   From these verses, it is seen that Kochchenganan was an emperor, one who slew valiant enemies and killed both the Kongu king and the Vanji king in battle.

   Thus, it becomes clear that the Vanji king (Chera king) who opposed this Chola was killed in battle. There is no mention anywhere in *Kalavazhi* of Kanaikkal Irumporai (the Chera king in question).

(2) The aforesaid verse 74 is found in the *Tamil Navalar Sarithai*, an anthology compiled in the seventeenth century presenting histories of poets and the verses they composed, under the title *Song written by Seraman Kanaikal Irumborai to Poigaiyar when he was beaten in battle by Chenganan*. What is the reason for the difference between this and the footnotes from *Purananuru*?

(3) Footnote to verse 74 indicates that Kanaikal Irumborai died in prison. However, in the *Tamil Navalar Sarithai*, it is indicated that 'Moved by the song Poigaiyar composed in *Kalavazhi Narpathu*, Chenganan frees him and grants him kingship.' Considering that both these statements differ from each other, novelist-Pandita NM Venkataswamy Naattar says, 'The one who died was Kanaikal Irumborai, while the one imprisoned and later granted kingship should be considered as a different Chera king.'

Thus, it is inappropriate to define the reign of an emperor like Kochchenganan with irrelevant footnotes that confound even scholars.

2. Thirumangai Alwar mentions that Kochchenganan built seventy Shiva temples. However, there is no evidence that any king built a Shiva temple or a Tirumal temple during the Sangam period. A time when a single king built numerous Shiva temples must have been one in which Shaivism was at its peak. There is no evidence to suggest that such sentiments were widespread during the Sangam period. It is known that many religions coexisted peacefully in the Tamil region during Sangam era. In such a peaceful state, a king building seventy temples would have been disastrous.

   After the Sangam period and before Appar, Buddhism and Jainism spread widely in the Tamil region due to the intervention of foreign rulers like the Kalapiras and Pallavas. The Velvikudi copper plates clearly indicate that religious persecution under the

Kalapiras posed a threat to the Brahminical land rights granted by the Pandya rulers of the Sangam period.

Murthy Nayanar was persecuted in Madurai during the reign of the Kalapiras. In the Chola kingdom, devotees of Shiva like Dandi Adigal and Nami Nandi Adigal had debates with the Jains. It must have been only in the later period, when religious disputes took place and the spirit of Shaivism emerged, that kings like Kochchenganan tried to promote Shaivism by building many temples.

3. The following are the remarks made by Thirumangai Alwar about Kochchenganan:

    (1) King of Kongu Nadu, the Chola of the South who ruled the world (Comparable to Sundarar's phrase *Thennavalai Ulakanda Chenganan*).
    (2) The southern Tamil *Vadapulakon.*
    (3) The Chola King with the divine sword, over whose royal crown a raven crawls.
    (4) Chenganan Kocholan, who mastered the art of kingship.
    (5) The Chariot expert, Kocholan, who was clothed by his general.

These references show that he was (1) a victorious king who slew many people in battle, (2) the conqueror of Kongu Nadu, (3) the victor of the land north of the Chola kingdom (Tondai Nadu), and (4) a ruler with a mighty elephant force and an excellent cavalry.

Being referred to as the *Kalal* king, the *Viral* king and the *Padai* King, it can be inferred that those who opposed him were powerful enemy kings. The crushing defeat of the enemies is evident as Chenganan triumphed over them with his 'divine sword'. If it is true that Chenganan fought with many kings during the Sangam period, then there should be some facts about it in the books of the time. If not, there should at least be some indication of their identity. Historians suggest that Kochchenganan belonged to a later period than Senguttuvan (200–250 CE). In that case, who were the 'Kalal-Viral-Padai' kings who fought with him at that time?

It can be inferred from *Manimekalai* that Tondai Nadu was under Chola rule during the Sangam period. Even if it is said that he won the northern territories beyond that, who was the enemy king?

In short, (1) Sangam texts do not prove that this king won over many enemies; (2) but references suggest that he fought and emerged victorious against many kings; (3) There is no evidence that there was such a king even in the late Sangam period; (4) He built many Shiva temples. Due to these four reasons, the idea that Kochchenganan may have belonged to the post-Sangam period holds strong.

4. According to Sekkizhar, Kochchenganan performed religious deeds in Thillai. It is worth noting that 'Thillai' is not mentioned in Sangam literature as a place of worship for Shiva. It gained importance during the period of Kochchenganan, who settled there till his death and built many mansions. Hence, it would not be wrong to say that 'Thillai' became an important centre of Shiva worship well after the Sangam period.

5. Kochchenganan's father's name was Subhadevan and his mother's name was Kamalavathi. These names should have been mentioned by the first minister of the Chola Empire, Sekkizhar, with proper evidence. These names are pure Sanskrit names. There is insufficient evidence to suggest that royal families of the Sangam period used

such names. Punitavati is the name of Karaikal Ammaiyar who is believed to have lived around sixth or fifth century CE, preceding the Sambandar period. This name Punitavati when compared with the above mentioned name Kamalavathi, has some similarities.

Due to these many reasons, it can be concluded that Kochchenganan does not belong to the Sangam Period. He has been praised by poets such as Appar and Sambandar. Therefore, his period must have been after the Sangam era but before the time of Appar and Sambandar, that is, his period was approximately between CE 300 and 600. Let us examine the most appropriate timeframe for his life within this span.

Kochchenganan Period

According to the Velvikkudi Charter, after the Sangam period, the Pandya kingdom was under the rule of the Kalapiras. It is evident that Kadungon took possession of his country from the Kalapiras. However, it is not known how long the Chola Kingdom remained under the Kalapira rule. Nor is it clear who ruled the Chola Kingdom after Achuthan, the Kalapira ruler mentioned by Buddhadatta in the early fifth century. By the mid-fifth century, a Pallava named Kumara Vishnu had recaptured Kanchi... According to the *Vellore Palaya Pattayam,* his son Buddhavarman was like the *Vadava* fire to the vast ocean- like Chola army. The first Nandi Varman, believed to have reigned in the early sixth century, issued a charter from Kanchipuram. Around CE 575, a Pallava ruler Simha Vishnu recaptured Kanchi. Both the Velvikkudi Charter and the Kasakudi Charter state that he defeated the Cholas, the Malavars, the Kalapiras and others, extending Pallava rule up to the banks of the River Kaveri. These references suggest that Kanchipuram was not under Pallava control after Kumara

Vishnu and before Simha Vishnu's reign, indicating that the city may have constantly changed hands. Furthermore, there is no evidence to suggest that Kalapiras ruled the Chola kingdom after Achutha Vikkandan until Simha Vishnu's conquest of the region. In light of these Pallava sources, it can be inferred that the predecessors of Simha Vishnu neither ruled the Tondai region continuously not maintained a permanent presence in Kanchi.

By the mid-fifth century BC, Buddhavarman became crucial in confronting the ocean-like Chola army; At the end of the 6th century, Simha Vishnu had conquered the Cholas. Considering Buddhavarman's wars, it can be concluded that after the period of Achutha Kalapiran (3rd century CE), the Cholas had an ocean-like army; they fought with the Pallavas. Thus the Chola, who kept an army like an ocean, namely Kocholan, can be traced back to the Sangam period. He was a king who defeated many; he had a large army of elephants and cavalry, as evidenced by both the battlefield and the hymns of Tirumangai Azhwar. It seems that the Chola king subdued the Kalapiras who had conquered his country and went on to fight and win against Buddhavarman in the northern field as well. Thirumangai Azhwar called him *Vadapulakkon* and this seems to be what he was referring to.

Thus it can be said that the period of Kochchenganan corresponds to the time of Buddhavarman, around the mid-fifth century. The period of *Kalavazhi*, which sings about Kochchenganan, is believed to be between CE 450–600. Rao Sahib S Vaiyapuri Pillai's opinion has also been considered here to support this conclusion.

Pugazh Chola Period

After considering many of the reasons mentioned above and taking a middle ground, we can conclude that this Kocholan is

Pugazh Chola (mentioned in the *Periya Puranam*), the one who lived in the medieval period and has been referred to above. Since his name is not in the Sangam texts and there could not have been such a Chola emperor in the Pallava period after Simha Vishnu, it is appropriate to describe this middle period as the period when the famous Pugazh Chola lived. Since a Kalapira emperor like Achutan and a Chola emperor like Kochchenganan Pugazh Cholan ruled the Chola land during the fifth and sixth centuries, the Pallavas could not conquer Chola Nadu!

If we consider Kochchenganan Pugazh Cholan and the Kalapira kings such as Kutruva Nayanar (Achuta Vikkandan?) as belonging to this transitional period (around 450–550 CE), then a part of what has been regarded as the 'dark age' in the history of South India may be seen in a new light. The view held by epigraphists like Venkaiah—that 'this dark period must have been the period when the Pallavas renounced Kanji and lived in the Telugu country, and the Cholas were in a phase of interruption'—is to a large extent validated by this.

From 600 to 850 CE

(1) The Pallava king Simha Vishnu (c. 575–675 CE) conquered the fertile Chola country nourished by the River Kaveri. In this campaign, he defeated the Kalapiras, Cholas, Pandyas, and other kings of the South, who opposed him, as recorded in the Vellore Palaiya copper-plate inscriptions. (2) An inscription of the Chalukyas also claims that they defeated the Cholas. They must have been the Renandu Cholas. (3) Mahendra Varman, the son of Simha Vishnu, inspired by the beauty of the Chola Kingdom built a cave temple for Shiva on the Tiruchirappalli hill, as per an inscription. That hill is described as the crown of the Chola country. (4) As per the Aihole inscription, Pulikesi II

allowed the Pallavas to enter the Kachi Nagar fortress, thereby benefiting the Cholas, Pandyas and Cheras. This event took place around 634 CE. 5) The inscription states that Mahendran's son Narasimha Varman I defeated many southern kings including the Cholas. (6) The Kooram inscriptions state that Paramesvara Varman I conquered the Chola country. (7) Paramesvara Varman was initially defeated by Vikramaditya I, who stayed at Uraiyur in Chola territory. Around this time, the 'Kathval' inscription was issued, dated 674 CE. In that inscription, Vikramaditya I claims to have defeated the Chola country. His son states that the Pallavas and Tamil kings attacked and defeated him. (8) The Udayendira inscription states that it was the Tamil king who besieged Nandi Varman II at Nandipuram. (9) His grandson, Nandi Varman III, defeated the Cholas and Pandyas at the Battle of Tellaru. (10) The Velvikkudi inscription states that the Pandya king Kochadaiyan Ranatheeran claimed to be a Chola and a Sembiyan. (11) In the Tiruchirappalli inscription, the first Varaguna Pandya (Maran Sadayan)—c. 765–816 CE—claims that he belongs to the lineage of the Chola–Pandya dynasty.

Renandu-Cholas

Copper plate inscriptions and a few stone inscriptions have been found that mention four kings who ruled the Kadappa-Kurnool regions in the seventh century CE. These rulers identified themselves as 'Renandu Cholas' and 'descendent of Karikalan'. In their territory, there were said to be 7,000 villages. Hyeon-sung, who visited this region in 639–640 CE, mentions in his notes that he saw the Chola country! However, it is not clear when the Cholas went to the northern region—Was it during Karikalan's time? Or did Simha Vishnu conquer the Chola Kingdom and send Chola descendants to administer the northern regions under his rule? Since Pulikesi claims to have conquered them, it is likely that the Cholas were subservient to the Pallavas, but still retained their own titles and authority. The lion was the royal emblem of these Cholas. The following is their genealogical line.

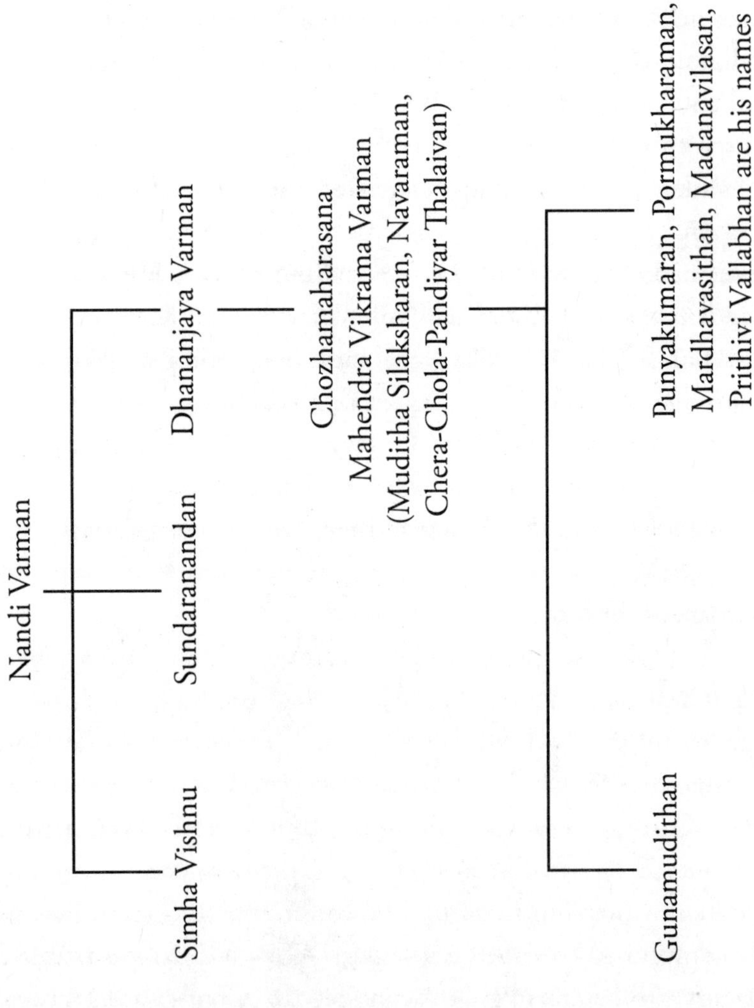

Many of these names are Pallava kings' names, aren't they? Nandi Varman refers to the first Nandi Varman. Simha Vishnu and Mahendra Varman are Pallava names. Hence, it seems that these Cholas adopted the names of their emperors! When Mahendra Vikrama Varman refers to himself as *Muthamil Vendan Thalaivan* (the Lord of three Tamil Kingdoms), it likely suggests that he had subdued the three Tamil Kings on behalf of the Pallavas. The last ruler, bore the name Punya Kumaran Prithivi Vallabhan, indicating a possible allegiance to the Chalukyas. His wife's name, 'Vasantha Pottri Chola Mahadevi' also reflects Chalukya connections.

Apart from the kings mentioned in this list, there was another ruler named Vikramaditya Satyaditya who bore the title *Chola Maharajadhiraja* (Great King of Kings of the Cholas). His wife was Ilanchozha Mahadevi. His status as an emperor is evident from his title. He ruled over the Renandu seven thousand along with the Siddhavur thousand.

In this way, many people in Telugu and Kannada regions also claimed to be descendants of Karikalan and governed those areas. Observing this, it is clear that the lineage of Sangam-era Cholas remained unbroken and continued to exist.

The Cholas and the Periya Puranam

References to the Cholas of this dark period can be found in notable works like the *Periya Puranam* and the *Thirumurai*. The *Tevaram* references, oral traditions passed down through generations in the Chola region, and the historical records that have survived from that era were utilised by Sekkizhar Peruman in composing the *Periya Puranam.* Thus, it is reasonable to classify the details in that text as belonging to this dark period without hesitation.

(1) Among the Kalapira rulers, one was Koottruva Nayanar, who preceded Appar. He conquered many regions and requested the Brahmins of Thillai to crown him. However, they refused, stating, 'We shall crown only the ancient Cholas, not newcomers.' Fearing his wrath, they fled to the Chera land.

(2) Around the sixth century CE, during the debates between Dandi Adigal Nayanar and the Jains in Thiruvarur, the arbitrator was the Chola king who resided there. Following Dandi Adigal's victory, the Jains, as per his words, were forced to leave Thiruvarur.

(3) Pazhayarai, located near Kumbakonam, had a Chola palace during Rajendra's reign. During Thirunavukkarasar's time, a Chola king ruled this city and had ministers. Upon learning of Thirunavukkarasar's fasting, he expelled the Jains and enabled him to find and worship the Shiva Lingam hidden by them.

(4) During Appar's era, Kungiliya Kalaya Nayanar visited Thiruppanandal. The Shiva Lingam there was leaning slightly to one side. Despite using elephants, the Chola king was unable to straighten it. Witnessing this, the saint himself attempted to straighten the Lingam and miraculously succeeded. The Chola king, impressed by his feat, revered and honoured him.

(5) It is most likely that the daughter of this Chola king was Mangaiyarkarasiyar, who became the wife of Nedumaran as this event is said to have occurred during Appar's era.

(6) Eyar Kon Kalikkama Nayanar was from Thirupperumangalam, located on the northern banks of the Kaveri River. He and his ancestors had served as military leaders under the Chola kings since ancient times. He lived during the time of Sundarar.

(7) During Sundarar's time, there lived a Velalar named Kodpuliar. He too was a commander in the Chola army. According to the *Periya Puranam*, he led a great army and went to war on behalf of his king.

(8) Sundarar, along with Cheraman Perumal Nayanar, went to meet the Pandya king. There, the king's son-in-law, a Chola prince was also present. The four of them visited several shrines together.

The Cholas and Vaishnava Literature

(1) Thondaradippodi Alvar was a contemporary of Thirumangai Alvar. He had once visited Uraiyur. According to the *Divya Suri Charitam*, Deva Devi said that she first saw him when she stepped out of the Chola palace in Uraiyur.

(2) Uraiyur Nachiyar, the daughter of the Chola king Dharma Varman, refused to marry anyone other than Thirumal (Lord Vishnu).

(3) Thirumangai is a prominent town in the Chola region. Thirumangai Alvar belonged to the Kallar clan. Initially, he served as a commander in the Chola army.

Conclusion

Based on records such as inscriptions, epigraphs, and literature, it is evident that the Cholas, during their period as minor rulers, built palaces in places like Uraiyur, Pazhayarai, and Thiruvarur. They engaged in excellent religious activities, had ministers and military commanders, and formed alliances with the Pandyas through marital ties. Despite their diminished power during this dark period, they continued temple-related works without fail.

TWO

Chola Uprising

Vijayalaya Chola–Aditya Chola (c. 850–907 CE)

The Battle of Tiruppurambiyam

Vijayalaya Chola ascended the throne of Uraiyur in 850 CE. Like his predecessors, he remained subordinate to the Pallavas. At that time, Nandi Varman III, the Pallava emperor, defeated the Pandya king Varaguna, who had gradually advanced up to the Tellaru region, and completely routed him. Vijayalaya or the Chola king who preceded him supported the Pandya in this war. Later a war took place between the Pallavas and Pandyas at Kudamooku (Modern Kumbakonam). In that battle, Srimaran Srivallavan, the son of Varaguna I, emerged victorious. Then Nandi Varman's son Nirupatunga Pallavan defeated Srimaran's forces on the banks of the Arisil River. After Srimaran, in 862 CE, his son Varaguna II launched an attack against the Pallavas. At that time, a Pallava named Aparajita Varman, along with his grandfather—the Ganga king Prithvipathi—waged a fierce war. In this war, Vijayalayan joined the Pallavas and fought on their side. The Mutharaiyars (descendants of Kalapiras) who ruled Tanjore supported the Pandyas. In this battle Prithvipathi lost; however, the Pandya king also suffered defeat and retreated. Aparajitan became the victor. So, Vijayalaya Chola, who had joined him, captured Tanjore from the Mutharaiyars. Aditya Chola, the son of Vijayalayan, who played a major role in the Battle of Tiruppurambiyam, became the ruler of a part of the Chola country. The Tiruppurambiyam battle took place around 880 CE.

The Significance of This War

This war brought about great changes in the history of Tamil Nadu. The Pandya nation that lost in this battle had no way to revive. Even before this, severe defeats at places like Tellaru and Arasilaru had already diminished the reputation of many Pandya rulers. All these combined to shatter the very lifeline of the Pandya Empire.

What was the condition of the Pallavas? Due to continuous wars with the Western Chalukyas and later with the Rashtrakoodas in the North and also due to unending wars in the south starting from the time of Varaguna I, and continuing for three generations, the Pallava Empire was in turmoil. The Rashtrakoodas conquered the northern part of the Pallava Empire and the southern region was conquered by Aditya Chola, who had recently risen to power.

Vijayalaya Chola (850–880 CE)

He was the founder of the later Chola Empire, which would go on to be regarded as one of the great empires of India. He defeated the Muttaraiyars and captured Thanjavur; the Thiruvalangadu copper plate inscriptions state that he built a temple for the goddess Durga there.

1. An inscription from Tiruchirappalli states that 'Vijayalayan granted a small village named Vijayalaya Chaturvedi Mangalam, bearing his name, as a Brahmadeya'.

2. A later inscription of Vikrama Chola reveals that there was an inscription from the fourth year of Vijayalaya Chola at Keelputtur, in North Arcot district.

From this it can be inferred that his rule may have extended into parts of Tondai Mandalam. However, this king was still subordinate to the Pallava ruler of the time. Even so, he had the right to mark his regnal years.

Aditya Chola (880–907 CE)

Since an inscription from his twenty fourth regnal year has been found, it can be said with certainty that he ruled for twenty-four years. He rose to prominence due to the previously mentioned battle of Tiruppurambiyam. The Thiruvalangadu copperplate states that 'He defeated Aparajita Varman in battle and captured Tondai country'. The Kanyakumari inscription says, 'Aditya Chola leapt upon Aparajita Varman who was seated on a big elephant, killed him, and earned the title Kothandaraman'. From these details, it is clear that Aditya Chola defeated Aparajita Varman and captured Tondai country. This event can be roughly dated around 890 CE.

Aditya and Ganga King

Prithivipati, the Ganga king, fought alongside Aditya Chola in the Battle of Tiruppurambiyam and died. His son, also named Prithivipati, acknowledged Aditya Chola's rise to power and became his friend. According to an inscription dated to the twenty fourth regnal year of Rajakesari Aditya Chola, he (the younger Prithivipati) gave a silver vessel to Thakola Peruman (a deity). In the inscription, Aditya Chola's supremacy is acknowledged.

Adityan and Pallavar

An inscription refers to Adityan's wife's mother as *Kaadupattigal.* So it is clear that Chola Mahadevi was a Pallava heir. Aditya Chola renewed the temple grants that had been made by the medieval Pallava king Kandasishya to the deity of Thirukazhakkundram. Adigal Kandan Marambavaiyar, the wife of Nandi Varman III, had previously made several grants to temples. She herself made a donation to the Pidari temple there during the eighteenth regnal year of Aditya Chola.

Aditya and Kongu Nadu

After Aditya Chola was crowned at Thanjavur, he went on to conquer Kongu Nadu and annexed it to his country. The book *Kongudesarasakal* states that he also captured the city of 'Thazhakadu'. Although copperplate inscriptions from the reign of Adityan's son, Paranthakan I, have been found in Kongu country, Paranthakan himself does not claim to have conquered the region in his inscriptions. This suggests that Adityan himself had already conquered Kongu country before his son's time. The Anbil plates which state that 'Adityan built Shiva temples all along the banks of Kaveri (from Sakasyama to the sea)' strengthens this assumption.

Aditya Chola and Cheran

The Chera king during the time of Adityan was Thanuravi. An inscription from Thiruneithaanam confirms that he was a friend of Adityan. The inscription states that 'Cheran and Adityan jointly granted the right to rule, along with privileges like a palanquin, palace, and elephant, to Vikki Annan, the husband of Kadamba Mahadevi,' and that he was also given the title 'Sembiyan Tamizhavel' (a prestigious Chola title). From this it can be inferred that this warrior must have performed some heroic deeds on behalf of both the Chera and Chola kings. It is also said by scholars that Parantaka I, Aditya's son, married a Chera princess, the daughter of Thanuravi, and that Thanuravi may be the same as Kokandan Ravi. It is likely that Vikki Annan, a commander of the Chera army captured the Kongu country from the Pandya king on behalf of the Chola King, and for this reason, both the Chola and Chera kings jointly honoured him.

Aditheswaram

Adityan died near Kalathi in Tondai Nadu. His son Paranthakan built a temple at the place where he died. It came to be known as 'Kothandarameswaram' and 'Aditheswaram'. He arranged to give alms to a thousand Brahmins at this temple during the festive season.

Religious Status of the Cholas

The Cholas were traditionally Shaivites over successive generations. The descendants of Vijayalayan also followed this religious path. Vijayalaya Chola built a temple for goddess Durga at Thanjavur. His son Adityan built many Shiva temples. His son, Paranthakan I, was an exemplary son who first built a temple for his father, showing his devotion and reverence. In later periods, the Chola kings actively supported and promoted Shaivism, guided by their religious leaders. As a result, Shaivism spread not only across Tamil Nadu but even up to the banks of the Godavari River, gaining widespread influence and prestige.

THREE

Paranthaka Chola I (c. 907–953 CE)

Paranthakan Family

Paranthaka Chola I, Aditya Chola's son is said to have had around twelve wives. Among them were Kokkilan Adigal, the Chera King's daughter, and others.

His children included (1) Raasadhithan (2) Kandaradhithan (3) Arikula Kesari (4) Uttamaseelan and (5) Arinjayan. His daughters included Veera Mahadevi and Anupama.

Veera Mahadevi was married to a minor king named Govinda Vallavarayan. Anupama was married to a Mutharaiyar chieftain of Kodumbalur. Rasadhithan's mother was Kokkilan Adigal; Arinjayan's mother was the daughter of the Chera King, and the prince named Arikula Kesari was married to Bhuthi Adichha Pidari, the daughter of the King of Kodumbalur.

Through these alliances, both the Chera King and the Mutharaiyars became reliable allies of Paranthakan.

Along with them, the Ganga king Prithvipati II, was also a close friend of Paranthakan. Paranthakan Chola bore the title of '*Parakesari*'.

The Pandya Country War

Paranthakan I had to fight against several powers—the Pandyas, the Eezhas (Sri Lankans), the Banars, the Vaithumbas, and finally, the Rashtrakoodar. Among these, the first major war was against the Pandyas. During Paranthakan's time, the Pandya country was ruled by Rajasimhan II. Paranthakan, with the desire to capture the Pandyan country, started a war. In this war, Paranthaka's friend Cheran, the Mutharaiyars and other minor kings helped him.

Rajasimhan II defeated the Tanjore king at Neyypur, fought a fierce battle in Kodumbalur and burnt down the city of Vanchi. According to a Rajasimhan copper plate, 'He defeated the king of South Tanjore at a place called Naval'.

It is understood that the Pandya War lasted for several years. Therefore, it is natural that both sides faced victories and failures.

It is worth noting that the references to this war in the Pandya's Chinnamanur charter, in the Ganga king's Udayendra charter, and in the historical chronicle of Mahavamsam, are almost the same.

In the first battle, Rajasimhan was defeated and lost control of Madurai. Paranthakan took possession of Madurai, adopting the title *Madurai-konda Kopparakesari* (Kopparakesari who seized Madurai).

Having lost Madurai, Rajasimha sought help from Kassapan V of Sri Lanka (who ruled c. 913–923 CE). The Sri Lankan king gathered a large army and sent it to the Pandyan country. With the support of this army, Rajasimhan once again opposed Paranthakan.

A fierce battle took place at Vellur. On the Chola side, the Paluvettaraiyars and a minor king named Kandan Amudanar joined the war effort. One division of the Chola army was commanded by Senni Perarayan. The Chola king defeated the army in a fierce battle. Just as Raghava (Rama) of old had defeated the Lankan armies, having similarly defeated the Lankan forces, he began calling himself '*Sangrama Raghava*'. Finally, the Lankan general, Chakka Senapati, gathered the rest of his army and prepared for a final battle. However, during that time, a deadly epidemic struck the army. Chakka Senapati died, and many soldiers perished. The surviving Lankan troops retreated to Eezham (Sri Lanka).

The battle of Vellur is estimated to have taken place around 915 CE. Due to severe defeat in this war, Rajasimhan fled to Sri Lanka. The entire Pandya country came under Chola rule.

The Pandya dynasty, established by Kadungon after defeating the Kalapiras in c. 575 CE, was destroyed by Parantaka Chola in c. 915 CE.

Eezham War

The king of Eezham honoured Rajasimha with a private residence. However, realising that it was futile to stay there, Rajasimha left his royal clothes, ornaments, and his crown in Lanka and went to the Chera country, his mother Vanavan Mahadevi's homeland. This is also confirmed by the Thiruvalangadu copperplate inscription.

Paranthaka Chola desired to crown himself in Madurai. He learned that the Pandya crown and other regalia were in Sri Lanka. Immediately he sent emissaries to the king of Lanka asking for them. But the Lankan king refused to give them.

Infuriated, Paranthakan sent a large army to Lanka. A fierce battle took place between the Lankan army and the Chola army. The Lankan commander died in the war. Immediately the Lankan King Udayan IV (c. 945–953 CE) retreated to the coastal city of Roganam. The Chola army followed him there; but not knowing how to enter the city, they became confused and, overtaken by fear, retreated.

War with the Banas

The land from Bunganur to Kalathi, north of the River Palar, was ruled by Banas for a long time. The land they ruled was known as Paanapadi or Perumpaanapadi. During the Pallava period, they were located near Anantapur. As the Chalukyas grew in strength, they were forced to come south.

Vijayaditya II ruled Paanapadi until around 909 CE. His grandson belonged to the period of the Rashtrakooda king, Krishna III. Between these two, Vikramaditya II and Vijayaditya III (Kandan the Praised) ruled.

The Ganga king Prithvipathi II was a friend of Paranthakan. At Paranthakan's command, he fought and defeated these two Panar kings. The Chola Singhapuram inscriptions state that Paranthakan conferred on him the title *Panathirasan* and left Paanapadi under his rule. The defeated Panar king surrendered to the Rashtrakooda king.

War with Vaithumbas

The Vaithumbas ruled over a region called 'Renandu Elayiram' 'Renandu' refers to the country including the districts of Kadappa and Kurnool. The Vaithumbas spoke Telugu. They maintained a friendship with the Banas. So they fought alongside the Banas against the Kangars and Tulambars. In AD 915 Paranthakan defeated the Vaithumbas and captured the country. So the king of Vaitumbas sought refuge with the Rashtrakooda king

War with Vengi Nadu

Vengi is the land between the Krishna and Godavari rivers. After the fall of the Pallavas, it extended to Nellore. Maran Parameswaran, one of Paranthakan's chieftains, defeated a person called Seetpuli, destroyed Nellore and returned. On his return, he donated land to the deity of Thiruvotriyur for his victory. The date of his donation was around CE 941. Seetpuli was the commander of the army under Eastern Chalukya king Bhima II.

Beginning of Troubles

The Ganga king, Prithivipathi II, died in CE 924. Since his son, Vicky Annan, had died earlier, he had no son to inherit the throne. At that time, the Rashtrakooda emperor Krishna III's brother-in-law, named Bhutuga II—who had married Krishna's sister Revaka —became the Ganga king without opposition. Thus, the newly ascended Ganga king being a relative of the Rashtrakoodas, along with the fact that the Banas and the Vaithumbas had aligned themselves with the Rashtrakoodas, became a hindrance to Paranthakan's empire.

Paranthakan's Precaution

Since Paranthakan was a skilled political strategist, he had made prior arrangements to protect his empire. In the region of Tirumunaippadi, located in the central part of the kingdom, at a place called 'Gramam' near Tirunavalur, Paranthaka's eldest son Rasaditha was stationed with a large army. That army was commanded by Vellankumaran, a commander from the Chera country. In CE 943, he built a temple for Shiva on the banks of the Pennai river. Tirunavalur came to be known as Rasadhithapuram. Rasadithan's younger brother Arikula Kesari also supported him. From this prior arrangement, it is evident that Paranthakan anticipated the trouble that could arise from the Banas and Vaithumbas.

Battle of Takkolam

A fierce battle took place in CE 949 between the Rashtrakooda king Krishna III and the Cholas. Before that, once Rasaditha had defeated Krishna. But the subsequent battle at Takkolam was intense. Takkolam is located about six miles southeast of Arakkonam. Rasaditha fought fiercely against the enemy. However, the new Ganga king Bhutuga II suddenly pounced on Rasaditha who was sitting on an elephant and killed him. Due to this, the Chola army lost the war. Krishna III honoured his brother-in-law by granting him Vanavasi 12000 and Belvolam 300. [sv1]

Due to this battle Paranthakan lost Panappadi, Tondai Nadu and Vaitumba Nadu which he had previously won. Inscriptions of Krishna are found in these places. Some charters state that Bhutugan II entered and caused destruction in Chola Nadu as well. It is evident from some charters that Krishna proclaimed himself as the one who 'conquered Kanchi and Tanjore'. Bhutugan claimed to have erected a victory pillar at Rameswaram. However, south of Puducherry, no inscription or charter of Bhutuga or Krishna has been found so far. Be that as it may, there is no doubt that the great empire built through the hard-fought wars of Adityan and Paranthakan had crumbled.

Award Names

Paranthakan bore many names. Since he destroyed Madurai, he was called Madhurantakan; since he conquered the Sinhalese country, he was called Singhalantakan. The Kanyakumari inscription states that he was known as Vira Chola because of his bravery against Krishna in the first battle. He also held titles such as *Cholakula Perumanar* (Lord of the Chola lineage), *Veera Narayanan* (Valiant Narayana), *Samara Kesari* (Lion of Battle), *Vikrama Singhalan* (Valiant Lion), *Kunjaramallan* (Wrestler of Elephants), *Chola Sikhamani* (Jewel among Cholas), *and Sura Sikhamani* (Jewel among Warriors).

Religious Activities

Paranthakan granted many villages like Veeranarayanapuram completely to Veda Scholars. He was a great devotee of Lord Shiva. The Leiden charter states that he covered the Puliyur Chitrambalam (temple) with gold. This is also supported by Vikram Chola's inscription as well. He ruled the country for forty-six years; he implemented several reforms in the Uthiramerur assembly. He was renowned for performing *yamagarbam* and *tulabaram*. The Thiruvalangadu copper plate refers to him as 'a beetle living in the lotus feet of Lord Shiva'. Many temples were constructed during his time; several temples left incomplete by Aditya Chola were completed during his time. His son Rasadithan built the Kotanda Rameswaram near Kalathi (Rasadithan's name was Kothandaraman) and Aditheswaram at Keezhaipakkam near Arakkonam. His wife's name was Irairavan Devi Ammanar. He constructed the Veeranarayana Lake (Veerana Airi–Veeranatham Eri) near Kattu Mannarkudi in his own name. He established Veera Narayanallur (Veeran Nallur) and Veera Narayana Chaturvedi Mangalam. He also built a temple for Alandeswar in Kattu Mannarkudi.

FOUR

Descendants of Paranthakan (CE 953–985)

Descendants of Paranthakan

By examining the Thiruvalangadu inscription, the Leiden Grant and other sources, it is clear that the descendants of Paranthakan held royal authority both during and after the reign of Paranthakan.

Kandaradhithan (949–957 CE)

Since Rasadhithan, who was earlier in line, passed away in the Battle of Thakkolam, Kandaradhithan ascended the throne after Paranthakan. He issued inscriptions under his name even while his father was alive. He bore the title Rajakesari. He married Sembiyan Mahadevi, the daughter of Mazhavaraiyan, and had a son named Uttama Chola (Madhurantakan).

He established a town named 'Kandaradhitha Chaturvedi Mangalam' on the northern bank of the Kaveri and passed away. His idol can be seen in the temple at Konerirajapuram. He had another wife named Veera Narayani. This Chola king attempted to reclaim the Tondai country from the Rashtrakooda king and seemingly achieved some success.

Kandaradhithan was a great devotee of Shiva. He is likely the one who composed hymns in Thiruvisaippa, praising Chidambaram. In that Thiruvisaippa, it is mentioned that Paranthakan conquered the Pandya kingdom and Sri Lanka, and gilded the Perambalam with gold. In the same work, Kandaradhithan refers to himself as *Koyil Vendan* (King of Uraiyur) and *Tanjai Koon* (Thanjavur King). An inscription designates him as the deity who emerged from the West. He established a village named Kandaradhitha Chaturvedi Mangalam on the northern bank of the Kollidam River, to the west of the sacred site of Tirumazhapadi.

His wife, Sembiyan Mahadevi, was an ardent follower of Shaivism. She lived even during Rajarajan's reign and was praised by many, including her husband, son, daughter-in-law and notable figures like Sundara Chola. She transformed many temples that had received the Tevaram hymns into stone temples; donated garments, silver vessels and ornaments to several temples; and granted lands as endowments to various temples. The temple renovations and services she undertook were numerous.

Arinjayan (956 to 957 CE)

He was the younger brother of Kandaradhithan. Since Kandaradhithan's son, Mathurantakan was still a child at the time, Arinjayan ascended the throne. However, he had a very short reign and passed away soon after. He held the title *Parakesari*. He had several wives, among whom Viman Kundaviyar and Kodhai Pirattiyar lived for a long time and undertook many religious works. There are differing accounts regarding Viman Kundaviyar's lineage; some suggest she was the daughter of a Chalukya king Viman, while others assert she was the offspring of a minor king named Arayan Adityan Viman. Arinjayan died at a place called Aroor, near Melpadi. An inscription indicates that Rajaraja I, his grandson built a *pallipadai* (memorial temple) at that spot to honour his ancestors. It is believed that Arinjayan died in the attempt to reconquer Tondai Nadu, having engaged in a battle during the campaign. The Thiruvalangadu inscription describes him as 'one who was like fire to his enemies (forest of foes)' making it clear that he was a vicious warrior. He ruled for only one year before he passed away.

Paranthakan II (c. 956–973 CE)

He was the son of Arinjayan, born to Kalyani, the daughter of the Vaithumba Chief. He bore the title of Rajakesari, and was known as *Madurai-konda Rajakesari* (Rajakesari who conquered Madurai). As soon as he ascended the throne, he confronted Veerapandiyan, who was ruling the Pandyan territory independently. A fierce battle took place at Sevur. The river ran red like blood; many elephants perished. Adityan II, Paranthakan's son, though a boy at the time, participated in the battle. The Leiden inscription, states that he 'played with Veerapandiyan', indicating his boldness in the battle; while the Thiruvalangadu inscription calls him, 'Adityan who took the head of Veerapandiyan', thus crediting him with Veerapandiyan's death.

After the Sevur battle, a minor king from Kodumbalur named Paranthaka Siriya Velar, allied with the Cholas, marched into the Pandyan territory, and chased Veerapandiyan into the forest. He also held off the Lankan troops supporting Veerapandiyan, and then proceeded to Lanka, where he fought a fierce battle and died on the battlefield in 959 CE.

Several individuals supported Aditya Karikalan against Veerapandiyan. Among them was the previously mentioned Velar. Another was a minor king of Kodumbalur named Poothy

Vikrama Kesari. He had two wives Katrali Pirattiyar and Varaguna Perumanar. An inscription says that the latter was a sibling of the Chola king (possibly Adityan II). Since the names Paranthakan and Adityan appear in the names of both his sons, it becomes as clear as a gooseberry in one's palm (i.e. absolutely clear) that the Chola kings both gave and took brides from the Kodumbalur regional rulers.

An inscription credits Vikrama Kesari with defeating the Pallava—though some scholars suggest the word 'Pallava' might be a scribal error for 'Vallabha' of the Rashtrakooda dynasty. Paranthakan II like his father and grandfather, sought to capture Tondai Nadu with Vikrama Kesari likely participating in this endeavour as well. The fact that inscriptions of Parantaka II and Aditya Karikalan are found in abundance in Tondai Nadu, while those of Rashtrakooda king Krishna III are fewer in number, suggests that Tondai Mandalam, which had been lost during the later years of Parantaka I, was gradually reclaimed by his successors.

Paranthakan II passed away in his palace at Kanchipuram, earning him the title *Ponmaaligai Thunjiya Thevar* (the Lord who passed away in the Golden Palace) signifying that during his rule, Tondai Nadu was once again under Chola dominion.

Among the wives of Paranthakan II, two are particularly notable: one is Vanavan Mahadeviyar, the daughter of Malayaman, she climbed her husband's funeral pyre and performed sati. The Thirukovalur inscription of Rajaraja I indicates that he was a child at the time of his father's (Paranthaka II's) death.

The other one is Cheran Mahadevi. Vanavan Mahadevi's children included Aditya Karikalan, Rajarajan, and Kundavai. It was during this king's period that a scholar named Puthamithiran authored the grammatical work *Veerasozhiyam*. Kundavai later installed idols of her parents in the Periya Kovil (Brihadeeswarar temple) at Thanjavur.

Aditya Karikalan (956 to 969 CE)

He did not officially ascend the throne but he assisted his father in governance. Numerous inscriptions were issued in his name. Even while his father Paranthakan II was still alive, Karikalan was murdered.

What was the reason behind his murder? Since Uttama Chola (also known as Madurantakan), son of Kandaradhithan, had not reached an appropriate age at the time of his father's death, his uncle Arinjayan ruled the kingdom briefly. After him, his son Paranthakan II became the king. Following him, the rightful heir was the valiant Aditya Karikalan. However, if Aditya were to be crowned, Madurantakan—Aditya's uncle—would never have the chance to become king in his lifetime. Aware of this, Madurantakan, it is believed, orchestrated a plot to have Aditya Karikalan assassinated. The Chola nobles urged Arulmozhi Varman (Rajaraja) to claim the title, but he declined, aware of Madhurantakan's ambitions. Instead, he accepted the role of crown prince and helped administer the country. Only after Madhurantakan's reign ended did Rajaraja become the king as per the agreement made between them.

Uttama Chola (969 to 986 CE)

He was the son of Kandaradhithan. Even before he ascended the throne, the entire Tondai Mandalam region, extending up to Kanchi, was already under Chola dominion. The abundance of inscriptions attributed to Aditya Karikalan found in places such as Uttaramerur, Kanchipuram, Thakolam, and Thiruvanamalai, focusing on land transactions, charitable acts, temple constructions, and political affairs, suggest a period of stability in Tondai Nadu during Adityan's rule. Numerous inscriptions and a collection of copper plates from Uttama Chola's era have been discovered. He bore the royal title *Parakesari*. Many inscriptions mention only the title Parakesari without specifying the ruler's name, and some scholars infer from supporting evidence that such inscriptions belong to his reign. Chola coins from this period are considered among the oldest. A gold coin attributed to his reign was discovered. It bears identical imagery on both sides: a tiger seated and facing a fish on the right. The name 'Uttama Chola' is inscribed in Grantha script around the coin. According to numismatist Elliott, this gold coin weighs between 40 and 60 *kunrimani* (traditional weight units).

Politics

The inscriptions from Uttama Chola's reign provide valuable insights into the political landscape of his time. During his reign, a high ranking official named Ambalavan Pazhuvur Nakkan played a key role in Chola administration. He hailed from Kuvalalam (Kolar). He undertook the renovation of the ancient temple at Visaya Mangalam, a village on the banks of the Kollidam River, which had been praised in the hymns of the saint Appar. In recognition of his contributions, Uttama Chola conferred upon him the title *Vikram Chola Marayar*, which subsequently led to Uttama Chola being referred to as 'Vikram Chola'. During the reign of Rajaraja, this same official was also known as *Mummudi Chola Marayar* and *Rajaraja Pallavarayan*.

Uttama Chola's Family

Uttama Chola had several wives. Among those, worth mentioning are Arul-pattan Thana Thongi, Mazhapadi

Thennavan Mahadeviyar, Vanavan Mahadeviyar, the daughter of Vizhupparayan, and the daughter of Pazhuvettaraiyar. An inscription states that all of them jointly donated money to the temple priestess in Sembiyan Mahadevi village for conducting the birthday worship (puja) of their mother-in-law, Sembiyan Mahadevi.

The chief queen was named Uraththayan Sorappaiyar (a Kannada name). She was also known as Akka Mahadeviar and respectfully referred to as 'Mootha Nam Pirattiyar' (Our elder lady/princess). She bore the title 'Tribhuvana Mahadeviar' as well.

All of Uttama Chola's wives made various donations to the Shiva temple located in the village named after their mother-in-law—Sembiyan Mahadevi—situated in the Thanjavur region. This clearly shows the great affection and reverence this royal family held toward Sembiyan Mahadevi.

It is not known exactly how many children Uttama Chola had. However, inscriptions mention one son by the name of Madurantakan Kandaradithar, who was responsible for overseeing temple affairs during the reign of Rajaraja Chola.

All the kings discussed so far ruled only for a brief period and passed away quickly. Yet, it was through their significant efforts that the Tondai Mandalam (northern Tamil region) was reclaimed and brought back under Chola control. However, the Pandya country was not yet annexed into the Chola empire. It was Rajaraja Chola I, who succeeded them, that expanded the Chola kingdom and firmly established the Chola Empire as a major power.

FIVE

Rajaraja I (985–1014 CE)

Birth Date of Rajaraja I

Rajaraja Chola I, was born to Sundara Chola (Paranthakan II) and Vanavan Mahadevi. He ascended the throne on June 25, 985 CE.

In the inscription at Rajarajeswaram Temple (Brihadeeswarar Temple) in Thanjavur, there is a reference to a festival called *Udayar Rajaraja Devar Thiruchathaya Thiruvizha*. Similarly, in the inscription at Thiruvaiyaru Ulaga Mahadevi Eswaram Temple, there is a reference to a festival called *Udayar Thingal Sathaya Vizha*. At Thiruvotriyur Varaha Perumal Temple in Chengalpattu, an inscription mentions that every year, starting from the Sadaya Nakshatra (star) in the Tamil month of Avani, a festival called *Rajarajan Thiruvizha* was celebrated for seven days. These inscriptions make it clear that Sadaya Nakshatra was regarded as his birth star.

An inscription at a Sivan temple in Thirunandikarai of the Chera country mentions that Rajaraja donated the village of 'Muttam' to conduct a festival on his birthday, confirming that he was born on the Sadaya star day of the *Aippasi* month. This event is beautifully detailed in the Thiruvalangadu inscriptions.

His Greatness

Among the Cholas who followed Vijayalaya, Rajaraja was the one who firmly established and strengthened the Chola empire. The empire he built lasted for nearly two centuries, a testament to the solid foundation he laid. Rajaraja, having learned about governance under his father and uncle, planned his strategies well in advance. After ascending the throne, he implemented them with precision, achieving significant success. One of his notable achievements during his reign was making his son Rajendra a great warrior, which eventually led to the conquest of Kedah through naval expeditions. Rajaraja's reign is often considered the golden age of Chola history, as art, sculpture, drama, music, and literature flourished. The spread of the Shaivism also reached its peak during his rule.

Chola Empire

Rajaraja was the one who assembled a mighty army to build the Chola Empire. His military forces achieved all of their objectives without any hindrance. He was also the architect of a strong political system. The advanced governance structure during his time was very similar to modern-day systems. The Chola kingdom, which had been affected by attacks from the Rashtrakoodas, expanded under Rajaraja's rule, stretching from the Krishna River in the north to Sri Lanka in the south and to the Arabian Sea in the west.

His Military Skill

Rajaraja's military skills deserve high praise. His divine presence was his greatest asset. Statues of Rajaraja and Queen Koperundevi, are enshrined in the Thiruvaisalur temple. Rajaraja was an expert in military affairs, highly knowledgeable in governance, and deeply devoted to Shaivism. He has left an indelible mark on Chola history, which has been well recorded thanks to him.

His Historical Records

Before Rajaraja Chola, there were many inscriptions of many rulers. In those only the royal lineage and a few qualities of the king would be briefly stated. But Rajaraja completely changed this approach. In the inscriptions issued during his reign, he systematically recorded the military campaigns and events of his rule in chronological order. His first victory at Kandalur Salai is the first one mentioned in his inscriptions. Each subsequent victory was mentioned in this manner. Thus, Rajaraja's rule and the victories won during his reign have been meticulously chronicled in inscriptions, providing a clear picture of his achievements.

Rajaraja was also the one who had a preamble for inscriptions or copper plates. This introduction made it easy to identify the record as belonging to him. It begins with the poetic phrase: 'Like the Goddess of Fortune herself...'

His heroic son, Rajendra, used a different introduction in his own inscriptions and copper plates. Likewise, future rulers followed their own variations of this tradition

Surrounding Regions

During Rajaraja's reign, the Chola Empire extended from Tondai Mandalam in the north to the northern border of the Pandya country in the south. To the north, the Eastern Chalukyas ruled as far as Nellore, while the Pandya kingdom remained independent in the south. To the west, existed the Chera country, Ganga country, Kodagu, and other minor kingdoms. To the northwest, the Western Chalukyas, who had overthrown the Rashtrakoodas, established a new empire at Rattapadi and ruled from there. In

Sri Lanka, Mahinda V was the reigning monarch.

War with the Cheras and Pandyas

Rajaraja ascended the throne in 985 CE and led a military campaign against the Cheras in 989 CE, defeating the Chera king Baskara Ravi Varman. The leader of Rajaraja's military expedition was Rajendra Chola, also known as Panchavan Marayan.

Victory at Kandalur

Rajaraja destroyed the Chera naval fleet at Kandalur in 989 CE. However, since Rajaraja's inscriptions begin appearing in Chera and Pandya countries from 993 CE onward, it is evident that it took around four years to conquer these two kingdoms, establish Chola rule, and bring about political stability in the region.

War in the Kudamalai Region

The Kudamalai region, including Udhagai, was invaded by Rajaraja's forces. He captured this area around 1008 CE.

Kollam and Western Coastal Regions

After successfully conquering Kollam and the western coastal regions, and bringing these territories under his control, Rajaraja earned the title 'Keerthi Parakram Chola'.

Gangapadi

Gangapadi refers to a large region of present-day Mysore. Its capital was Talakad. Its rulers stood against the Chola Empire, having ruled Gangapadi for several centuries dating back to the Pallava period. Rajaraja first captured Tadigaipadi and later conquered the entire Gangapadi region.

Nolambapadi

Nolambapadi comprised territories in present-day Tumkur, Sira, Chitaldurg, and districts like Bangalore, Kolar, and Bellary all part of Mysore region. It was ruled by the Nolamba Pallavas. During Rajaraja's reign, this territory was incorporated into the Chola Empire.

Telugu Region

To the north of Tondai Mandalam, the rule of the Eastern Chalukyas extended up to Nellore. Rajaraja sent Paraman Malapadiyar from Karugudi with a large army to capture King Bhima. He successfully brought the regions of Sittpulinadu and Baginadu into the Chola Empire.

Eastern Chalukya Region

During Rajaraja's reign, the Eastern Chalukya kingdom was in turmoil. King Sakti Varman was driven out by another faction of the kingdom claiming kingship. He sought refuge with the Chola Empire. In 999 CE, Rajaraja captured Vengi and reinstated Sakti Varman as king. He also gave his daughter Kundavai in marriage to Vimaladitya, who was Sakti Varman's relative. Through these two acts, the Eastern Chalukya country became an integral part of the Chola Empire.

Kalinga Region

Rajaraja's conquest of Kalinga is mentioned on two inscriptions found on the Mahendra Hills. In those, it is inscribed that Rajendra defeated Vimaladitya, the king of Kuluta Nadu, and erected a victory pillar on the peak of Mahendra Hill. Some have mistakenly identified the Vimaladitya mentioned here as the same Eastern Chalukya Vimaladitya mentioned earlier.

Eezham (Sri Lanka) Region

According to inscriptions dating from 993 CE, Rajaraja conquered the Eezham region (Sri Lanka) and renamed it *Mummudi Chola Mandalam* (the region of the three-crowned Chola). During this campaign, Polonnaruwa was made the Chola capital, which was renamed as Jananatha Mangalam. Here he built a new Shiva temple.

Western Chalukyas

The Western Chalukyas regained control of the region called Rattapadi in 975 CE from the Rashtrakoodas. After 992 CE, Satyashrayan, a Chalukya ruler, fought against Rajaraja but was defeated by the Cholas.

Maldives Conquest

Rajaraja deployed a large naval fleet to conquer the Maldives (Pazhantheevu Pannirayiram). As a result, he earned the title *Seyankonda Chola*. Following this, the Tondai Mandalam region came to be known as *Seyankonda Chola Mandalam*.

Minor Kings

Kandan Maravan of the Pazhuvettaraiyar dynasty was a minor king. Rajaraja brought him under his rule. Kandan Maravan built a temple for Thiruthottam Udaiyar in Melapazhuvur.

In the Kadappa region, a man named Nanamarayar, the son of Vaithumbarayan Thukkarai, made donations to the temple at Thiruvallam (in North Arcot).

In 993 CE, a king named Mummudi Vaithumba Maharasan made donations to a temple at Rettipaanayam.

A minor king, Kalukkiviman, and his wife Veemayan Vambavai donated lamps and materials to the temple at

Thiruvaiyaru. It is unclear which specific region this minor king ruled. However, many such minor kings existed within the Chola Empire.

A king named Maravan Narasimha Varman, from the Bana dynasty, ruled near a place called 'Sambai' in the South Arcot district. He excavated a lake in that area.

Administrative Officials

Among the notable administrative officials mentioned in inscriptions, one is Maha Dandanayaka Pinjavan Marayan. Some researchers say he was Rajaraja's son, Rajendra, while others disagree. Another important official was Kandaradhithan, the son of Uttama Chola (Mathurantakan), who was in charge of overseeing temple constructions across the kingdom. Some mistakenly believe he was the Kandaradhithan mentioned in the Thiruvisaippa hymns. Paraman Malapadiyar, known as the *Mummudi Chola*, was a military commander who conquered the regions of Sittpulinadu and Baginadu.

Another notable commander was Senathipathi Sri Krishnan Raman, who was from Amangudi. He was responsible for constructing the circumambulatory corridor and the mandapam in the Brihadeeswara Temple.

Senathipathi Kuravan Ulakalanthan bore the title *Rajaraja Maharajan*. He played a critical role as a tax assessor across the Chola Empire, ensuring taxes were collected and managed efficiently.

Ulakalavitta Thiruvadigal Saathan, another official, was also engaged in this task. Eerayiravan Pallavaraiyan, another *Mummudi Chola*, was an important officer responsible for political revenue collection. Thiruvaiyan Sankaradevan, a descendant of the Ganga dynasty who ruled Kolar, was another high-ranking official. He built the 'Thiruvai Easwaram' temple in Thiruvallam in honour of his father.

Among these were officials like Krishnan Raman, Eerayiravan, Paruthikkudaiyan Velan, Uttama Chola, and Mathuranthaka Muvendha Velan, who are said to have served as ministers. Other key officials included Rajendra Singa Muvendha Velar, and the custodian of the Kanchi Gate, Udhayadhivakaran Rajaraja Muvendha Velar, who served alongside senior administrators.

According to the Anai Mangalam inscription, officials responsible for political administration included Parakrama Chola Muventha Velan of Aruran Aravanaiyan, Tathan Senthan's son Sembiyan Muventha Velan, and Meenavan Muventha Velan, along with other prominent figures like Arunkundram.

Various officials under Rajaraja's rule included tax officers responsible for calculating and recording taxes, budget planners who allocated expenditures, scribes who documented orders, and dispatch officers who reviewed incoming orders and issued responses. There were also officials in charge of dividing and monitoring regions, assessing benefits and harms, overseeing courts, and currency officers. These positions were documented in numerous inscriptions.

It has also been recorded that the ancient Pandiyan country inscriptions, originally in old scripts (*Vatteluttu*), were rewritten in modern Tamil during Rajaraja's reign. His political system was as advanced and organised as modern governance systems. He conducted surveys across the entire country, dividing tax-exempt lands and arranging for taxes to be levied based on the productivity of different land types. To ensure proper tax collection, he appointed several officials. A high-level administrative council was established to oversee all categories of taxes. There were separate officials for each district and some overseeing all districts. The political system was incredibly well-structured and organised.

The local councils managed the village administration efficiently. Well-trained armies were stationed in each district, with border areas protected by military forces. The famed navy was unparalleled in its might. In summary, Rajaraja can be rightfully considered one of the greatest emperors who established a vast empire in South India.

Religious Policy

Rajaraja was a devout follower of Lord Shiva, and the *Periya Kovil* (big temple known as the Brihadeeswara Temple) he built stands as testimony to his devotion. However, like other great emperors of India, he respected and treated all religions within his vast empire equally.

The sculptures on the big temple walls and the Vishnu temples he built in Mysore, along with the donations he made to these Vishnu temples, show his inclusive and harmonious mind-set. He also contributed resources to construct a Buddhist Vihara in Nagapattinam, demonstrating his support for diverse faiths.

During his reign, some subordinate kings contributed to Jain temples. This clearly indicates that Rajaraja allowed his subjects and subordinate kings the freedom to follow the religion of their choice.

During his reign, many temples became centres of learning, and several new Shiva temples were constructed. Many temples received support from various patrons, and temple activities flourished greatly.

The Big Temple

The Brihadeeswara Temple in Thanjavur stands as a grand testament to Chola rule and showcases the artistic and architectural brilliance of Tamil Nadu. Rajaraja Chola was the one who first envisioned and completed the construction of such a grand temple with a unique design.

The temple's main tower is small, but the dome built above the sanctum is quite large. The dimensions and architecture of the temple are proportionate and harmonious. This temple is officially known as Rajarajeswaram, and from this, it is inferred that the king was called Rajaraja.

In 1004 CE, Rajaraja made several donations to the Thillai Chidambaram temple, and as a result, the temple priests conferred on him the title 'Rajaraja'. This name can be found in inscriptions from his nineteenth year of reign.

Therefore, it is believed that the construction of the big temple began in 1005 CE. Several donations were made for this temple from his twenty-third to his twenty-ninth year of reign. Thus, it is likely that the Big Temple was built between his twentieth and twenty-third years of reign, taking approximately four years to complete.

An inscription from his twenty-fifth regnal year reads, 'On the 275th day of the twenty-fifth year of the reign of Rajaraja Devar, lord of Rajarajeswaram, a copper pot was placed atop the Vimanam as a finial. The pot weighed 3083 palams, and was crafted using 2926 kalanju of refined gold, as measured and certified by the goldsmith Adavallan.' This indicates that the main activities related to the temple were completed by his 25th year of reign.

Temple Structure

This temple is located within the small fort of Sivagangai. After the first tower, there is another grand tower built by Rajaraja.

Upon entering, there is a vast outer platform approximately 500 feet long and 250 feet wide, paved with black stone and red bricks. On it stands a massive single stone Nandi, along with a pavilion built to protect it.

Opposite the Nandi is the main temple tower, and next to it is the Goddess's shrine. The temple complex consists of six sections—the inner sanctum, the artha mandapam, the maha mandapam, the sabha mandapam for Tyagaraja, the dancing hall, and the music hall.

The temple has seven entrances, each with guardian statues (*Dwarapalakas*) standing seven meters high and three meters wide. The first entrance is known as the *Keralanthagan Thiruvayil*, while the second is referred to as the *Rajaraja Thiruvaasal*. The temple's inner entrance is called the *Thiru Anukkan Thiruvaasal*.

There are additional entrances on the south and north sides of the tower, each with stairways. The southern entrance is known as the *Vikraman Thiruvaasal*, presumably named after Vikrama Chola in later times.

Below the southern entrance is a sculpture of Goddess Lakshmi, and under the northern entrance is the figure of Goddess Saraswati, both appearing with grace and beauty. In earlier times, it was customary to ascend the steps on either side of the Thiru Anukkan Thiruvaasal to reach the inner sanctum. These features were integral to the temple's construction. Therefore, due to its elevated position above the surrounding land and its design, this temple can be classified as a true *Maadakkovil* (raised temple).

The straight steps now found directly in front of the Thiru Anukkan Thiruvaasal were likely added in later times during the reign of King Sarabhoji.

The temple's length is 265 meters, and its width is 132 meters.

Siva Lingam

The Siva Lingam in the sanctum is enormous. When the base of the lingam was being anointed with sacred medicinal paste and bound using the traditional method of Adi Saivars, the procedure could not be completed properly because the base *(Avudaiyar)* was so large that the paste melted and the binding didn't hold. Rajaraja was concerned about this situation. To alleviate his worries, the Saiva sage Karuvur Thevar appeared and successfully completed the binding by perfectly aligning the lingam with its base. This incident is narrated in the Karuvur Puranam.

Karuvur Thevar also composed a hymn (*pathigam*) in praise of Rajarajendran of Thanjavur, which has been included in the ninth *Thirumurai* (a sacred Tamil Saiva canonical text).

It is believed that the great sage attained samadhi within this temple. In the western Thiruchutru (circumambulatory path) of Rajarajeswaram, there is an east-facing platform, near which stand a neem tree and a vilva tree. Later generations built a small shrine on this platform, housing a statue of a yogi. Even today, this shrine continues to be a place of worship for many devotees.

Tower Gateways

This grand temple features three gateways in accordance with ancient customs. According to the *Periya Puranam,* the three gateways in temples were named as Thoranam Vayil (ornamental gateway), Thirumaligai Vayil (palatial gateway), and Thiru Anukkan Vayil (Anukkan's sacred gateway). However, Rajaraja renamed these gates as Keralanthagan, Rajarajan, and Anukkan Thiruvayil respectively.

Tower–Base–Finial Pot

The temple's tower stands 75 meters tall; it has a wide base and gradually tapers to the top. At the summit, lies a platform made from a single block of black granite, weighing 80 tons. Placed on top of this platform, on the finial tier of the vimana, is a copper pot (cheppukudam) that weighs 3083 palams. Covering this copper pot is a gold plate, weighing 2926.5 kalanju. The tower is referred to as *Dakshina Meru* (Southern Meru). According to the *Brighu Samhita* composed by Varahamihira, temple towers are classified into twenty types such as Meru, Mandara, Kailasa, Gajaprishta (elephant-back), Rishabha (bull-shaped), Simha (lion-shaped), and so on. Among these, the vimana here follows the Meru type and, being located in South India, is referred to as the Dakshina Meru. The presiding deity is called Vidangar, which translates to 'the one who is self-manifested'.

The tower is square-shaped and has thirteen tiers. The base of the tower weighs 80 tons. It is said that this stone was taken to the top of the Vimanam by building a ramp extending from a village called Sarapallam, located about four kal (old Tamil measure) away from Thanjavur. At each corner of the square base are two Nandi statues, each measuring six and a half feet in length and five and a half feet in width.

Thiruchutru Maaligai (Circumambulatory Corridor)

A major part of this was constructed by the chief commander Krishna Raman, who belonged to the Mummudi Chola dynasty. He completed this work in accordance with the directives of Rajaraja. In the circumambulatory corridor, there are temples dedicated to the eight directional guardians. One can take delight in the exquisite stone carvings of these directional deities.

For each of these temples, copper finials made from sheets of gold were donated by Isana Sivapanditar, the spiritual preceptor of Rajaraja. However, only stone finials are seen today. The existing Pillaiyar temple was built during the Maratha reign. The Murugan temple is also a later addition.

It has been a long-standing tradition to build a temple for

Chandeeswaran in the circumambulatory path. He is recognised as the overseer of the temple, a role established in ancient times. Consequently, all temple activities were conducted in his name.

This was also evident during the reign of Rajaraja Chola. Even today, devotees visiting the temple customarily stop at the shrine of Chandeeswaran before leaving and symbolically clap their hands together, saying: 'We are not taking anything that belongs to Shiva; please witness our empty hands.' This gesture reflects the enduring custom.

The Amman Temple

The original Amman temple must have been located in the Sivagangai garden, to the north of the main temple. It is said to have been destroyed during the Nayak era. The current Amman temple was built at a later date.

Given this, it is evident that the northern side of the present-day Brihadeeswara Temple must have been more spacious in earlier times.

The Great Nandi

The Nandi statue in the grand temple is carved out of a single stone. It stands 12 feet tall, 19.5 feet long and 8.5 feet wide. The current Nandi mandapam dates back to the Nayak period.

Sacred Images

Several divine images (*tirumeni*) were installed in this temple by Rajaraja Chola, his queen, and others. A few of them are mentioned here:

Among them is one Shiva Lingam, from which Shiva appears with four arms, with Brahma and Vishnu standing beside him (with a boar's face). This is the sacred image of the deity described in the Linga Puranam.

Another idol depicts Brahma performing a ritual alongside Vishnu, who stands with four arms in a blessings pose. This is the Kalyanasundara image.

In another image, among four disciples, with a tiger and a snake by their sides, atop a two-peaked mountain crowned with nine Palmyra trees and their 42 branches, sits Dakshinamurthy beneath a banyan tree. At his divine feet rest rabbits, and he holds a veena in his four arms.

There is also an image of Sandesa Prasada Devar rising with his consort and offering his blessings in the form of a garland to Sandesa.

Additionally, there is an idol representing the five forms of deities emerging from Sadashiva, including Brahma, Vishnu, Rudra, Mahesha, and Sadashiva.

Furthermore, there is an idol of a Nayanar in his divine form, a notable figure from ancient times. During the time of Kadavar Kon (the third Nandi Varman Pallava, 840–865 CE), there was a temple dedicated to him at Kumara Marthandapuram in Thirunageshwaram. Statues of the saints Appar, Sambandar, Sundarar, and others have been installed in this temple. However, there is no idol of Thiruvathavurar (Manickavasagar), indicating that *Thiruvasagam* had not yet been included in the Saiva canon (*Thirumurai*) during Rajaraja Chola's time. Conversely, any claim suggesting otherwise is a misconception.

If we study the inscriptions in the great temples of that period, we clearly understand that processional vehicles (*vahanas*) for deities were not yet in use at that time.

Inscriptions of the Brihadeeswara Temple

The majority of the inscriptions in the temple date back to the time of Rajaraja Chola. They provide detailed information about the various idols consecrated during his reign, as well as the lands, the vessels, emblems and ornaments donated for their worship. They also include records of arrangements made for supplies ranging from salt to camphor.

The inscriptions of Rajaraja and his sister Kundavai have been inscribed within the central passage of the temple tower. Inscriptions relating to Rajaraja's wife and children are found carved in the corridor (Tiruchuttru Maligai) surrounding the temple. This clearly shows the high regard he held for his sister.

Among the inscriptions in this temple, sixty-four are from the era of Rajaraja, twenty-nine from Rajendra, one from Kulothunga Chola I, one from Vikrama Chola, three from the period of Konerinmai Kondan and a few later inscriptions from Nayak and Maratha periods.

Thirty-Five Temple-Endowed Villages (Devadana Sitrurkal)

To ensure the uninterrupted operation of the Brihadeeswara temple, 35 villages were granted, as mentioned in the inscriptions. The largest of these towns spanned over 1000 acres. Four of these towns ranged between 500 to 1000 acres, three towns from 300 to 400 acres, seven towns from 200 to 300 acres, six towns from 100 to 200 acres, and three towns from 50 to 100 acres. Six towns had an extent of 25 to 50 acres, with two towns covering less than 25 acres.

Inner Shrine Paintings and Sculptures

The inner circumambulatory wall of the grand temple features two layers of painting. The outer layer features Nayak-period frescoes. Beneath them, the Chola-period paintings from the time of Rajaraja can still be seen.

Rajaraja's profound devotion to Shaivism and his broad religious outlook are evident in the many images and sculptures found throughout the grand temple's vimanam (tower) and other parts of the complex, which depict themes from both Saiva and Vaishnava Puranas. This is further emphasised by the 343 surviving Nandi statues found on the temple's four sides, despite many having fallen from the tall surrounding walls or being taken away by others.

On the northern side are striking images of Gangadhara (Shiva bearing the Ganges), Kalyanasundara (Shiva in his divine wedding form), and Mahishasura Mardini (Durga slaying the buffalo demon). Additionally, the temple features figures of Nagakanniyars and preceptors of various religions.

Reason for Constructing the Temple

The Siva-linga deity known as *Ulagalanda Iswarar* is enshrined in a linga form on a platform located within the Sivaganga fortress, in the Sivaganga sacred tank. This may be the very deity referred to by Apparswamy as *Tanjai Tanikulaththar* (the Lord of Tanjai's sacred purifying tank). Alternatively, there could have been an ancient stone temple at this site from earlier times, which was later expanded into the current temple by Rajaraja Chola as an expression of his expansive Saiva devotion.

Arumugam Temple and Others

This temple belongs to the period of the Nayak kings. It is notable for its design, resembling a chariot pulled by elephants and horses. The Ganapati temple dates back to the time of Sarabhoji Maharaja. The Nataraja shrine is also from a later period.

Velaikkar Troops

It is essential to understand the details regarding this troop. These warriors were known for laying down their lives wherever they were stationed. There were fourteen such divisions. These soldiers, having vowed, 'I shall do this; if not, may I meet ruin,' faithfully executed their words. If due to their negligence any harm befell the king, they would give up their own lives. Since even he (Murugan) protects his devotees from harm, the *Tiruvaguppu* describes him as a Veḷaikkaran (royal guard). Then what more can be said of the excellence of those who bear that title?

The Sanskrit term 'Vel' means an 'agreement' or 'contract.' In Tamil, it becomes '*velai*'. Those who entered into a formal agreement with the king—pledging to guard him and, if necessary, to sacrifice their lives—were known as Velaikkarar. Many such Velaikkarar groups were organised into separate regiments.

Relationship with the Chinese

Rajaraja Chola expanded maritime trade; in 1015 CE, he sent a delegation to China laden with precious goods. A mediator translated their speech for the Chinese emperor. The emperor provided them accommodation in a guesthouse adjacent to his palace. During their visit, they attended the birthday celebration of the Chinese emperor. He bestowed numerous gifts upon the Chola delegates and honoured them greatly. This account is found in Chinese records.

Titles and Honours

Rajaraja Chola held numerous honorific titles. Titles such as Rajaraja, Mummudi Chola, and Sayangonda Chola were used not only as royal titles but also as names of regions and settlements. In addition, Rajaraja was referred to by titles like Cholendra Simhan (Lion among Cholas), Sivapadasekaran (He who adorns the feet of Shiva), Kshatriya Sigamani (Jewel among warriors), Jananathan (Lord of people), Nikarili Chola

(Incomparable Chola), Rajendra Simhan (Lion-like Rajendra), Chola Marthandan (Sun of the Chola lineage), Rajasrayan, Raja Marthandan, Nithya Vinodan (Eternal delight), Pandya Kulasani (Enemy of the Pandya clan), Keralantakan (Destroyer of the Keralas), Singhalantakan (Destroyer of the Sinhalese), Ravikula Manickam (Gem of the Solar dynasty), Telunga Kula Kalan (Yama to the Telugu race). We can verify that these names were commonly recorded in inscriptions.

These titles were also used in naming settlements, as attested by inscriptions. For example, in Thirukalithittai, located in the Thanjavur district, several neighbourhoods bore names such as: Arulmozhi Deva Cheri, Jananatha Cheri, Nithya Vinodha Cheri, Rajakesari Cheri, Nikarili Chola Cheri, Azhagiya Chola Cheri, Singhalantakan Cheri, Kundavai Cheri, Chola Kula Sundara Cheri, Rajamarthanda Cheri, and Rajaraja Cheri.

Family

Rajaraja Chola had multiple wives. In inscriptions alone, fifteen of them are mentioned. These include Ulaga Mahadeviyar, Chola Mahadeviyar (daughter of Thittai Piraan), Abimanavalliyar, Trailokya Mahadeviyar, Panchavan Mahadeviyar, Prithivi Mahadeviyar, Ilada Mahadeviyar, Meenavan Mahadeviyar, Nakkan Thillai Azhagiyar, Kaadan Thongiyar, Koothan Veeraniyar, Ilankon Picchaiyar. Rajaraja referred to them as 'our women' in the inscriptions. Among them, the name of Ulaga Mahadevi is the first mentioned in the inscriptions.

When Rajaraja Chola performed the Tulabharam ceremony in Thiruvisanalur, the chief queen Thandisakti Vidangiyar entered the sacred hall (*Iraniyakaruppam*) and offered forty-five copper coins for preparing sweet Pongal for Lord Perumal of Thiruvisanalur temple. This same queen also established a learning centre in Thiruvaiyaru and named it 'Ulaga Mahadevicharam' after herself.

An inscription recording this states, 'Udaiyar Sri Rajaraja Chola's queen, Thandisakti Vidangiyar, the esteemed Ulaga Mahadevi...' This clarifies that Ulaga Mahadevi is indeed the one who entered the sacred hall. In the Thanjavur Big Temple (Brihadeeswara Temple), both Rajaraja's and Ulaga Mahadeviyar's images have been enshrined, indicating clearly that she was his principal queen. Rajendra Chola was the son of Thirubhuvana Mahadevi, who was also known as Vanavan Mahadeviyar. Ilankon Picchaiyar was the daughter of Vallavaraiyan. Vallavaraiyan is the husband of Kundavai, Rajaraja Chola's beloved sister. Thus, Picchaiyar was Rajaraja Chola's maternal niece.

Rajaraja Chola had three daughters. One was Kundavai, who married Vimaladithan of the Chalukyas. The other was Madhevadigal, who is referred to in the Thiruvalanchuzhi inscription as 'the woman who administered justice' (*natuvir pen*). The name of the third daughter remains unknown.

Rajaraja Chola held his ancestors in the highest regard. He constructed a temple at Melpadi for his grandfather Arinjayan and named it 'Arinjikai Iswaram'. He also built a hall in Thirumukkoodal and named it after his grandmother, Sembiyan Mahadevi.

Compilation of the Sacred Hymns

The histories of the Nayanmars and the recitation of the *Tiruppadigams* in temples had already become widespread during the Pallava period. Vijayalaya Chola and the succeeding Chola kings, transformed the temples praised in the hymns into stone temples. The local communities of that era laid down various conditions for the temples. The *Tiruppadigams* (sacred hymns) were requested to be recited in the temples.

Aware of the widespread influence of the Nayanmar traditions and *Tevaram* recitations, Rajaraja resolved to compile and organise the *Tevaram* hymns. The king, having heard from scholars that the person fit to assist with this was Nambiyandar Nambi, a great Saiva Brahmin living in Thirunaraiyur, went to Thirunaraiyur. He expressed his desire to compile the hymns. Nambi was a devotee of Polla Pillaiyar; he indicated that the hymns were preserved in a chamber to the west of the sanctum in the Chidambaram temple, under the seal of the three saints (Appar, Sambandar, Sundarar). Immediately, the king travelled with him to Chidambaram. The Thillai Brahmins said that they would open the sanctum only if the three saints came in person. Rajaraja arranged for a procession of the idols of Appar, Sambandar, and Sundarar, in order to bring out the *Tevaram* manuscripts from the sacred chamber.

Some manuscripts had been destroyed by termites. The surviving hymns were organised and categorised by Nambi; the compositions of Thirugnanasambandar were grouped into the first three *Thirumurais* (books), those of Thirunavukkarasar (Appar) into the 4th, 5th, and 6th *Thirumurais*, and the hymns of Sundarar into the 7th *Thirumurai*.

The recitation of these hymns became an established practice in every temple. The appointment of forty-eight individuals for reciting the *Tirupathigams* in the great temple of Thanjavur indicates that Rajaraja Chola, known as Sivapada Sekaran, made significant efforts to spread the *Tevaram* hymns across the land. That the *Tirumurai* was organised during his reign is also unmistakably clear. Some scholars claim that this compilation did not take place during his reign, but rather later. However, such a claim is untenable, as made clear through the research writings of the scholar Ulaganatha Pillai.

Rajaraja Chola attained undying fame in the Saiva world. There is no doubt that his name will endure as long as the *Tevaram* hymns are known.

The greatness of this king, who combined deep religious devotion with exceptional political wisdom and asserted the might of the Tamil rulers not only to the southern kings but also to others, is known to all. His name holds a place of distinction both in history and in the realm of Shaivism.

SIX

Rajendra Chola (1012–1044 CE)

Birth

Rajendra Chola, also known as Parakesari, was the only son of Rajaraja Chola. He was born to Queen Tribhuvana Mahadeviyar, who was known as Udaiya Pirattiyar Thambiran Adigal Vanavan Mahadeviyar, on the auspicious Thiruathirai star day in the Tamil month of Margazhi. Beyond this, there is no information about his early years. However, the inscriptions that do exist are only related to his reign, bearing the title *Thirumanni Valara.*

Name

The Thiruvalangadu inscriptions reveal that Rajaraja's original name was 'Arulmozhi'. These inscriptions also indicate his birth name as Madurantakan.

Upbringing

The kings descending from Vijayalaya had a palace at Pazhaiyaarai. Rajaraja's sister, Kundavai, resided there, along with their grandmother, Sembiyan Mahadevi, the wife of Kandaradhithan.

Both women were deeply devoted to Lord Shiva. It is believed that Rajendra was nurtured and raised under their guidance.

Crown Prince Rajaraja ascended the throne only after the demise of his father Parantakan II, his brother Aditya, and his uncle Madurantakan. Therefore, he should have already been an older man by the time he was crowned in 985 CE. Consequently, his son Rajendra would have been a young adult at that time. That is why, even in an inscription from Rajaraja's fourth regnal year (988 CE), Rajendra Chola Deva is already mentioned by name.

Political Involvement

Rajaraja ruled for nearly thirty years, during which Rajendra actively participated in various battles alongside his father. By the time Rajendra ascended the throne, he must have been around fifty years old. Earlier records indicate that Rajendra, as a prince, played a pivotal role in Rajaraja's military campaigns.

Co-Rule and Transition

Rajendra, by then skilled in warfare and governance after decades of experience, began co-ruling with his father towards the latter's old age. Rajaraja formally crowned Rajendra as king during his lifetime. This co-regency is further supported by inscriptions from Thirumukkudal, which mention Rajaraja making a religious endowment during Rajendra's third regnal year.

State of the Empire

When Rajendra ascended the throne in 1012 CE, the Chola Empire stretched as far north as the Krishna and Tungabhadra rivers. In newly conquered territories, skilled and trustworthy officials were appointed to oversee administration. Some regions retained their previous rulers under Chola suzerainty. Well-trained soldiers were strategically stationed in these areas, ensuring stability and allowing the emperor to focus on future conquests.

Crown Prince Rajadhiraja

Rajendra Chola, in a remarkable display of political acumen, crowned his son Rajakesari as co-ruler in the seventh year of his reign (1018 CE). This unprecedented arrangement saw father and son govern together for nearly twenty-five years, a testament to Rajendra's innovative approach to leadership. While Rajendra undoubtedly retained ultimate authority, Rajadhiraja played a significant role in the administration of the empire.

Rajadhiraja's influence extended across the vast empire, as evidenced by his inscriptions. His twenty-sixth-year inscription from Thirumazhapadi states: 'Just as his father's royal white umbrella offered its protective shade, so too did Rajadhiraja's umbrella spread over the empire. He ruled the empire of Rajendra which spanned from the Ganges in the north to Eezham in the south, from Mahodayapuram in the west to Kadaram in the east.'

This highlights the significant portion of the empire overseen by Rajadhiraja during this period of co-rulership.

This unique arrangement, where a son was crowned while his father still reigned, allowed Rajadhiraja to gain invaluable political experience and administrative skills under his father's guidance. This rare achievement demonstrates Rajendra's exceptional political foresight and his ability to groom a capable successor.

Rajadhiraja was not Rajendra's eldest son. However, Rajendra appointed him as the crown prince, recognising his exceptional abilities and potential. This decision underscores Rajendra's wisdom in assigning royal duties based on individual merit rather than mere birth order. This co-rulership was a notable event in South Indian history.

Prince Sundara Chola

Rajendra also entrusted the governance of the Pandya region to his other son, Sundara Chola. In inscriptions, this prince is referred to as Sadaya Varman Sundara Chola Pandiyan, reflecting his dual identity as both a Chola prince and a ruler of the Pandya region. He later expanded his control to the Chera country, earning the title 'Chola Keralan'.

While the emperor's title and fame were recorded in inscriptions, the actual administration of various regions was delegated to his sons and other trusted officials. By appointing his own family members as regional rulers, Rajendra ensured smooth and efficient governance across the vast Chola empire.

Military Campaigns

Rajendra's military campaigns can be categorised into three types: (1) those he conducted as a prince, (2) those he led as the king, and (3) those conducted by his son, Rajadhiraja, during his reign. The first category has already been covered in the account of Rajaraja's reign. We will now explain the second category—campaigns led by Rajendra himself as emperor.

- Conquest of the Deccan: In his third regnal year, Rajendra conquered Idaithurai Nadu (present-day Raichur district), Kollippaakkai (near present-day Hyderabad), and the formidable Mannai kadakkam, the former capital of the Rashtrakoodas and later the Western Chalukyas. This significant victory is commemorated in Thiruvotriyur with a mandapam named *Mannai Konda Chola* (the Chola who captured Mannai).
- The Eezham War: During Rajaraja's reign, Mahinda V, the king of Eezham (Sri Lanka), who had been defeated, attempted to reclaim his lost territories. Rajendra swiftly responded with a powerful army

and decisively defeated Mahinda. He captured the Eezham king, his queens, and numerous symbols of royal authority, including the crown of Rajasimha Pandiyan. This victory brought the entire island of Eezham under Chola control.

- Southern Campaigns: Despite having already subdued the Pandya region, Rajendra undertook further campaigns in the south. He defeated the Pandyan king and re-established his son Sundara Chola as the ruler of the region. He then crossed the mountains and conquered the Chera country, defeating the ruling king.
- Chalukya War: In his ninth regnal year, Rajendra launched a campaign against the Chalukyas, capturing seven and a half lakhs from Jayasimha's Rattaipadi region. This significant victory is celebrated in the Thiruvalangadu inscriptions with ten verses in a poetic style.

In 1016 CE, Jayasimha, the younger brother of Vikramaditya V, began to rule the Chalukya kingdom. He captured the regions of Pallari and Mysore and boasted of having defeated the Cheras and the Cholas. However, Rajendra met Jayasimha at a place called Muyangki (also known as Musangi) and defeated him.

Some say that Muyangki refers to Uchangi Durga in the Pallari district, while others believe it refers to 'Maski' in the Hyderabad region.

The Ganga Conqueror

In Rajendra's 11th year, his campaign in the northern regions is mentioned. Thus, in 1023 CE, he must have led an expedition towards the north. During this campaign, Rajendra's military general conquered several territories. Rajendra met this general on the banks of the Godavari River.

The army chief first won Chakrakottam, also known as

'Chitrakota', located 12 km away from Rajapura, the capital city of Bastar Samsthan in Madhya Pradesh. In this area, there were also locations like Madhuramandalam (known as 'Madhuvan' in Odisha), Namanayakolam, and Panchapalli.

In the city of Adhi, he captured Indradhan and also the forest-rich Oottar region of Kosala. Inscriptions from Thiruvalangadu indicate that Rajendran captured the king of Oottar and acquired various treasures from his brother.

Later, he conquered the territories of Danmapalan's Dandaputhi, the realm of Ranasuran in the southern region, and eastern Bengal under Govindachandran. Dandaputhi is situated between Oottar and Bengal on both banks of the Swarnarekha River. This can be regarded as 'land granted to a commander to enjoy (or govern) in return for military protection.' In Bengal, one region was called Rada. This is the same region referred to in inscriptions as the land of Lada.

Historical Significance

The kings who ruled over these three countries were, more or less, well-established figures in history. Therefore, these names are not fictitious. Mahipalan ruled over Bengal but fled the battlefield out of fear of confronting the Chola king. Immediately afterward, the Chola army chief captured the elephants and treasures belonging to the king and reached the banks of the Ganges.

The waters of the Ganges were brought back over the heads of the defeated kings. Whether this is an exaggeration or a truth remains unknown. Rajendran rejoiced upon meeting the returning army chief on the banks of the Godavari River.

The northern military campaign must have lasted for approximately two years. Rajendra Chola did not desire to rule over the northern regions he conquered. That was not the reason for his expedition. Instead, he aimed to purify the newly established city of Gangaikonda Cholapuram and the canal called Cholaganga with the sacred waters of the Ganga. It was to bring back the Ganga water that he sent his armies northward. The local rulers would not permit foreign armies to pass through their lands. Moreover, Rajendra may have also wished to earn the fame of having conquered the northern territories. These seem to be the reasons behind the wars.

The Bengali Tamil King

The military chief or political leader involved in this campaign (a person from Karnataka) settled in western Bengal. His descendent was a man named Samanta Sen, who later became the first king of the Sena Dynasty that ruled Bengal.

The one who ruled Mithila was also a southerner of this kind. Many Saiva Brahmins from the Ganges coastal regions settled in Rajendran's Kanchi and Chola territories during Rajendran's reign. A knowledgeable and capable person would be revered in any nation.

Kadaram and Others

Rajendran crossed the sea, bringing news about Kadaram as noted in his thirteenth inscription. Therefore, he must have conquered it between 1024–25 CE. In this attempt to cross the sea, Rajaraja first defeated the king of Kadaram and seized his elephants, wealth, and resources. Later, he captured many countries and towns and ultimately gained possession of Kadaram itself. Now let us see which countries and towns he acquired.

Sri Vijaya

This refers to 'Palembang', located on Sumatra Island. It flourished as a significant trade centre in the Malay Archipelago from the eighth to thirteenth centuries CE. The Chinese referred to it as 'Sri Vijaya'. This area thrived as a central point for east-west trade routes.

Kadaram

The term 'Southern Kadaram', indicates that this was a coastal region. In northern languages, it was known as 'Kadaham', while in Tamil it is referred to as 'Kazhagam' and 'Kadaram'. The term 'Kazhagam' appears in *Pathupattu*, indicating that Tamil merchants had long been engaged in maritime trade with Kadaram; Chinese traders did so too. According to their records, 'Kedah' in south-eastern Malay Peninsula likely corresponds with 'Kadaram'.

Other Regions

Mayirudingam, Ilankasokam, and Malaiyur are regions in Malay Peninsula; Mappappamai and Thalaithakolam are located near the Isthmus of Kra. Mathamalai is known as 'Temiling' or 'Tembeling', located in southern Malaysia where the Kuantan River meets the Sea. The exact location of 'Valaipandu' is unknown. 'Pannai' refers to a place called 'Panei' or 'Panay', located on Sumatra's southern coast.

Ilamuri Desam

It is a region in northern Sumatra referred to as 'Lamuri' by Arabs.

Manakkavaram

This is the ancient name for the Nicobar Islands. The forests and towns here were under the Sri Vijaya Empire according to Chinese texts. They served as significant trading points where Chinese and Tamil ships met and exchanged goods with Malay countries.

Reasons for Conquest

It remains unclear why Rajendran Cholan conquered these areas that aided Tamil commerce. Perhaps it was to protect the rights of the Tamil merchants settled there or maybe to suppress the arrogance of the Sri Vijaya ruler. The reason is unknown. It does not appear that these territories were under the Chola control; therefore, the above mentioned reasons might be the appropriate explanation.

The wars waged by Rajadhiraja

Since the wars waged by Rajadhiraja took place during the reign of Rajendra Chola and were carried out in support of his father, they should also be considered as wars waged by Rajendra himself. Now, let us look into the details of those campaigns.

Ceylon War

After the initial war in Ceylon during Rajendra's reign, Rajadhiraja had to wage war in Lanka again in 1042 CE. Vikramabahu ruled for thirteen years and died. According to inscriptions, he died fighting against the Cholas. After him, Kitti ruled for eight days; then, Mahalan Kitti ruled over the Rohana country for three years. He fought against the Cholas, was defeated, and committed suicide.

His son, Vikrama Pandyan—son of the Sinhalese king and a Pandya princess—fled to the Thula Country, and later returned to conquer Rohana, where he became king. He died in a battle against Jagadheepalan. According to the Mahavamsa, this Jagadheepalan was a royal prince from Ayodhya. He had fled from a country called Kanyakubjam; his name is stated to be Veerasalamegan in Chola inscriptions.

The Cholas defeated the king of Lanka and killed him. They imprisoned his sister and wives, and humiliated his mother. Vikrama Pandyan's son was Parakraman. The Cholas defeated him as well.

War with the Pandyas

In the Pandya country, Sundara Pandyan was ruling a portion of the land as a minor king. He gathered an army and incited a rebellion. Rajadhiraja defeated him in battle and drove him out of the country. The exact year in which this happened is not known.

War in the Hill Country

According to his official eulogy (*Meipugazh*) Rajadhiraja waged war and achieved victories over several kings who ruled the hill regions. He marched from the Pandya region towards the Kandalur Salai (highway); along the way, he attacked and killed the king of Velanadu and liberated the ruler of Koobhanadu (present day South-Travancore).

There was a region near Elimalai called 'Iramakudam', also known as 'Eli Nadu'. The king of that region was referred to as 'Moovar Thiruvadi'. Rajadhiraja defeated him and drove away the Chera king. These events are recorded in inscriptions starting with the phrase *Thingal Ertharu...*

Western Chalukya War

Towards the end of Rajendra's reign, the Western Chalukyas once again waged war against the Cholas. In 1042 CE, the Chalukya king, Jayasimha II, died. His son, Somesvara I, ascended the throne. He was also known by names such as Agavamallan and Thiralokyamallan. In Chola inscriptions, he is referred to as Agavamallan. This led to the onset of war.

Rajadhiraja confronted the Chalukya army, killed key commanders like Dandapayan and Gangadharan. Somesvara's sons, Vikramaditya and Vijayaditya, along with their general Sangamayan, fled from the battlefield. They disappeared. Rajadhiraja seized the enemy's treasures and set fire to the camp.

In the three major fords—Siruthurai, Perunthurai, and Daivapeemakasi—he bathed elephants and engraved the Chola tiger emblem over the Chalukya boar insignias carved into the rocks.

Realizing that he could not defeat the Chola, Agavamallan sent some envoys to negotiate with Rajadhiraja. The Chola king seized two of them—he branded one with the *'Aingudumi'* and adorned the other in women's attire; he then mockingly named them 'Agavamallan' and 'Agavamalli' respectively, and sent them back.

Agavamallan later suffered a major defeat at a place called Poondi. Rajadhiraja then captured the great city of Kalyanapuram and established his authority there, taking the title of 'Vijaya Rajendran'. He plundered the city, taking several valuable objects including a notable gateway guardian statue. An inscription on its pedestal reads; 'Victory to the illustrious king Sri Vijaya Rajendra Devar, who brought back the gateway guardian from Kalyanapuram'. This statue was originally kept at the Airavateshwara temple in Darasuram but is now housed in the Big Temple in Thanjavur.

Gangai Konda Cholapuram

This was a grand city newly established by Rajendra Chola. Today, it remains a small town in the Udayar Palayam taluk of the Tiruchirappalli district.

Rajendra Chola constructed this city to commemorate his victorious northern campaign and his conquest of the lands up to the banks of the Ganges! The ancient inscriptions found here refer to him as Veera Rajendra Chola Devan. Similar to the big temple (Brihadeeswara Temple) in Thanjavur, he built a beautiful temple called 'Gangai Konda Someswaram' in this city; he also constructed a magnificent lake called 'Chola Ganga'.

After bringing the sacred Ganges water from the north, Rajendra met his returning victorious generals and army on the banks of the Godavari River. On his return journey, he stayed and worshipped at various places along the way, eventually reaching his newly built capital city. There, he purified the city, temple, and lake with the Ganges water. This Ganga expedition was celebrated and well-received by the people.

City

There is no adequate evidence to understand the layout of the city. A palace called 'Chola, Keralan' existed there. The palace had a staff quarters, called Thirumanjanthar Velam. There was also a large market.

About a kilometre from the temple, there is a fortified mound called 'Maligai Medu'. It is said that the Chola palace stood there. Remains and symbols of the building can be seen beneath the mound. If this site were to be excavated, many important clues could be discovered.

On the southern bank of the lake, there is a small town named Gangaikonda (Chola) Puram. It is surrounded by a forest. Within the forest, there are many beautiful but ruined old structures. These resemble the mounds marking the remains of the ancient city of Babylon. During prosperous times, the Chola Ganga must have contributed immensely to fulfil the water needs of the city. The large area lying in ruins now must once have been a lush green landscape.

Gangai Konda Someswaram

It received this name because it was built by the king who conquered the Ganges. Its structure is similar to the grand temple built by Rajaraja. This temple had six towers. Though this temple is smaller than the grand temple, its sculptural work is far more splendid. This magnificent temple is now in ruins. The circumambulatory corridors (prakarams) are no longer visible. Of the towers, only the lower tower remains, but it is now in ruins. The inner sanctum and the surrounding walls are only partially visible at present.

Vimana

This resembles the vimana of the big temple in Thanjavur. It is 170 feet tall and the base measures 100 square feet; it has nine tiers. Of these, the first two tiers stand upright, one on top of the other. The others incline slightly as they rise. On all four sides of the vimana, there are entrances and balconies.

The vimana is adorned with beautiful lotus designs all over. At the top of the vimana, there is a single stone spire, similar to the one found on the Big Temple's vimana. Its *kalasam* (finial pot) is currently missing.

Sivalingam

The sivalingam here is as large as the sivalingam in the Thanjai Big

Temple. It is made from a single stone. It is said that it was struck by lightning and has now split into two. The great deity of this Sivalingam has been specially praised in a hymn by Karuvur Devar. This hymn is included in the ninth Thirumurai. It is said that when the lower anicut was constructed across the Kollidam River, parts of the temple precincts and circumambulatory paths were broken and taken away. Simple villagers tried to stop this, but it was of no use. Those who opposed were punished. Promises were made to replace the broken stone wall with a brick wall. However, it was not fulfilled.

Today's View

Thirumadhil (The Sacred Fort Wall)

Its length is approximately 200 meters; the width is 150 meters. Its thickness is 1 meter, and it is entirely made of stones. Adjacent to the *thirumadhil*, there used to be a two-storeyed cloistered hall (*Thiruchuttru Maaligai*). Today, only a portion of it can be seen.

Within the cloister, many shrines are found; the Chandrasekarar temple lies in ruins. All these shrines (except for the small shrine of Chandikeshwara) are of later origin. The Amman temple appears to have been relocated and constructed inside (the complex) at a later period.

At both front corners of the *Thirumadhil* and at the centre of the rear wall, semi-circular structures resembling guard rooms (*kaavarkoodam*) are believed to have existed—traces of such structures can be seen.

Directly in front of the inner sanctum, lies a large Nandi statue made entirely of red stone. The height up to its head is 20 feet, and up to the back is 12 feet. To its right side, directly opposite is an exquisitely constructed lion-faced well. The steps leading to the nearby well are arranged in a straight line. At the top of the steps is a lion carved from red stone. If one enters through the opening in its belly, one can descend the steps and see the water in the well. It is said that there are about 30 steps under the water and 20 above. All the steps are made of black stone.

Inner Sanctum

The length of the temple is 340 feet; the width is 100 feet. Inside, the Maha Mandapam is 175 feet long and 95 feet wide. Between the deity's chamber and this mandapam, there is the Ardha Mandapam, which has beautiful gateways with steps on both the northern and southern sides. The main entrance to the temple is on the eastern side. In the Maha Mandapam, there are 140 stone pillars arranged in eight rows. The central portion of the hall is about 18 feet high and the two sides are about 16 feet. The entire space is roofed with stone slabs. The Ardha Mandapam consists of large square stone pillars arranged in two rows.

Vimanam (tower)

It has a height of 186 feet. The base of the temple is square shaped, measuring 100 feet on each side and the height is 35 feet. Above that, there are two upper storeys, and above these, the structure has eight more tiers.

Lingam

The lingam has a circumference of 13 *muzham* (cubits); the pedestal has a circumference of 30 cubits; the height of the lingam is about 4 meters. There are small stone pillars to support the pedestal, which has split into two. The inner circumambulatory passage (*thiruchuttru*) surrounding the sanctum is 3 meters wide. It is constructed at a height of 6 meters above the temple floor.

Ardha Mandapam

On the pillars of the Ardha Mandapam, several dancing sculptures are carved. They depict various dance poses. Facing the lingam, there are six rows of sculptures on the opposing wall (like the sculptures on the wall of the Kanchi Vaikundha Perumal temple). These illustrate (1) the history of Chandeeswarar, (2) the marriage of Thadathakai, (3) the battle between Parthiban and Paraman (Siva), and (4) the history of Markandeyan. All of these are presented as lifelike carvings.

Maha Mandapam

This kind of mandapam can be said to be the foundation for later thousand-pillared mandapams. Here, a stone statue of Sambandar is seen in great beauty, and also seen is a remarkably crafted statue of Durgai Amman. The arrangement of the nine planetary deities is unique and innovative.

The Sun god (Surya) is depicted on a chariot. The eight directional guardians (*Ashtadika palakas*) are around him. Above him, the Navagrahas are arranged. At the centre is a lotus pedestal (Padma Peedam). All these are sculpted from a single round stone. In the two rooms of the Maha Mandapam, there are several idols of various deities along with the *kalasam* (finial pot) of the Vimanam.

Door Guardians

There are majestic *Dvarapala* (entrance guardian) statues that stand about 4 meters tall. The first two statues are found in the tower ruins. The remaining ten are positioned at various entrances—the temple entrance, the Ardha Mandapam entrance, the entrance to the sanctum, and at the northern and southern entrances.

Sculptures

The sculptures that adorn the Vimanam and the intricate carvings on the temple's exterior are exquisite. Scholars say that these sculptures are not only superior to the ones found in other South Indian temples but also excel the renowned sculptures of Savakam (Java), which were influenced by the South Indian tradition. In the southwest corner is a sculpture of Sabapathi, to the west is Lingodbhava Arunachaleshwaran, to the south is Vinayagar, and to the north, near the northern gateway is the divine image of Siva (known as *Chandeshwara Arulpur Murthi*) blessing Chandeshwara with grace.

In addition, there are numerous Ganas (divine attendants), Apsaras (celestial dancers), and Rakshasa figures everywhere, adding grandeur to the temple's majestic appearance. Most of these sculptures are stylistically rooted in the sculptural tradition of Mamallapuram from Narasimha Varman's period; yet they go beyond the foundation and illustrate the advancement of sculptural art.

Thus, it can be stated that this temple has achieved a distinct status in terms of beauty and sculptural skill among the temples of the Chola period.

Palace Mound

This site is believed to be the location of the palace. It spans a very vast area, but today it appears as a levelled paddy field. In the fields, there are platforms scattered here and there. Among them and in the fields, remnants of broken pedestals are found lying around. The bricks found here measure 38 cm in length, 20 cm in width, and 10 cm in thickness. Stones from the large palace mound were excavated and used to construct steps for the new junction pond. Debris with lime mortar traces is found in abundance. To the east of this mound, the remains of a long white stone wall are still visible. Along its course, the brick foundations can be seen clearly. A drainage channel for rainwater and wastewater from the old palace once existed here. The remnants of a kind of stone-built drainage structure can still be observed today. The stream behind the current temple is new, but on both sides, remnants of stone walls can be seen. The Palace Mound is about 2 km long from north to south and 1.5 km long from east to west.

Ancient City

It seems that Rajendran had established four Kali shrines at each of the four corners of the newly-built city as guardian deities. The western gateway Kali temple is five kilometres away, the northern gateway Kali temple is located two stones' throw (3-4 kms) away in a small village called Saluppai; it is located on the Chengamamedu. The eastern gateway Kali temple is similarly located about two stones' throw away. The southern gateway Kali temple is likewise situated about three to four kilometres away in the village called Veerarajam. There, a sacred pond is found where it is said the deity Brahadeeswarar used to give blessings. These indications suggest that the ancient city had a layout of nearly 6 square kilometres.

Surrounding Villages

Surrounding the temple, within a distance of two *kal* (stones) are several small villages. They include: Sunnampu Kuzhi (the place where lime was prepared for temple work), Kanakku Vinayakar Temple, Ponneri (a village associated with the Chola lake), Palli Odai, Pakalmedu, Saluppai, Chengamamedu, Muthu Silpa Madam, Chappodai, Manmalai (this is located three stone's throw away; the temple chariot was said to have been kept here; there is a place called *Thermedu* [Chariot mound] there), Meikaval Puthur, Veerasozhapuram, Vaan Tharaiyan Kuppam (this is now known as 'Vaanaduppu'), Kuyavan Pettai, Thotti Kulam, Kazhani Kulam, and Utkottai (this is located two stone's throw away). The village known as Paranai Medu is located seven stones' throw away from the temple. It is said that cotton bales were stacked there, tied up and transported to the temple tower (*vimanam*).

Tunnel

A tunnel seems to have existed connecting the palace and the temple. Its remnants can be still seen in the stream that lies between the temple and the palace mound. A portion of the brick-wall foundation is visible in the stream.

The Temple's Land and Revenue

The temple possesses 365 *kaani* (about 1.5 acres) of land. Each kaani yields an income of ₹5-10-0 (i.e., 5 rupees, 10 annas, and 0 paise—in the old currency system). Despite this, due to a lack of proper supervision, this historically famous temple remains in a state of neglect. If this condition continues, there is no doubt that its glory will fade away. It is the duty of the trustee of religious endowments to entrust the temple's administration to knowledgeable and devoted individuals to maintain the temple in good condition.

Wells

There are wells located within a stone's throw of the temple on all four sides. Old bricks are found in abundance; black stones are also being recovered.

Temple Tower (Gopuram)

The tower, which has collapsed now, is said to have been nearly 25 meters high. It was entirely made of black stonework; above it, there were seven *kalasams* (sacred pots) made of stucco. It is said that the tower collapsed around seventy-five years ago when explosives were used to obtain stone for building a dam. The debris has not been removed; the entire inner corridor of the temple is overgrown with thorny bushes, and it is in such a state that walking without footwear is impossible.

Chola Gangam

This is an artificially excavated lake, now called 'Ponneri'. It is currently a raised ground. This lake, located north of the village, is 25 km long from north to south and has high banks. There is a distance of sixty *kal* between this lake and the Kollidam River. From there, a large canal was dug. The water that flowed through it partially filled this lake. Another canal brought water from the Vellar River. Since these canals brought water from two rivers—one from the north and one from the south—the lake was always full, appearing like a sea. The banks of these canals can still be seen today. This lake once provided water to Tiruchirappalli and South Arcot. Many agricultural lands benefited from its flow. But today, this great lake lies in a state where it merely reminds us of its ancient glory. It has now become a dense forest. A local tradition says that later invaders ruined it. This lake is currently undergoing restoration work. If it regains its ancient state, it will bring prosperity to the land.

In a flat area without mountains or hills, constructing strong banks for a length of 26 km and harvesting water by cutting a 100 km long canal are no small feats. Rajendra Chola's sole goal for undertaking and executing such a great task could only have been the welfare of his people, through which he himself would find happiness. Wasn't Tamil Nadu truly blessed to have had such a great emperor?

Royal Titles

Rajendran had many titles. Among them are Maruranthagan, Uthama Cholan, Vikrama Cholan and Veera Rajendran, which were titles held by both his ancestors and descendants. Titles specific to him include Mudikonda Cholan, Gangaikondan, Kadaramaikondan, and Panditha Cholan.

Royal Family

The royal family seems to have mostly resided in Pazhaiyarai. During that time, Pazhaiyarai was known as 'Mudikonda Chozham'. A temple was built there for Rajendran's first wife, Panchavan Mahadevi. Rajendran had several wives. Among them notable were Panchavan Mahadevi and Thirubuvan Mahadevi also known as Vaanavan Mahadevi. Mukkokkizhan Adigal and Veera Mahadevi are also notable. Veera Mahadevi ascended the funeral pyre along with Rajendran. This great emperor had many children. As far as we know, Rajadhirarajan, Rajendradevan, and Veera Rajendran are his children. It is unclear whether Sadayavarman Sundara Cholan was one of these three or another one. Among his daughters, one was Arulmozhi Nangai, referred to as Pranar. She presented an expensive pearl umbrella to the Thirumalapadi temple during the early reign of Rajadirajan. Another daughter was Amanga Devi. Rajarajanarendran, the son of Kundhavai (daughter of Rajaraja) and Chalukya Vimaladitya, married Amanga Devi, the daughter of Rajendra. Their son became the great emperor Kulothunga I. Rajendran's mother was Vaanavan Mahadevi. Rajendran made a statue for his mother and installed it in a temple located in a place called 'Sembiyan Mahadevi' in Nagapattinam, and made endowments for its worship. Arranging for the worship of the deceased in temples was not a common practice. This mother was a devout follower of Shiva, and therefore, her form may have been worshipped!

Rajaraja Vishayam

This book seems to have been about Rajaraja; it was read during special occasions. The person who read it to the king was Narayanan Pattadithan. The king granted him land. This text is no longer available now. If it were still in existence, wouldn't it be possible to understand the history of Rajaraja in detail and enjoy it?

King's Teacher

During the time of Rajaraja, the great scholar Sarvasiva Panditar Rajarajendra was a person of great esteem in the Big Temple. Orders were issued that he and his disciples, wherever they were, should be annually granted rice measured and given as *Acharya Bhoga* (teacher's honorarium). Another teacher was Lakulisa Panditar. He belonged to the Kalamukha sect of Shaivism. Many from this sect were renowned scholars at that time. They safeguarded some of the educational institutions.

Buddhist Monastery

A Buddhist monastery that was initiated in Nagapattinam during Rajaraja's time gained prominence during Rajendra's reign. It was built by Maravichayothungavarman, a king of the Sri Vijaya kingdom, belonging to the Sailendra dynasty. It was constructed for the Buddhists of his country to worship in Nagai. Responding to his request, Rajaraja granted land and support for the construction of the monastery. It was completed during

Rajendra's period. The king of Sri Vijaya named it after his father as 'Choodamani Varman Vihara'. The village named 'Aina Mangalam' was donated to it as *Pallichandam* (a land grant for a Buddhist temple). The inscription recording this donation is known as the Leiden Grant. The name 'Leiden' comes from the city of Leiden in the Netherlands, where this copperplate was taken and preserved, hence the name.

Sino Relations

Earlier, just as Rajaraja sent an embassy to China with gifts, Rajendra sent an embassy to the Chinese emperor in 1033 CE. Chinese texts state that the Chinese emperor welcomed them and fulfilled their requests. This indicates that the Chola kingdom maintained strong maritime trade relations with China.

Territorial Divisions

During the time of Rajendra, various regions were known by distinct names: Tondai Nadu–Sayankonda Chola Mandalam, Pandya Nadu–Rajaraja Pandya Mandalam, Sri Lanka–Mummudi Chola Mandalam, Gangapadi–Mudikonda Chola Mandalam, and Nulambapadi–Nikarili Chola Mandalam. The Chola Mandalam, Malai Mandalam, Kongu Mandalam, and Vengi Mandalam retained their ancient names.

Political Officials

There were many officials to conduct the administration. They were categorised as *Karumigal* (executors) and *Paniyalar* (functionaries). Among the executors, there were senior (*Perundharam*) and junior (*Sirudharam*) officers. These officials managed various divisions related to politics and efficiently conducted governance. High-ranking officials received land or its revenue from the king according to their qualifications.

During Rajendra's reign, three individuals were instrumental in the victories he achieved. One was Arayan Rajaraja. He was renowned for his exploits in the Chalukya wars. A stone inscription states that the Vengi king fled on hearing that he was coming with an army! He earned titles such as *Nalumadi, Bhiman, Samandha Paranam, Veerabhooshanam, and Edirthavar Kalan*. He had been a Chola commander since the time of Rajaraja.

Krishna Raman was another military leader from Rajaraja's time. His son was Marayan Arulmozhi. He was the one who assisted in building a temple for Goddess Pidari at Kolar in 1033 CE. He held the title *Uttama Chola Brahmarayan*.

The king granted titles based on merit. Ministers and heads of departments received titles. The high-ranking officials were given the title *Muveenda Velan* along with their designation or award, while those who excelled in their field received titles like *Marayan* and *Perarayan*.

Inscriptional examples include: *Vachiya Marayan* (Marayan in charge of musical instruments) and *Nirutha Perarayan* (Chief of dance or performance).

Vallavaraiyar Vandiyathevan, the husband of Rajaraja's sister Kundavai governed the regions surrounding Brahmadesam in present-day North Arcot district. He had other wives as well—Kunthala Devi and Kuntha Devi. Princess Kundavai resided in the palace at Pazhaiyarai. Vandiyathevan was likely the chief among the vassal lords (*Samanta Thalaivan*). The region named after him extended as far as Salem.

In the South Arcot district, Yadava Bhima, who bore the title *Chola Miladudaiyar*, ruled as a feudatory in 1016 CE. An inscription from 1023-24 CE mentions another chieftain named Gangaikonda Chola Miladudaiyar, who donated lamps to a temple in Kalathi.

Sankalvar was a small king who ruled Mysore. Kongalvar was also a small king. As years passed, the Kongalvars began to claim descent from the Chola dynasty; similarly, some Telugu-Kannada lineages also started asserting that they were descendants of the Cholas.

Armies

The Chola king had elephant corps, cavalry, and infantry; but there is no mention of chariot corps. Not a single inscription indicates that any warrior brought a chariot to the battlefield. It is recorded that the kings and commanders fought mounted on elephants or horses. The infantry was referred to as *Kaikkola Perum Padai* (the great army of the Kaikkolars—an elite warrior group). Each branch of the army was further divided into several divisions. Inscriptions mention terms like *villigal* (archers) and vaalpetra Kaikkolar (sword-wielding Kaikkolars), suggesting that weapons such as bows and arrows, spears, and swords were used in warfare. The Chola army was stationed in all the conquered territories. The Chola navy had notable glory; it transported warriors across the sea to countries like Sumatra and Malaysia; it gained fame for enhancing maritime trade.

Coins

During his reign, Rajendra Chola issued coins in his own name. They are referred to as *Rajendran Maadai* (Maadai—an old Tamil term for coin) and *Rajendra Chola Kasu* (Chola coin of Rajendra) in inscriptions.

Education

Rajendran was known as *Pandita Chola* (the learned Chola). This implies that he must have attained great expertise in Tamil. His true fame (*mei pugazh*) has been described with deep scholarly appreciation in many inscriptions. Therefore, it appears that there were some Tamil scholars in his court. Amita Sagara who composed *Yapparungalam Karikai* and Gunasagara who wrote a commentary on it are considered to have lived during this period. The renowned Saiva saint Karuvur Tevar was also from this period. Rajendran's son, Veerarajendran, was a Tamil scholar as well, and a poet named Veera Chola Puthamithirar (possibly named after him) lived in this time. It is likely that Nambiyandar Nambi, who compiled the *Tirumurai*, lived during Rajendran's era and had associated with him.

Sanskrit (Vadamozhi)

The Sanskrit inscriptions and copper plate grants related to Rajendran are composed in epic style. Notably, Narayana Kavi, who composed the Thiruvalangadu copper plates, was a distinguished Sanskrit scholar. In the South Arcot district, there is a town called Ennayiram, known as *Rajaraja Chaturvedi Mangalam*. A major Sanskrit college was established there. Likewise, a Sanskrit college also existed at a place called Thiribuvanam.

Royal Distinction

Rajaraja established the Chola Empire; Rajendran further enriched and expanded it. He achieved victories across the sea and spread the glory of the Cholas far and wide. Rajaraja built temples to affirm his devotion; Rajendran not only did that but also constructed a new city and a remarkable reservoir.

Just like his father, Rajendra was a devout Shaivite, yet he respected other religions as well. He expanded maritime trade. His bronze statue is found in the great temple of Thanjai. Rajendran conducted himself generously with all religions. During his twenty-fourth year of reign, he granted land to the Rajendra Chola Vinnagaram built by the Chera king Rajasimhadeva at Mannarkovil in the Tirunelveli district. This great emperor who ruled in an unparalleled manner passed away in 1044 CE.

SEVEN

The Children of Rajendran (1044–1070 CE)

Introduction

After the great emperor Rajendra Chola, his three sons ruled one after the other. During their respective reigns, they governed the empire that had been left by their father. To preserve this empire, they had to wage several wars. Notable among these were the wars fought against the Western Chalukyas.

During one such fierce battle, Rajadhiraja Chola was killed. This caused the Chola army to falter. At that time, Rajendra Chola Devan (younger brother of Rajadhiraja) who was stationed in the rear, immediately ascended the throne on the battlefield itself. With heroic vigour, he fought and won the battle.

While these wars in the north were taking place, in the south, the rulers of Lanka, the Pandyas, and the Cheras formed an alliance and rose in rebellion to restore their sovereignty. These three sons of Rajendra, in turn, periodically quelled such chaotic situations to ensure that the empire remained stable. Ultimately, they sought the assistance of the Chalukyas to preserve the Chola Empire for another century; that is, they established the lineage of Kulothunga Chola I, also known as Chalukya Chola Rajendra.

Administration Method

Professor Neelakanta Sastri has delineated the periods during which Rajendra Chola and his successors ruled as follows:

- Rajakesari – Rajadhiraja Chola ruled from 1018 to 1054 CE.
- Parakesari – Rajendra Chola Devan II reigned from 1052 to 1064 CE. (His son Rajakesari – Rajamahendran was a prince during his reign and passed away between 1060-1073 CE.)
- Rajakesari – Veera Rajendran ruled from 1053 to 1069 CE. (He was also known by the names Veera Cholan and Karikala Chola.)
- Parakesari – Adhirajendra Chola reigned between 1069 and 1070 CE (He was the son of Veera Rajendran.)

Rajadhiraja (1018–1054 CE)

Rajadhiraja ruled the Chola Empire along with his father for twenty-five years. He participated in all the wars that occurred during his father's reign. After his father's death, he ascended the throne and immediately crowned his younger brother Rajendra Chola Devan as the crown prince.

Chalukyan War

(1) Around 1044–45 CE, either at the terminal stage of Rajendra Chola I's life or shortly after his death, a war broke out between the Cholas and the Western Chalukyas. In this war, Rajadhiraja completely defeated the Chalukyas and many of the small kings who came to aid the Chalukyas; he even destroyed the Chalukya Royal palace located at Kambili. (2) A fierce battle occurred at a place called 'Pundur' on the left bank of the Krishna River. In

that battle, many subordinate rulers and women of Someshwara (the Chalukya king) were captured. Pundur was destroyed; it was ploughed over using donkeys; the palace at a place called Mannandhippai was set on fire; and a victory pillar engraved with the tiger emblem was erected.

Koppam War (1054 CE)

A fierce battle took place between Rajadhiraja and the aggressive Someshwara I of the Western Chalukya dynasty at a place called Koppam (now known as Chitrapur) on the right bank of the Krishna River. Both sides fought fiercely. The enemies specifically targeted Rajadhiraja, aiming their arrows at him. What happened? The royal elephant he was riding was killed; the valiant warrior Rajadhiraja himself became the target of the enemy arrows and was killed. Immediately, the enemies shouted in victory and charged forward. The Chola warriors, shaken by the situation, fell back. Seeing the chaos, Rajendra Chola Devan, who was behind, shouted 'Do not fear, do not fear!' and charged ahead; the Chola warriors rallied together; they donned their battle gear and fought with the intention of avenging their fallen comrades. As before, the Chalukyas aimed many arrows at Rajendra Chola Devan to bring him down. However, it was in vain. The Chola warrior killed Jayasimha, the younger brother of the Chalukya king, as well as Pulikesi, Dasapanman, Nanni Nulamban, and others.

The feudal lord Vaniraivan, the heavily armed Duththan, Kundamaiyan, some princes, and the Chalukyan Agavamalla fled from the battlefield. The elephants, horses and chariots of the enemies, along with treasures such as the royal umbrella, priceless swords, royal insignia, noblewomen, and other valuables—all fell into the hands of Rajendra Chola. Immediately, Rajendra did something that no one else had done before. Though his body was still wounded by the enemy's arrows, he crowned himself as the emperor of the Chola Empire on the battlefield itself. Later, Rajendra went to Kolhapur, where he established a victory flag and returned to Gangaikonda Cholapuram.

Since Rajadhiraja died while riding an elephant, he earned the title 'the Lord who died on an elephant'—a title by which he is referred to in later inscriptions.

Family

Rajadhiraja was born under the Poorva Phalguni star. He ruled from Gangaikonda Cholapuram. One of his wives, known as Thirailokkiyamudaiyar, was called Pirattiyaar. The names of his other wives are not known. His eulogy mentions that he appointed his uncles, brothers, and children as political officials. However, it is unclear who they were or what became of them.

Titles

Rajadiraja held various titles, including Vijayarajendra (a title associated with Kalyanapuram), Veerarajendra Varman, Agavamalla Kulantakan, and Chola who conquered Kalyanapuram among others.

Minor Rulers and Officials

During Rajadhiraja's reign, there were many who served as both minor rulers and high officials of the empire. One of them was Rajadhiraja Neelaganga Rayar, known as 'Dandanayakan Chola Kumaran Paranthakamarayan.' Another was Pillaiyar Chola Vallabha Devan, the husband of Panjavan Mahadeviyaar, while in the Kadappa region, there was Dandanayakan Appimayan, who ruled over the Maharasapadi Elayiram (a region or administrative division). Pillaiyar Vasuvardhana Devar, also known as Chalukya Rajarajan, was another official. His wife was Ammanga Devi, the daughter of Rajendra and the sister of Rajadhiraja. In 1050 CE, she donated 300 golden coins, known as *Rajaraja Madais*, to the temple at Thiruvaiyaru in the Vengi region.

Senapati Rajendra Chola Mavali Vanarayan was another significant official. There was also Ulagalandha Chola Brahmamarayan, a notable figure. He was also known as 'Adhikarigal Parashrayan Vasudeva Narayanan'. He is identified as the spiritual teacher (Gurudevan) of Rajadhiraja. Since he was called 'Ulagalandhan', it is believed that land surveying might have taken place during the reign of Rajadhiraja.

In the twenty sixth year of Rajadhiraja's reign, Tirukkalukkunram was called 'Ulagalandha Cholapuram' (the city of the Chola who measured the world).'

Personal Virtues

It would not be an exaggeration to say that Rajadhiraja spent his entire life in battles. He spent twenty-six years alongside his father and ten years as the sole ruler, a total of thirty-six years in warfare. He seems to have been born a warrior!

It would not be wrong to say that the Chola Empire remained strong due to the military prowess of this great warrior. Realising his extraordinary strength even in his youth, Rajendra Chola bypassed his eldest son and made Rajadhiraja his crown prince. He shone as an unmatched warrior even during his father's reign. His inscriptions begin with phrases such as *Thingaler Peravalar* and *Thingaler Tharu* (both poetic honorifics, roughly meaning 'he who flourishes like the moon' or 'he who gives like the moon').

Rajendra Chola Devan (1052–1064 CE)

Crown Prince

Rajendra Chola Devan became the crown prince in 1044 CE. From that time onwards, he had been managing political affairs along with his younger brother, Rajadiraja. He held the title 'Parakesari'.

Emperor

In 1054 CE, Rajadhiraja died in the Battle of Koppam. Immediately, Rajendra, with great valour, fought the battle, destroyed the enemy army, captured their treasures and resources, and crowned himself king on that very battlefield, as previously mentioned.

War in Eezham

According to Rajendra Chola II's inscription dated 1055 CE, 'Rajendra sent a large army to Eezham (Sri Lanka). That army defeated Veerasala Meghan and captured the two sons of Maanabarana, the ruler of Eezham'. This indicates that Eezham was under Chola control. A further evidence, an inscription of Rajendra Chola was found at Sangili Kanadarava, which further attests that Eezham was under his rule.

Chola Coins in Lanka

Chola coins discovered in Lanka bearing the names of Rajadhiraja and Rajendra Devan, are further evidence that a large part of Eezham was under the Chola Empire. However, the southern district of Rohana remained independent.

Rohana Rebellion

In 1058 CE, a person named Kitti, known by the name

'Vijayabahu', became the ruler of the Rohana province and initiated a war against the Cholas. However, during Rajendra Devan's reign, his efforts proved unsuccessful.

PART III

ONE

Kulothunga I (1070–1122 CE)

The History of Kulothunga's Coronation (1070 CE)

Birth and Childhood

Ammanga Devi, the daughter of Rajendra Chola, married Rajaraja Narendra. On an auspicious Poosam day in 1043 CE, she gave birth to a son. He was named Rajendra after his maternal grandfather. According to the Eastern Chalukya tradition, he was also named Vishnuvardhana VII.

Family Background

Rajaraja Narendra had a half-brother named Vijayaditya VII, born to his father Vimaladitya's younger wife. Rajaraja Narendra ruled the Vengi region from 1018 to 1039 CE (for twenty-one years). During this period, Vijayaditya served as his assistant and governed the land. Vijayaditya had a son named 'Sakti Varman'. Kulothunga received the title of crown prince, lived with his father and assisted in administration.

Confusion

In 1060 CE, Rajaraja Narendra passed away. However, the crown prince Kulothunga did not immediately take up rule of Vengi. He entrusted the kingdom to his uncle and headed north, aiming to capture regions such as Vairagaram and Chakrakottam. His focus remained entirely on the Chola Empire. Meanwhile, Vikramaditya VI sent Chamundaraya with a large army to capture Vengi. Realising this, Virarajendra marched directly from Koodal Sangamam, defeated the enemies, reclaimed Vengi, and handed it over to Vijayaditya.

Athirajendra

Virarajendra died in 1059–1070 CE. His son Athirajendra ascended the throne with the title 'Parakesari'. The credit for crowning him goes to Vikramaditya VI of the Western Chalukya dynasty. Upon Virarajendra's death, Vikramaditya came to Kanchipuram, then proceeded to Gangaikonda Cholapuram, where he crowned his brother-in-law Athirajendran. He stayed there for a month, and then returned to his country, believing his brother-in-law would rule without fear.

Crowning

After he left, there was turmoil in the Chola country. In that chaos, Athirajendran was killed, and the country suffered greatly. Upon learning of this, Kulothunga, who had been fighting at Chakrakottam to the north of Vengi, returned to the Chola country. In 1070 CE, he crowned himself as the emperor of the Chola empire at Gangaikonda Cholapuram, entrusting the rule of Vengi to his uncle, Vijayaditya VII.

Chakrakottam Campaign

Toward the end of Virarajendra's reign, Kulothunga I led a large army to the north of Vengi. In the central province, at a place called Vairagaram, he captured a large number of elephants and set fire to the place. He defeated Taravarshan in battle and forced him to pay tribute. Chakrakottam, now known as 'Chitrakootam,' is located in central India, about 25 miles west of Jagdalpur. An inscription from Kuruspal states *Chakrakotteeshwaranam.... Taravarsha Name Nareswara* (meaning The lord of Chakrakotta, the king named Taravasha) which confirms that Taravarshan was indeed the ruler of Chakrakottam.

War with the Chalukyas

This great war took place between Vikramaditya VI and Kulothunga I in 1076 CE. After learning that his cousin Athirajendra was killed and Kulothunga had become the Chola emperor, Vikramaditya was disturbed. He realized that both the Chola empire and the Vengi region were now under the rule of a single king, which was not favourable to him. At that time, both Vikramaditya and his brother, Somesvara II, experienced great internal conflict. As a result, Vikramaditya left Kalyanapuram with his younger brother Jayasimha. Thus, the Rattapadi kingdom was divided into two parts, one ruled by Somesvara II and the other by Vikramaditya VI. Recognising this internal conflict, Kulothunga allied himself with Somesvara II. This led to a full-blown war.

Tripuvanamalla Pandyan, Kadambakula Jayakesi, the Devagiri Yadava king, and Hoysalas such as Eriangar supported Vikramaditya.

Vikramaditya launched the first attack and marched up to Kolar. Kulothunga confronted him and chased him as far as the Tungabhadra River. Battles took place along the way at places like Alatti and Manalur. Ultimately, a fierce battle ensued on the banks of the Tungabhadra River. Somesvara was defeated in this battle, captured by Vikramaditya, and lost his kingdom.

Vikramaditya, who sought to defeat Kulothunga, ultimately conquered his brother and brought the entire Rattapadi region under his control. Jayasimha ruled the southern part of Rattapadi with Vanavasi as its capital. In this war, a significant portion of the Mysore region came under Kulothunga's control. His inscriptions found there confirm this fact. The epic poem *Parani* mentions that Kulothunga captured herds of elephants in Navilai. The Vikrama Chola *Ula* (panegyric) states that he reached the western sea and also conquered Vanavasi.

Separation of Sri Lanka

Vijayabahu, who ruled the southern part of Sri Lanka, attempted to take control of the northern part in 1070 CE. During that period, there was much unrest in the Chola empire, as Kulothunga was trying to bring peace after assuming the throne. Therefore, he could not focus on Sri Lanka. Seizing this opportunity, Vijayabahu marched and attacked Polonnaruwa, defeating the Chola forces and capturing and killing their commander.

However, soon after, a large Chola army arrived from the mainland and reached Eezham. A great battle took place at Anuradhapura. Vijayabahu fled south. During this time, the Cholas incited a rebellion among Vijayabahu's supporters. Nevertheless, the capable Vijayabahu subdued the rebellion and expelled its leader, who had been influenced by the Cholas. He then went to Tamblagramam, built a fort, and raised a new army. He sent two large armies to attack the Chola forces from two sides.

One army attacked Anuradhapura, while the other attacked Polonnaruwa. After fierce battles, Polonnaruwa fell, followed by Anuradhapura. Thus, the Chola rule, established by Rajaraja

Chola in Sri Lanka, collapsed in 1076 CE. Vijayabahu crowned himself at Anuradhapura and immediately began to uphold and promote Buddhism, following the traditions of his ancestors.

Pandya Region

The Pandyas had always been a source of trouble for the Cholas. In 1070 CE, when the empire began to decline, there was great unrest in the Pandya country. All the laws and political structures established by the previous Chola rulers were disregarded in Pandya Nadu. Chera Nadu also followed Pandya Nadu's example. At this time, Kulothunga returned after completing the northern campaign against the Western Chalukyas. He became aware of the chaotic situation in the south. He was not worried about Lanka because it was across the sea and posed no immediate threat. However, Pandya Nadu was adjacent to Chola Nadu. If it became independent, it would threaten the Chola empire. Kulothunga also knew that the Pandyas were vengeful and would certainly seek revenge for their past defeats. Therefore, he decided to first subdue the Pandya Nadu.

Pandya Nadu War

Kulothunga dispatched an enormous army—horses like waves of sea, elephants like ships, and infantry forces flowing like water. The army moved southward as if the northern sea was rushing to swallow the southern sea. Five Pandya rebels fled into the dense forest fearing the Chola army. The Chola army destroyed the forest, conquered the Pandya region, and erected victory pillars in all directions. The five Pandyas were driven into hiding in the cruel mountain forests. The Chola army also seized the pearl-harvesting places and the sacred Tamil Pothigai hills. Delighted by this grand victory, Kulothunga rewarded his soldiers by granting them villages throughout Pandya Nadu and stationed a garrison at Kottaru.

The *Vikrama Cholan Ula* (a royal eulogy) states: 'Kulothunga destroyed the Pandya dynasty, subdued the Chera pride, and twice blocked ships on the Kandalur coast.' The *Kalingathu Parani* (a war poem) adds: 'Kulothunga's army defeated the Pandyas and drove the Cholas away, capturing the important port cities of Salai and Vizhinjam.'

Thus, Kulothunga conquered both the Pandya and Chera regions and established peace. He appointed local chieftains to rule these regions peacefully and stationed his garrison in various places. However, he did not interfere in the governance of these local rulers. It can be said that they largely retained autonomy. All Kulothunga expected from them was submission and the payment of tribute. This is evident from the fact that Kulothunga's inscriptions are few in these regions.

Southern Unrest

Fifteen years after the above-mentioned events, unrest arose again in the south. In this turmoil, Velnadu (Southern Thiruvananthapuram) stood out. To quell this disturbance, Kulothunga sent a general named Naraloka Veeran, who also had another name—Kalingarayan. Several inscriptions mention him. This great warrior suppressed the unrest, defeated the enemies, and restored peace in the southern region.

The Eezham Connection

Kulothunga, desiring to establish friendly relations with the autonomous ruler Vijayabahu, sent a diplomatic delegation. At the same time, Vikramaditya (of the Chalukyas) also sent an embassy with valuable gifts. Vijayabahu welcomed both parties and honoured them. First he sent the Chalukya envoys back along with his own emissaries. However, when they entered Chola territory, the Chola people cut off the noses and ears of the Eezham envoys and sent them back.

Upon learning this, Vijayabahu became enraged. He summoned the Chola envoys and said, 'Let your king come and fight me one-on-one. Otherwise, let the armies of both sides battle and determine the strength.' He then dressed the envoys in women's clothing and sent them back to the Chola kingdom. He despatched a fleet of soldiers by ships to attack the Chola country.

Two commanders were to lead the fleet. At that time, however, the Tamil Velaikkara troops in the Eezham army rebelled, stating they could not fight against their own people. They killed the two commanders, looted Polonnaruwa, kidnapped the king's sister and her three children, and set fire to the royal palace.

Vijayabahu fled to the southern province. After hiding his wealth, he returned to Polonnaruwa with a strong force, fought fiercely, and drove away the enemies. He then captured their leaders, tied their hands, and burned them alive as revenge.

However, Vijayabahu did not stop there. In his forty-fifth year of reign, he assembled a proper army and waited on the southern coast of Lanka, expecting the Chola king to confront him. When the Chola king did not come, he returned in frustration. This event is said to have occurred around 1088 CE.

After these events, Kulothunga became friends with Vijayabahu. He gave his daughter Suryavalliyar in marriage to Veerapperumal, a Sinhalese prince aligned with the Pandya faction in Eezham.

Relationship with China

Just as Rajaraja and Rajendra had sent envoys to China to boost maritime trade, in 1077 CE, Kulothunga sent a delegation of seventy-two people to the Chinese kingdom. They took as gifts for the Chinese emperor items such as glassware, camphor, rhinoceros' horns, ivory, perfumes, cloves, cardamom, and many other items. The emperor warmly welcomed them and gratefully received the gifts. In return, he honoured them by giving 81,800 copper coins.

Relationship with Kadaram

The *Parani* states that Kulothunga destroyed Kadaram. Kulothunga's inscriptions indicating that the valuable goods were sent as gifts from overseas countries. One inscription mentions that the king of Cambodia presented Kulothunga with a valuable stone.

In 1020 CE, the king of Kadaram (Srivijaya), requested Kulothunga to issue a donation order for two small villages to be dedicated as revenue sources for two Buddhist monasteries built in Nagapattinam. These monasteries were named Rajaraja Perumpalli and Rajendra Chola Perumpalli. The individuals who came from Kadaram to receive this charter were Raja Vidyadhara Sri Samantan and Abhimanotunga Samantan. The charter was issued by the king from the royal court in Pazhayarai, seated on a throne named 'Kalingarayan'. The gifts brought from Kadaram were adorned on elephants standing at the palace gates.

An inscription found in Sumatra reveals the existence of a Chola trading group known as the *Disai Ayirathu Ainnurvar*. The name of this group means 'A hundred merchants from a thousand towns, from all directions'. These references suggest that Kulothunga had a close relationship with Srivijaya and that maritime trade was conducted smoothly between them.

Vengi Region

While Kulothunga was in the process of stabilising Chola rule, in 1072-3 CE, Yasakarna Deva, the Haihaya King who ruled Tripuri, attacked Vengi. In one of his inscriptions, he states, 'I defeated the mighty Andhra king and presented several ornaments to Lord Bhimeshwara in Draksharama'. The Andhra king referred to here was none other than Vijayaditya VII, Kulothunga's uncle. There is no evidence to suggest that Yasakarna conquered or annexed Vengi, though he did invade it.

Prince Ruler of Vengi

Jayasimhan, who ruled Vengi, did not have good relations with Kulothunga. It appears that King Rajaraja of the Western Ganga dynasty acted as a mediator between them. Jayasimhan's inscriptions indicate that he fought against Kulothunga on behalf of Vijayaditya. The details are unclear. This Ganga king married Kulothunga's daughter, Rajasundari.

Jayasimhan died in 1076 CE. Immediately, Kulothunga sent one of his sons, Rajaraja Mummudi Chola, to govern Vengi. He ruled the region for one year and then left. In 1077 CE, another prince, Veera Chola, began his rule over Vengi, which lasted for six years.

From 1084 to 1089 CE, another son, Rajaraja Chola Kangan, ruled Vengi. He was Kulothunga's eldest son. In 1089 CE, Veera Chola was again sent to govern Vengi, and he ruled until 1092-93 CE.

From 1093 to 1119 CE, another prince, Vikrama Chola, ruled Vengi. He later became the Chola emperor after Kulothunga.

The First Kalinga War

This war occurred in the twentieth year of Kulothunga's reign (in

1096 CE). It was fought between the Chola prince who ruled over Vengi and the king of Southern Kalinga.

In this war, Telugu Bheeman, a minor king of Kollanu (Elluru), supported the king of Kalinga. As a result, Vikrama Chola had to fight both of them simultaneously. Parakramapandya, a subordinate of the Chola empire, moved north to assist Vikrama Chola, and together they conquered Southern Kalinga.

Bheeman was captured. Southern Kalinga refers to the region between the Godavari River and the Mahendra Mountains, an area that was part of the Vengi kingdom.

With the king of this region captured and subdued, Southern Kalinga became a peaceful country. Kulothunga's inscriptions from 1098 CE have been found in this region, particularly at Simhachalam and Draksharama.

Second Kalinga War

This took place around 1111 CE. It is mentioned in the inscriptions of Kulothunga and described in greater detail in *Kalingathu Parani*.

First, let us see what the inscriptions say:

> The Chola army crossed the Vengi region; the enemy sent an elephant corps to stop the Chola army. All those elephants were killed. The Chola forces set fire to the Kalinga country; it killed all the valorous warriors of the Kalinga army. Their heads rolled on the battlefield, and vultures devoured them. Ultimately, northern Kalinga was subdued.

The Kalinga king was Ananta Varman. He did not acknowledge the Chola king and did not pay tribute. Therefore, the Chola king sent his commander Karunakara Tondaiman with a large army. The army that accompanied that commander crossed the rivers Palaaru, Ponmugari, Pazhavaaru, Koliyaaru, Vadapennaaru, Vayalaaru, Mannaaru, Kundriyaaru and also crossed the Krishna; after that, it crossed the Godavari, Pambai and Godamai rivers, reaching the Kalinga territory. There, they looted several towns while setting fire to some cities.

Upon hearing about the army's movements, the Kalinga king became enraged and gathered his troops. At that time, a minister named Engarayan advised him with ample evidence to consider peace, explaining the strength of the Chola army. The king did not heed the advice. Ultimately, a battle occurred. The Kalinga king was defeated. Karunakara Tondaiman could not capture him, so he returned to the Chola country with much wealth.

Although the poet Jayamkondar seems to have exaggerated certain events in his account, the inscriptions confirm that the expedition and victory are indeed true reports.

Who was Ananta Varman, the Kalinga king? He was the son of Rajaraja Ganga and Rajasundari, the daughter of Kulothunga.

But so what? Royal arrogance does not care for kinship, does it? The reason is not appropriate. Northern Kalinga was not under the Chola rule. There is also no evidence that the Cholas conquered and ruled northern Kalinga.

It is more plausible that the king of North Kalinga, driven by territorial ambition, tried to capture South Kalinga. This information reached Kulothunga from the Kanchi palace. He immediately sent Tondaiman to assist the prince of Vengi. This reason seems to be appropriate.

Alternatively, it can also be said that both the First and the Second Kalinga War were instigated by the intrigues of the Chalukyan Vikramaditya.

With the goal of removing Vengi from Chola control, he may

have incited several petty kings against the prince of Vengi. This incitement attempt may have borne fruit around 1118 CE.

Vengi Kingdom

Realizing that his end was near, Kulothunga summoned Vikrama Chola from Vengi in 1118 CE. Immediately, unrest broke out in the Vengi region. This is confirmed by Kulothunga's forty-eighth regnal year inscriptions and by those of Vikrama Chola. Kulothunga's inscriptions have been found at Draksharama up to his forty-eighth year. There are no inscriptions from Vengi after Vikrama Chola received his title. From then on Guntur seems to have become the northern boundary. A reference to this palace situation can be seen in the inscriptions of Uttama Chola. From this, one can clearly understand that Vengi had been separated.

However, many inscriptions from the forty-fifth to the forty-eighth regnal years of Vikramaditya have been found in Vengi and places like Draksharama. These inscriptions belong to local rulers of Vengi region. Among these, one states that it was the regnal year of Vikramaditya, and that these minor rulers were subordinate to his empire.

An inscription states that in 1118 CE, Ananthapalaiyan, a chieftain of Vikramaditya, ruled Vengi. Another inscription dated 1120 CE, referring to a grant by his wife to the Bhimeshwara temple, also mentions Vikramaditya's regnal year. The inscriptions from Draksharama refer to Vikramaditya's rule up to 1132–3 CE. A relative of Ananthapalaiyan governed Kondapalli in the Krishna region in 1127 CE, and Nanbirasa, known as the king of Kollippakkai, ruled the territory south of the Krishna River in 1131 CE.

From these evidences, it appears that the Vengi kingdom, which had been a rightful part of Kulothunga's Empire, was captured by Vikramaditya at the end of his reign in 1118 CE. This outcome shows that Vikramaditya achieved his original goal—namely, to separate Chola country and Vengi into distinct kingdoms.

The Separation of Gangapadi

The region comprising the forts of Hassan and Kadur in Mysore, as well as the Nagamangala taluk, was first ruled by the Hoysalas. The Hoysalas had been around since the time of King Rajaraja. The first king among them was Thirumagaman (1022–1040 CE). His son was Vinayaditya. His grandson was Eriyanga. Vinayaditya ruled from 1040 to 1100 CE.

In 1100 CE, King Pittiga Vishnuvardhana ascended the throne. He recovered Thalaikadu from the Cholas in 1116 CE, and hence prefixed his name with the title *Thalaikadu-konda* (meaning 'he who conquered Thalaikadu'). An inscription of his reveals that, in that same year, he brought the whole of Gangapadi under his rule.

Gangapadi had been under Chola rule for a long time. It bordered Kongu country; it was under the oversight of the Adiyamans, who ruled Kongu Nadu. The Adiyamans served both as Chola army leaders and subordinate rulers under the Cholas. Vishnuvardhana's general Gangarasa invited the Adiyaman ruler to surrender.

When the Adiyaman refused, war broke out. Chola army leaders like Damodaran, Narasimha Varman and others fought, but in the end, they were defeated.

As a result, Gangapadi came under Hoysala rule. Kulothunga's inscriptions have been found in Gangapadi only up to the year 1115 CE. Under the Cholas, the region was called Rajarajapuram. Therefore, it is true that Gangapadi changed hands in 1116 CE.

Foreign Relations

During Kulothunga's reign, the great Chola empire had close ties with foreign countries. The ties with Kadaram and China have already been discussed earlier.

An inscription found in the temple at Gangaikonda Cholapuram indicates the connection the Chola empire had with the northern regions.

It praises the Kanauj king Madanapalan or perhaps his son Govinda Chandra. The inscription starts with a reference to the forty-first regnal year of Kulothunga, followed by the praise of the Kanauj king, and finally outlines the reason for the inscription. The exact nature of the relationship between Kanauj and the Chola kingdom is unknown.

The people of Kanauj were sun worshippers and sun worship had a special place in the Chola realm during Kulothunga's rule. A copper-plate grant of Govinda Chandra mentions that a Chola named Vagishvaraksitha was a disciple of Sakyaraksithar from Odisha. The copper-plate grant of Govinda Chandra (the Kanauj king) dates back to 1129 CE.

The king of the Cambodian country showed a precious stone to Kulothunga and later gifted it to him. An inscription dated 1114 CE in the Chidambaram temple indicates that Kulothunga placed it on the wall facing the inner shrine at the Chidambaram temple.

The Chola Empire

Under Kulothunga's rule, the Chola Empire remained as it had been for forty-five years (until 1115 CE). Only the Eezham province to the south had separated from the empire. Gangapadi was separated in 1116 CE. In 1118 CE, a large part of the Vengi region also came under the rule of the Western

Chalukyas. Towards the end of Kulothunga's time, the northern boundary was marked by Kadappa and Kurnool regions. In the Kadappa region, Nandalur was known as 'Kulothunga Chola Chaturvedi Mangalam'.

Gangaikonda Cholapuram was the primary royal capital of Kulothunga and remained his most important city. Next was Kanchipuram. From the Abhisheka Mandapam there, the king issued many prestigious edicts. Another important palace was in Ayiraththali (Pazhaiyarai), which had been developed and maintained by Rajendra Chola I. Thirumazhapadi was considered a significant and prosperous city, well-suited for royal residence.

Vassal Kings

Several minor kings are mentioned in the inscriptions that surfaced from Kulothunga's rule.

1. In the northwest hilly region of the South Arcot fort, a group of chieftains called Chethirayar ruled. Their capital was Kiliyur.
2. According to inscription 1.29 of 1908 (A.R.E), Periya Udaiyan Rajarasan, known as Chandran Malayana Rajendra Cholan, ruled in Thirumunaipadi as a feudatory of the imperial Cholas. He had some chieftains under him. They included the likes of Malayakularasan.
3. The western part of North Arcot and the eastern part of Mysore formed a region called Mulvai Nadu. It was ruled by a chieftain named Ganga Nulamban.
4. In Vengi, a minor king known as 'Kongan' was the chief of the northern region. He was prominent, and his lineage ruled the region peacefully for a long time. The inscription states that Kulothunga regarded this Kongan's son as his own son and honoured him.
5. A minor king named Pothappi Kama Sodi Maharajan ruled

Kadappa. His military chiefs included Ramannan and Pekkada Bhimayan.

6. Another minor Telugu king from the Pallava lineage referred to himself as Maha Mandaleshwaran and Kanchipureswaran.

Ministers and Military Commanders

There were many ministers and commanders under Kulothunga's rule, but only a few were especially prominent. Among them:

- One was Gnanamurthi Pandithan, also known as Maduranthaka Brahmadhirajan. He hailed from Nalur, belonging to the Vatsa gotra. He served as one of the military commanders of the Chola king.
- Another was Bharadvaja Mantra Narayanan. He was also known by the title 'Veera Santhosha Brahma Chakravarthi'. He appears to have ruled over Tiruppattur as a local chieftain and also served as a minister under Kulothunga.
- Karunakara Tondaiman was both a highly celebrated commander and minister. He belonged to the Pallava dynasty and was praised in the *Kalingathu Parani* by Jayamkondar with epithets like 'King of the Vandaiyars, the Lord of Kings, Minister, and World-renowned Karunakaran'. He also served during the reign of Vikrama Chola, which is confirmed by Vikrama Chola's inscriptions. His native village was Vandai, which an inscription identifies as Vandalanjeri in the Thirunaraiyur region of the Kulothunga Chola Valanadu in the Chola kingdom. Today it is known as 'Vanduvancheri'. His wife's name was Azhagiya Manavalani Mandaiyazhvar. She made donations to several temples. Karunakara Tondaiman's brother was Senapati Pallavarasar. His emblem was the ancient Nandi flag of the Pallavas. He also participated in the Kalinga war, as mentioned in *Parani*. The *Thiruvarur Ula* (a temple chronicle) notes that

Karunakaran was deeply devoted to Lord Siva of Thiruvarur, undertook many temple renovations there, and finally merged with the feet of the Lord. Among the names of Lord Thyagaraja, one is Karunakara Tondaiman, which is said to have originated from him, highlighting his devout Shaivism.

- Araiyaan Maduranthakan alias Kulothunga Chola Kerala Rasan was another distinguished military commander. He governed Muzhaiyur in Manni Nadu of the Chola kingdom. He earned the title 'Kulothunga Chola Keralarajan' by leading his army to victory in the war against the Chera kingdom. He was also in charge of the standing army (*Nilaipadai*) stationed in Kottaru (present-day Kottar). He constructed a temple there called Rajendra Choleswaram for which Kulothunga himself provided land. It is evident that this chief was also a great devotee of Shiva.
- Kalingarayan, also called Manavi Koothan, was a highly distinguished military commander. He was the head of the town Manavil, one of the twenty-four divisions in the Tondai region. He established himself as a commander under Kulothunga, and led campaigns against regions such as Pandya Nadu, Venadu, and Malainadu, gaining widespread fame. His achievements brought enduring glory to the Chola dynasty. Recognizing his skills, Kulothunga honoured him with the title 'Kalingarayan'. He also held a prominent position during the rule of Vikrama Chola.
- He was a great devotee of Shiva, showing profound love for Lord Nataraja of Chidambaram. He undertook many renovations at the Chidambaram temple: he gilded the roof of the Thillai Ambalam (dancing hall); he constructed the hundred-pillared hall, a grand circumambulatory mansion, a mandapam for reciting the Tevaram hymns, and the Sivakama shrine; he donated villages such as Thyagavalli to the temple as devadana (land grants to temples); he had the hymns of the three Tamil Shaivite saints (Moovar

Tevaram) inscribed on copper plates and preserved them at Thillai Chidambaram. At the Thiruvathigai temple, this valiant commander, built the Kamakottam shrine and gilded it with gold; established a dance hall; built a sacrificial hall (Yagasala); and donated lands as devadana. These noble acts of temple service were many, and verses (venpa) that praise these contributions are inscribed at both the Chidambaram and Thiruvathigai temples.

Titles of the King

The King bore several honorific titles including Rajakesari, Kulothunga Choladevan, Tribhuvana Chakravarti, Rajendran, Vishnuvardhanan, Sarvalokashrayan, Parantakan, Perumaan Adigal, Vikrama Cholan, Kulasekara Pandya Kulantakan, Abhayan, and Sayadharan. He was also known by the name Thiruneetru Cholan (sacred ash wearing Chola). A village was named after him using this title. He earned the title 'Sungam Thavirtha Cholan' (The Chola Who Abolished Taxes).

Other notable epithets of Kulothunga Chola found in literary works like the *Kalingattu Parani* include: Ulaguyya Vandhan (He who came to uplift the world) and Virudaraja Bayankaran (Virudaraja, the Fearsome). These titles reflect his power, piety, and the admiration he earned during his reign.

Territorial Divisions

During Kulothungan's rule, the vast Chola kingdom was divided into several *Mandalams* (regions): (1) Chola Mandalam, (2) Jayamkonda Chola Mandalam, (3) Rajaraja Pandya Mandalam, (4) Mummudi Chola Mandalam, (5) Vengai Mandalam, (6) Malai Mandalam, and (7) Adhirajarasa Mandalam.

Of these, Chola Mandalam included the Thanjavur and Tiruchirappalli districts along with part of the southern Arcot district; Jayamkonda Chola Mandalam encompassed a significant part of the southern Arcot district, as well as Chengalpattu, North Arcot, and Chitoor districts. Rajaraja Pandya Mandalam encompassed the territories of Madurai, Ramanathapuram, and Tirunelveli among other districts. Mummudi Chola Mandalam consisted of the northern parts of Ceylon. Vengai Mandalam referred to the region of the Western Chalukyas (Chalukyas of Vengi). Malai Mandalam consisted of Travancore, Kochi, part of the Salem district, and the Malabar district. Adhirajarasa Mandalam consisted of the Coimbatore district and a significant portion of the Salem district, also known as Kongu Nadu.

During the reign of Kulothungan, these mandalams were further divided into *valanadus* (larger divisions), and *valanadus* into *nadus* (smaller regions). He renamed many of these divisions by replacing them with names reflecting his own royal titles. For instance, he changed Kshatriya Sigamani Valanadu to Kulothunga Chola Valanadu. He divided Rajendran Singavala Nadu into two parts: the western region was named Ulaguyya Vanda Chola Valanadu ('The Chola Who Came to Uplift the World' Valanadu). The eastern part was named Virudaraja Bayankara Valanadu ('The Fearsome Hero King' Valanadu).

In general, these valanadus were bounded by two rivers, as confirmed by stone inscriptions. Only the Jayamkonda Chola Mandalam, known also as Tondai Nadu, retained its traditional administrative setup of 24 kottams (subdivisions), just as it had during the Pallava times.

Politics and Governance

Kulothunga was an excellent political strategist; who clearly understood that winning the hearts of people was his primary responsibility. Hence, one of his first actions was to abolish the customs tax (*sungum*) that people paid annually to the king. This tax was primarily imposed on export goods. Because of this popular reform, people praised him by calling him *Sungam Thavirtha Cholan* (the Chola who abolished taxes). The poet Jayamkondar in the epic *Kalingathu Parani* also praises him as *Taviraadha Sungam Thavirthon* (the one who exempted the unavoidable taxes). It appears that this tax exemption was limited to the Chola heartland! An inscription dated to 1194 CE confirms that 'no taxes were collected in the Chola country'. An example of this policy's legacy is the Karundittai near Thanjavur, which came to be known as *Sungam Thavirtha Cholanallur* (Sangam Exempted Cholanallur). Furthermore, in his seventeenth and fortieth regnal years, Kulothunga ordered a land survey and after the measurements were completed, he levied only one-sixth of the yield as tax from the people. He also exempted certain lands from taxation altogether. These are among the finest achievements of his reign.

The King

Kulothunga was a great scholar. He was born in the Vengi region; being the son of Rajaraja Narendra, who had Nannaya Bhattana compose the Mahabharata in Telugu; he was well-versed in the Telugu language. It is said that he also possessed knowledge of Sanskrit. He had a good knowledge of Tamil, as noted by the author of *Parani*. He is described as 'one who spent his time with arts, poets, poetry, and music. Since he was called 'Patron of Poets', it seems that besides Jayamkondar, many other scholars often visited him! It appears that he also supported many scholars! He was a great warrior! He was a political expert who, as soon as he ascended the throne, brought peace to a large kingdom that was in a chaotic state. He abolished the customs tax and won the hearts of the people. He was a learned man who, by establishing political relations with foreign countries like Kadaram, China, and Kamboja, expanded trade. He was a noble man who tried to regain the lost Eezham country without sacrificing lives. In short, it would not be an exaggeration to say that he was one of the great emperors, alongside Rajaraja and Rajendra.

Religious State

This great emperor was a devoted Shaivite. The Cholas were traditionally worshippers of Shiva. He was a pure devotee who worshipped the Lord of Thillai with great love; however, he was a venerable person who respected other religions as well. His inscriptions are found in temples of all religions. The Perumal temple in Mannargudi was built in his name. Its old name was 'Kulothunga Chola Vinnagaram'. Furthermore, during this great man's time, many small kings constructed many Vaishnava temples and made donations. Kulothunga donated lands to the Rajaraja Perumpalli (Buddhist Vihara) in Nagapattinam in 1090 CE. The copper plates that refer to this are found in the museum in the city of Leiden in the Netherlands. These are known as the 'Leiden Copperplates'. Some small kings and private individuals of his time also made donations to Jain monasteries. Therefore, it can be understood that during Kulothunga's reign, all religions received their due respect and support. However, the king himself remained a devout Shaivite. The fact that he referred to himself as *Thiruneetru Cholan* (Chola of the Holy Ash) is enough to illustrate his commitment to Shaivism.

Royal Family

Wives

It is said that Kulothunga married Maduranthaki, the daughter of Rajendra Devan. She bore him seven children. Since these sons became princes of Vengi from 1077 CE onwards, and considering that Kulothunga ascended the throne around 1070 CE, it can be inferred that he married Maduranthaki around 1060 CE. Maduranthaki was also known as Kopperundevi. She was referred to as Bhuvana *Muzhuthudaiyaal* and *Avani Muzhuthudaiyaal* (meaning the one who possessed the whole world). She also had the name Deena Chinthamani. She passed away before the thirtieth year of Kulothunga's rule, after which Thiyagavalli became the chief queen.

Another wife was Ezhisai Vallabhi. She was called *Ezhulagu Udaiyaal* (She who owns the seven worlds), so perhaps she was referred to as *Ezhisai Vallabhi.* Another royal consort was Thrailokkiya Mahadevi. In 1072 CE, she arranged for a lamp to be lit in the Aarpakkam temple, for the well-being of her mother, Umainangai. Another one of Kulothunga's wives was Kadavan Mahadevi, known as *Chola –Chorudaiyaan Aana Kadavan Mahadevi.* She was a Pallava princess. There was another wife named Kamba Mahadevi, also known as Thiribuvana Mahadevi, who was a devotee of Vishnu. One more wife, belonging to the Chola clan, was called 'Chola Kulavalli', referred to as the 'wife of Aadiththan-aanda Kuttiyaar'. From what has been stated, it is known that he had seven wives: (1) Maduranthaki, (2) Thiyagavalli, (3) Ezhisai Vallabhi, (4) Thrailokkiya Mahadevi, (5) Kadavan Mahadevi, (6) Kamba Mahadevi, (7) Chola Kulavalli.

Siblings

From the Chidambaram inscriptions, it is known that he had two sisters named Kundavai and Maduranthaki.

Children

Kulothunga and Maduranthaki had seven sons and two daughters. Among the sons Rajarajan, Veera Cholan, Cholangan, and Vikrama Cholan are mentioned in inscriptions. The eldest among them was Cholangan; the next was Rajarajan, followed by Veera Cholan; the fourth son was Vikrama Cholan. Of these, the one who captured Kulothunga's heart was Vikrama Cholan. He is the one who ascended the throne after his father. Kulothunga also held a deep affection for Veera Cholan and sent him to rule Vengi twice.

Among the daughters, only the names of three are known from inscriptions: Rajasundari, Suriyavalli, and Ammangai. Rajasundari married Rajarajan, the king of Kalinga. Suriyavalli married a prince from Lanka. There is no record regarding Pillaiyar Ammangai Alvar, only her name is known.

It is noteworthy that Rajakesari Kulothunga ruled the Chola Empire for fifty-two years until 1122 CE. After him, Vikrama Cholan became the emperor of the Chola dynasty. The inscriptions of this Kulothunga begin with phrases like *Thirumanni Valara, Thirumanni Vilanga, Poomel Arivaiyum, Poomaruviya Thirumadanthai, Pugazh Mathuvilanga, Pugazh Soozhndha Punari,* and *Poomevi Valar.*

TWO

Vikrama Chola (1122–1135 CE)

Introduction

Vikrama Chola ascended the throne in 1118 CE and ruled alongside his father until 1122 CE. He was born under the Uthiradam star in the Tamil month of Aani. During the latter part of his father's reign, he was recognised as the rightful heir to the Chola Empire. It is noted that much of his rule was marked by peace without war. Inscriptions from the regions of Gangapadi and Vengi, which had earlier been lost, suggest that large portions of these two regions were reintegrated into the Chola Empire during his time.

Inscriptions

Vikrama Chola has two types of *meikeerthi*s (eulogistic preambles to inscriptions). One begins with *Bhumadhu* or *Bhumagal Punara* (meaning "when the earth goddess rejoiced" or similar); the other begins with *Bhumadhu Midainthu* (when the earth goddess trembled). The inscriptions beginning with *Bhumagal Punara* describe the renovations he carried out at the Chidambaram temple. The inscriptions beginning with *Bhumadhu Midainthu* relate to Vikrama Chola's military campaign in South Kalinga during his time as crown prince. Neither of these mentions other wars or events.

Literature

The work *Vikram Chola Ula* was composed by Ottakoothar, the court poet of Vikrama Chola. He also composed a *Parani* celebrating the king's south Kalinga campaign as referenced in *Rajaraja Ula* and *Kulothunga Chola III Ula,* which mention the Talisai verse of *this Parani*. However, the *Parani* itself has not yet been found. Therefore, his history must be reconstructed through the inscriptions and the *Ula*.

Vengi Country

Vikrama Chola left the Vengi country and returned to his father in 1118 CE. From that point, the region became a part of the great empire of Vikramaditya. The Vengi country was governed by the Velanandu chieftains, who accepted the rule of the Chalukyas and continued as feudatories. However, in 1126 CE, the great ruler Vikramaditya passed away. Immediately, the southern region of Vengi was incorporated into the empire of Vikrama Chola. The fact that minor rulers in places like Guntur and Kollipakkai, who had earlier acknowledged Vikramaditya's authority, began recording Vikrama Chola as their overlord in inscriptions serves as clear evidence of this change. The minor rulers of Velanandu also accepted Vikrama Chola as their emperor.

Gangapadi

Only the eastern part of Gangapadi was integrated into Vikrama Chola's empire. It is not specified when or how this integration occurred. An inscription from his second regnal year, found at

Sugatur in Mysore, states that one of his military commanders built a temple there. Another inscription from his tenth regnal year, found in the Kolar district, records the construction of a temple tower (*vimana)*. These two inscriptions indicate that at least the eastern part of Gangapadi was under the great Chola empire during Vikrama Chola's reign.

Flood Calamity

During the sixth regnal year of Vikrama Chola, large parts of the North and South Arcot districts were devastated by floods. As a result, in some places, public lands were sold to pay government taxes. The village assemblies of towns like Thiruvotriyur and Thiruvardhigai were involved in these sales. Due to the severity of the floods, the temple in Koviladi in the Thanjavur district was abandoned. An inscription states, 'Because the times were unfortunate, our village was destroyed, and the people fled and scattered'. These references indicate that a major flood calamity occurred in the Chola country during the sixth and seventh regnal years of Vikrama Chola.

Politics

Vikrama Chola's reign was largely peaceful. Like his predecessors, the king was enthusiastic about touring and inspecting his empire. Although Gangaikonda Cholapuram was his capital, he also issued royal orders from palaces in towns like Pazhaiyarai. In 1122 CE, Vikrama Chola appears to have been in the palace at Mudi-konda Cholapuram (Pazhaiyarai). The next year, he was at Kunivalanallur in the Chengalpattu district, issuing commands from the Kulakkarai Mandapam which was likely similar to today's travellers' bungalows. In 1124 CE, he was located in the palace at Veera Narayanar Chaturvedimangalam (Kattu Mannar

Temple) in the South Arcot district. In 1120 CE, he had stayed in a palace in the town of Thillai (Chidambaram). These records show that the emperor was deeply attentive to the governance of his realm, moving across the kingdom and monitoring its affairs directly.

Chieftains

Several minor chieftains are mentioned in inscriptions and a few are also noted in the *Vikrama Chola Ula*. Let us look at those mentioned in the inscriptions.

One such figure was a chieftain named Soorai Nayakan, the son of Naraloka Veeran, who received great honour from Kulothunga I. Soorai Nayakan was a chieftain of the Sambuvarayar lineage, ruling over a large part of the North Arcot region. He is described as Sengeni Naalayiravan Ammaiyappan alias Rajendra Chola Sambuvarayan. His wife made some donations to the Thiruvallam Mutt in 1123 CE.

As per usual practice, the rulers of Kovalur, known as Sethirayars, continued as chieftains. In Tondai Nadu, a chieftain from the Chalukya family ruled with Anaivari as his capital.

Among the southern chieftains, there was one named 'Pandinaadu Kondaan'. In the Ramanathapuram district, there was a chieftain named Sundan Gangaikondaan, who ruled over Sivapuri. He was also known as Dwarapati Velan; he was known to have had excellent sword warriors with him.

In the Telugu country, there were many chieftains, a few of whom were notable. In 1121 CE, a chieftain named Maduranthakan, also known as Pothappi Chola, ruled Pothappi. He bore the titles of Mahamandaleshwar and Vimaladitta Devan and claimed descent from Karikalan. The Pothappi Chola kings are noted for their extensive contributions to the temple at Kalathi.

In Velanadu a chieftain named Kongayan, also known as Second Kongan, is mentioned. His ancestors were loyal to the Chola Empire and had participated in the Southern Kalinga campaigns alongside Vikrama Chola.

Another ruler of a region within Kalathi Nadu was Katti Deva Maharajan, who bore the title Maha Mandaleshwaran. His forefathers had also held power during the reign of Rajendra Chola I. A chieftain named Nambaiyan ruled over Kollipaakkai.

Now, let us see who the chieftains mentioned in *Vikrama Chola's Ula* are:

- Karunagara Tondaiman, the chief.
- A man named Munaiyatharaiyan, who ruled the Munai Padi region. He was a commander, a chieftain, and also a minister.
- A man called Cholar Kon, who defeated the Kongars, Gangars, and Maharathars.
- Suddhamallan Vanakovarayan, who excelled in the art of warfare.
- Kalingarayan, a hero of Naraloka.
- Kadavarayan, who ruled near Senji; he was skilled in taming and controlling maddened elephants.
- A chieftain who ruled Vel Nadu; he governed the land peacefully without hardship.
- Anantapalan, who performed many charitable deeds from the Ganges to Kanyakumari; he made several donations to the Siva temple in Thiruvavaduthurai.
- Sethiyarayan, who destroyed the fortresses of the Karunadars.
- Adhikan, who ruled Thagadur and defeated enemies in the Kalinga war.
- Vaththavan, who caused destruction in the northern regions with his elephants.

- Nulambapallavan, who achieved victory in both Kottaru and Kollam.
- Thirikarththan, who defeated the kingdoms of Kongu, Kudagu and the Chera-Pandya rulers.

King's Titles

A title dearly loved by Vikrama Chola was *Thyaga Samudran* (Ocean of Sacrifice), as seen in both his *Ula* (royal proclamation) and inscriptions. *Agalankan* is another title, meaning 'One Without Faults'. Along with these, he also held many honorary titles that belonged to his father.

Royal Family

It is not known how many wives Parakesari Vikrama Chola had. Inscriptions mention four wives. One was Mukko Kizhan, and another was Thyagapathagai. The former served as the chief queen until her death in 1127 CE, after which Thyagapathagai became the chief queen. An inscription from Thirumazhapadi describing her states:

> She was like an ornament to all women, with curly hair, resembling a gentle doe, possessing pure virtues, said to be the mistress of the three worlds, fully blessed with the king's affection, and resplendent as she sat by the king's side.

In the same inscription, another wife, Tharani Muzhuthudaiyal, was described as;

> A woman among women, like a peacock in grace, celestial Arundhati among mortals, and like Goddess Lakshmi resting on the chest of Vishnu, she dwelled in the king's heart.

The third wife was Nambirattiyar Neriyaan Mahadevi. Inscriptions indicate that she had an *Agapparivaram*, referring to the retinue of female attendants traditionally assigned to a royal consort.

Vikrama Chola had a son named Kulothungan, who succeeded him as the next emperor of the Chola dynasty.

Religious Contributions

Since Gangaikonda Cholapuram became the Chola capital, the nearby Thillai city began to gain importance. From the time of Vijayalaya to Rajaraja Chola, the kings particularly revered Thiruvarur. Among them, it was Parantaka I who first glorified Chidambaram. From the time of Rajendra Chola, Thillai attained great prominence. During the reign of Kulothunga I, Chidambaram reached a highly elevated status. Lord Thillai was seen as the tutelary deity of the Chola dynasty.

During the reign of Vikrama Chola, the Thillai Peruman Temple flourished immensely. In 1128 CE, he generously spent a substantial portion of the tribute received from minor kings to renovate and expand the Thillai Peruman Temple and to carry out other religious works.

An inscription from Thirumazhapadi mentions this in detail:

> In the tenth regnal year, the pure gold treasures brought by minor kings were presented before the emperor. Engraved upon a jewel-studded golden plate was the prayer, 'May the king live long and protect the world!'
>
> The surrounding structures—including gold-covered halls, gopuram, gateways, and mandapams—of the Peruman Temple were richly adorned.

> The sacrificial altar was also made of gold. A temple chariot, adorned with pearl garlands and overlaid with gold, was also constructed. It was ordained that Lord Nataraja would be taken in procession on this chariot during the Purattasi and Uttiratadhi festivals. This event would be known as the 'Great Festival of Fame'.
>
> A grand avenue with shining mansions was laid, and it came to be named after the king.
>
> Ornate items such as golden ceremonial umbrellas (parikalam), golden kalpavriksha trees, and royal insignia were donated to the temple by the king. These renovations were completed in the tenth year of the king's reign, during the month of Chithirai, on a Sunday under the Hastha nakshatra.

This inscription clearly shows that Vikrama Chola was a devout follower of Lord Shiva and carried out numerous renovations at the Thillai Koothan Temple (Chidambaram Temple).

Later inscriptions reveal that the innermost enclosure wall of the Ponnambalan Temple was known as the *Vikrama Chola Thirumaligai* (Vikrama Chola's Mansion) and one of the streets surrounding the temple was named *Vikrama Chola Thiruveethi* (Vikrama Chola's Sacred Street).

Though Vikrama Chola was a staunch Shiva devotee, he is also noted for his renovations of the Thiruvarangam Temple (dedicated to Lord Vishnu). He constructed the fifth outer wall of this temple, as well as the Rama Temple and other structures, as recorded in the *Thiruvarangam Kovil Ozhugu* (temple chronicle). Doesn't this show that like his predecessors, he had an inclusive and harmonious approach to religion?

THREE

Kulothunga II (1133–1150 CE)

Royal Lineage

Kulothunga II was the son of Vikrama Chola. He ascended the throne in 1133 CE and co-ruled with his father for two years. When Vikrama Chola passed away in CE 1135, Kulothunga II became the Chola emperor. The *meikeerthi* (royal eulogy) found in the inscriptions of Kulothunga II rarely contains historical details, highlighting that there were no wars during his reign. His rule was marked by peace and prosperity, and the Chola kingdom continued to flourish as it had under Vikrama Chola.

Inscriptions

Opening phrases in Kulothunga II's inscriptions typically include titles such as: 1. *Bhoomannu Paavai* (the maiden who owns the earth) 2. *Bhoomaruviya Bhuviyelam* (the whole earth embraced by beauty) 3. *Bhoomevi Valar* (one who flourishes over the earth) 4. *Bhoomannu Padumam* (the lotus of the earth) 5. *Bhoomevu Thirumagal* (Lakshmi who dwells on the earth) 6. *Bhoomannu Yanar* (the lord of the earth)

Minor Kings

Notable among the minor kings under the reign of Kulothunga II were:

1. Vikrama Chola Sambuvarayan – He was Ammaiyappan Kannudai Perumal, son of Sengeni Ammaiyappan Sambuvarayan, who lived during Vikrama Chola's time. His name indicates a tradition where feudatories adopted names incorporating the reigning king's name.
2. In Thirumanikkuzhi, in South Arcot District, a ruler known as Kulothunga Chola Kadavarayan alias Mohan Aatkolli rose in rank over time, as revealed by his inscriptions. He made donations to Shiva temples in Thirunavalur, Thiruvadigai, and Thirumuthukundram (Virudhachalam).
3. A chieftain from the Bana lineage ruled Magadai Nadu (also referred to as Nadu Nadu). He was known as Rajaraja Magadai Naattaalvan.
4. A ruler of Malai Nadu, based in Thirukovalur was called Vikrama Chola Sethirayan. His son was known as Vikrama Chola Kovalurayan (Kovalan). Another was 'Kiliyoor Malayaman Kulothunga Chola Sethiyarayan'.
5. Thagadur Adiyaman, a ruler of Thagadur.
6. Some chieftains of the Nulamba Pallava lineage were active during this time.
7. In CE 1147, a chieftain named Siyagangan of the Ganga lineage made endowments to the Shiva temple in Kalathi.
8. The Yadavarayars, a lineage of minor kings, ruled the area surrounding Kalathi. This lineage of kings had been in power as minor rulers since the time of Veera Rajendra.
9. Among the minor kings of the Vengi region was Maha Mandaleswaran Pallava Deva Sodan.
10. Another branch of the Chola lineage was the Vellanadu Cholas. Kings and royal queens of this lineage undertook several renovation works

for the Shiva temples in Papadala, Draksharamam, and Kalathi.

11. In Kolanu, there was a Kadam Nayagan, who granted a small village as *Brahmadeya* (tax-free land) to the Vedic priests in 1142 CE. He also held the titles *Maha Mandalika Bhima Nayagan* and *Vengi Desa Chalukya Angakaran.*
12. Then there was another ruler known as Maduranthakan Pothappi Chola Sitharasan, who ruled over the Pothappi Nadu.

Titles

The titles of Kulothunga II include many honorary names, one of which was *Thiruneetru Chola*. This title was also held by Kulothunga I, leading some to mistakenly believe that Sekkizhar belonged to the era of Kulothunga I. Titles such as *Edhirilicholan* and *Kavikadinda Chola* were also honorifics carried by his predecessors. Kulothunga II was known as *Perambalam Pon Veynda Chola* (the Chola who adorned the Great Hall with gold), but his most notable title was *Anapayan* (the faultless one/he who does not falter). This title appears not only in his inscriptions and on state proclamations, but also in the name of his administrative officer who was known as *Anapaya Moovenda Velan*. Several villages were also named Anapaya Nallur in his honour.

Royal Family

The Thirumazhapadi inscription mentions two queens. Among them, the chief queen, Thiagavalli, was also known by the title *Bhuvanamuzhuthudaiyal* (the one who possessed the whole world). The other queen was called 'Mookkoakkizhar'; she was the daughter of a minor chieftain from Malaadu. No further information is available regarding his other wives or children, except for a son named Rajaraja, who was crowned in 1146 CE and ruled alongside his father. During Kulothunga II's reign, the

Chola capital remained Gangaikonda Cholapuram. However, Chidambaram gained significance during his time and came to be regarded as a major royal city where the king frequently visited.

Court Poets

In the court of Kulothunga II, the renowned poet Ottakoothar was a prominent figure. He was also active during the reigns of Vikrama Chola, Kulothunga II, and the latter's son, Rajaraja II, composing works in honour of all three. It's likely that Kulothunga II acquired his knowledge of Tamil from Ottakoothar. Although his name does not appear in any inscriptions, it would be incorrect to conclude he did not exist, as his works and compositions remain. Similarly, Sekkizhar of Kundrathur lived during this King's time. At the king's request, he composed the *Thiruthondar Puranam*, which will be discussed in further detail in another section. The *Thiruthondar Puranam* which is unmatched and unrivalled, along with the *Ula* poems by Koothar, and *Parani* are considered some of the finest literary works of this period. These writings provide valuable insights into the life and reign of Kulothunga II.

Religious Context

It is evident that Kulothunga II bowed his head in reverence at Chidambaram. During his reign, the city of Thillai flourished with unparalleled splendour. The city underwent significant renovations; temples were constructed with great grandeur. This is first noted in the king's seventh regnal year inscription, which is the Tiruppurambiyam inscription. In his third-year's inscription, he is referred to as 'Perambalam Pon Veynda Chola.' Therefore, it can be said that from the second year of his reign until the sixth, he was heavily involved in the renovations at Thillai. It is not clear whether this work was left unfinished during the reign of his father Vikrama Chola and completed by him, or if he initiated and completed the work entirely on his own. The temple renovations he conducted are prominently highlighted in the inscriptions. Kulothunga II, along with his queen, went to Thillai, witnessed the divine dance of Koothaperuman (the dancing Lord) and removed the Vaishnava deity, Govindaraja, from the hall of Thillai. He made many renovations: he constructed seven-tiered towers; he built for the goddess a grand palace surpassing even Mount Kailasa—her own birthplace—so that she would not be reminded of it. He covered several parts of the temple and notable locations in the city with gold. These very events are also briefly mentioned in the *Rajaraja Chola Ula* and in the *Thakkayaga Parani.* He is likened to a bee nestled in the lotus feet of Ponnambala Nathar (the Lord of the Golden Hall at Chidambaram). One inscription mentions that he made donations for rituals to be conducted for the idols of Appar, Sundarar, and Sambandar at Thiruvarur. From this, his deep devotion to Lord Shiva and his reverence for the three great Saiva saints can be understood.

An inscription mentions that Kulothunga II displaced Govindaraja Peruman from Thillai. The specific part of this record has been deliberately erased, while the other sections remain intact. At one point, an effort was made to unify Shaivism and Vaishnavism by worshiping Shiva and Vishnu together in the form of 'Sankara Narayana', blending the practices of both sects. However, later events did not support this unification. Kulothunga II's actions are among the significant events that marked a division between Shaivism and Vaishnavism. Aside from this incident, it can be concluded that his rule was exemplary in many respects.

FOUR

Rajaraja II (1146–1173 CE)

Politics

The reign of Kulothunga II ended in 1150 CE. However, it has already been stated that he crowned his son, Rajaraja II, in CE 1146 and ruled the country alongside him. Therefore, Rajaraja's reign is counted as beginning from 1146 CE. There is no mention of war in his inscriptions. Hence, it appears that his reign, like that of Kulothunga II, was a period of peace. Most of his inscriptions begin with the phrase *Perum Palan Poo Maruviya Thirumadum* (meaning 'the great ruler who transformed the land'). These inscriptions reflect his political integrity.

Extent of his Empire

In his seventh regnal year, a minor ruler named Kaduvetti from Kuvala Nadu (Kolar region) constructed a temple on a hill. An inscription records a donation made in Perumper, a place in Thagadur Nadu of the Nigarili Chola Mandalam (located in the Ganga country). The donor is identified as Thagadur Kilavan, and the donation was made in 1164 CE. This suggests that the Kongu region and parts of Gangapadi were within Rajaraja's dominions. Numerous inscriptions from Rajaraja's time have been found in the Vengi region, extending as far as Draksharamam. This suggests that Chola authority extended over Vengi as well. To summarise, the vast kingdom established during the time of Vikrama Chola continued to exist during the reigns of both Kulothunga II and Rajaraja II.

State of Governance

Following the reign of Kulothunga I, the central political structure of the Chola country weakened. There were numerous minor rulers. Although they showed nominal allegiance to the empire, they exercised complete autonomy within their territories. They began to both establish unity among themselves and engage in conflicts. The central authority could not restrain these developments. The emperor had to focus on countering the invasions of the Western Chalukyas, Hoysalas, and disturbances in the Pandya and Chera territories. Due to the need to pay attention to foreign invasions, there was insufficient time to regulate the minor rulers within the kingdom consistently. The minor rulers, aware of the emperor's predicament, continued to strengthen their military power. However, the village assemblies and town councils within the kingdom continued to perform their duties effectively. Nonetheless, the centralised administrative structure established by Rajaraja I showed signs of deterioration.

Minor Kings

Among the minor kings during the reign of Rajaraja II were:

1. A lord named Narasimha Varman, who constructed a Perumal temple at Tirukovalur. He was the ruler of Maladu 2000.

2. A portion of the Malai Nadu (country) was ruled by the Malaiyaman chieftains. Among them were Malaiyaman Periya Udayan, and Athimallan Sokkaperuman. The latter governed Kiliyur.
3. A chieftain of the Kadavaraya lineage administered Kudalur; he was known as 'Mohan, born to rule Kudalur' He also held the title of 'Rajaraja Kadavarayar'.
4. In the Chola region, one of the Pallavarayas governed areas around Karikai and Kulattur. He built a temple called Rajarajeswaram Udaiyar in Pallavarayanpettai. This same ruler safeguarded the Chola kingdom without disruption during Rajaraja's final years and even after his passing.
5. Nithavinotha Sambavarayan was one of the chiefs of Sengeni. His wife was Seerudaiyal. Another chief, Raja Narayana Sambhuvaraya, performed services in temples at Munnur and Acharapakkam. He was granted the title of Ammaiyappan Seeyan Pallavandan. There was a close relationship between these Sengeni chiefs and the Kadavarayars.
6. In the Pudukottai region, there was a lord named Kulothunga Chola Kadambarayan.
7. A ruler called Rajaraja Vangara Mutharaiyan, also known as Senthan and Koothaduvan, served as the guardian chief of Padikaval and resided in Thittakudi within the South Arcot district.
8. Among the minor kings of Telugu Nadu were two who claimed descent from Karikalan: one was Tribhuvana Malladeva Chola Maharajan, and the other was Jikkideva Chola Maharaja.

Apart from them, there were other minor kings such as Konarajendra Lokarasan, Konda Parumatti Bhutarasan, Kulothunga Rajendran Sodaiyan, and Kottari Errama Nayaka Sanaka Varman, who ruled regions spanning from Nellore to Vengi.

The King's honorific titles

In his *Ula* (courtly eulogy), this Rajaraja is seen bearing titles such as *Kandan, Veerathayan*, and *Virothayan*. In both the *Ula* and inscriptions, he is notably praised with the epithet *Cholendra Simham* (Lion among the Chola Kings). In inscriptions, he also held honorifics like *Raja Gambhiran, Edirili Chola, and Neriyudai Chola.*

Royal family

Rajaraja's chief queen was Avani Muzhuthudaiyal. His other wives were Bhuvana Muzhuthudaiyal and Tharani Muzhuthudaiyal. It is said that Rajaraja II did not have any children.

Crown Prince

Due to Rajaraja's lack of heirs, he adopted (Second) Rajadhiraja, the grandson of his grandfather Vikrama Chola, as his crown prince. Inscriptions indicate that Rajadhiraja's rule began around 1163 CE.

Therefore, it can be inferred that Rajadhiraja spent about ten years alongside Rajaraja, gaining insights into political governance. After 1163 CE, before Rajaraja's death, the Pandya kingdom experienced significant turmoil among its minor kings. One faction received assistance from the ruler of Eezham (Sri Lanka), while another received support from the Cholas. The details of these conflicts are elaborated in the section on Rajadhiraja's rule.

FIVE

Rajadhiraja II (1163–1179 CE)

Accession to the Throne

Rajadhiraja II was the grandson of Vikrama Chola. His birth name was Edirilipperuman. He had a younger sibling. Both children were brought from Gangaikonda Cholapuram to Ayyirattali Palace, where they were raised. On the day Rajaraja Chola II passed away, he crowned Edirilipperuman as his successor before his death. At that time, Edirilipperuman was just two years old.

Following the king's demise, chaos erupted in the Chola Nadu. Pallavarayan, the Prime Minister, immediately took the children and Rajamahadevi to Rajarajapuram, where he placed them under the protection of the guardians (Thakkars). For two years, Pallavarayan managed the affairs of the Chola kingdom.

When Edirilipperuman turned four, he was officially crowned with the title Rajadhiraja II. This event was commemorated and documented in the Pallavarayanpettai inscriptions.

However, when researchers examined these inscriptions alongside the regnal years of Rajaraja Chola II, they found discrepancies. According to their analysis, Rajadhiraja II became the heir apparent in 1163 CE, while Rajaraja II passed away in 1173 CE. Thus, they speculate that Rajadhiraja II received approximately eight to ten years of governance training under his predecessor.

Regardless of these debates, it is unanimously accepted that Rajadhiraja II succeeded Rajaraja Chola II. He was also known by the name Karikalan.

Pandya Kingdom Conflict

Within the first four to five years after Rajadhiraja II ascended the throne, a conflict arose between two royal claimants to the Pandya throne. One was Parakrama Pandyan, and the other was Kulasekara Pandyan. At that time, Parakrama Pandyan sought assistance from Parakrama Bahu (1153–1186 CE), the ruler of Sri Lanka.

In response, Parakrama Bahu dispatched a Sri Lankan military force led by Ilangapuri to aid Parakrama Pandyan. However, before the Sri Lankan troops could reach the Pandya kingdom, Kulasekara Pandyan captured Parakrama Pandyan in a city and laid siege to it.

In the ensuing battle, Parakrama Pandyan was killed. His son, Veerapandyan, fled to the hill country for refuge. Consequently, Kulasekara Pandyan became the ruler of the Pandya kingdom.

Ilangapuri's Campaign

Realising the situation, Ilangapuri defeated Kulasekara and attempted to restore the Pandya kingdom to the rightful heirs of the slain king. He entered the Pandya territory, captured Rameswaram, and destroyed the temple there. He seized a place called Kundukalam, built a fortress, and named it Parakramapuram after his king.

Hearing of these actions, Kulasekara sent two commanders with a massive army. However, these forces were defeated.

Subsequent battles took place in various locations, and Ilangapuri emerged victorious in all of them. In the final clash, Kulasekara, combining forces from Kongu Nadu, the scattered remnants of Parakrama Pandya's troops, and his own army, led the battle himself. Unfortunately, he suffered a crushing defeat.

Ilangapuri then consolidated his control over South Pandya Nadu. He brought Veerapandyan, who had taken refuge in the hill country, back into power. Veerapandyan was crowned king of the Pandya kingdom with gifts from the Sri Lankan ruler. Veerapandyan ruled the kingdom with Ilangapuri's support.

Ilangapuri continued his campaign, defeating Kanda Devan Malavarayan and Manava Chakravarti and installed his own governors in those areas. When Kulasekara, enraged at the desolation of his lands, regrouped his forces for battle, the local chieftains under Ilangapuri joined Kulasekara. Veerapandyan fled the throne and Ilangapuri summoned reinforcements from his king in Sri Lanka.

The new forces, led by Sagath Visayan, joined Ilangapuri, and together they decisively defeated Kulasekara. Veerapandyan was restored to the throne.

Later, Ilangapuri defeated Kurumbarayan and seized Tirupputhur. He entered Pon Amaravati, demolished the triple-jewelled palace and other structures, and returned to Madurai. Kulasekara, still determined, attacked Ilangapuri again at Seevilliputhur. The battle was intense, but Kulasekara faced another defeat and fled to a place called Sathaneri.

Learning of this, Ilangapuri pursued him to Sathaneri. To delay Ilangapuri's advance, Kulasekara attempted to breach the lake banks. However, this tactic failed, and he retreated to the Pazhaiyangottai fortress, and sent a plea for help to the Chola king.

First War with Sri Lanka

The Chola country was then ruled by Rajadhirajan II. His main ally was Peruman Nambi Pallavarayan, also known as Tiruchitrambalam Udaiyan. Pallavarayan marched into the Pandya kingdom with a massive army. Another ally, Narasinga Varma Rayan, joined the campaign. Together with the Pandya and Kongu forces, as well as the Chola troops, they attacked the Sri Lankan forces, who had been desecrating Pandya temples and looting villages.

Battles occurred in regions like Tirukkanapper, Thondi, Pasipon Amaravathi, Manamerkudi, and Manjakudi. Ultimately, the Sri Lankan forces were defeated and fled. Kulasekaran ascended the throne and began his reign.

Hearing about the atrocities committed by Ilangapuri, a minor chieftain named Edirilisola Sambhuvarayan approached a great sage, Gnanasiva Devar, also known as Umapathi Devar, seeking a solution. The sage prophesied, 'The Sri Lankan forces will soon perish; do not worry,' and conducted an intense Agora Puja for twenty-eight days. Eventually the news of the Sri Lankan forces' defeat spread.

In gratitude, the chieftain gifted the sage a village near Kanchipuram called Aarpakkam as an offering. This event is recorded as having occurred during the fifth year of Rajaraja's reign. Hence, the defeat of Ilangapuri likely took place in 1167 or 1168 CE.

Second War with Sri Lanka

After the first war, Pallavarayan, a close friend, chief minister, and valiant warrior of Rajaraja, passed away due to illness. He was succeeded by Annan Pallavarayan, also known as Vedavanam Udaiyan Ammaiappan. This new leader was skilled and held the king's trust. The Sri Lankan king, still bitter about his earlier defeat, strengthened his forces and began building ships in locations like Uraththurai, Pulaicheri, Mathottam, Valligaman, and Mattival. Hearing this, Pallavarayan provoked Sivallaban—the son-in-law of Parakrama Bahu, who had quarrelled with him—to go with an army and attack Eezham. Sivallaban joined forces with the Chola army and destroyed many of the targeted locations. They seized elephants, burned down twenty strategic pathways in the east and west, and seventy pathways in the north and south and destroyed many towns by fire. Many leaders were killed, and others were captured.

At this juncture, Parakrama Bahu, the Sri Lankan king, devised a strategy. He sent emissaries to Kulasekaran, reminding him of the historical alliance between the Pandyas and Sri Lankans against the Cholas. He sought to rekindle friendship with the Pandyas and urged hostility towards the Cholas.

Kulasekaran's Betrayal and Wars with Sri Lanka

Kulasekaran, who had been crowned with the support of the Cholas, betrayed them and turned against them. Influenced by the Sri Lankan king, he launched an attack on the Chola territories. Kulasekaran expelled key Chola allies, including the loyal Edagathar (from a village in Madurai Taluk) and Chola feudal chieftains like Rajaraja Karkudi Marayan, and Raja Kambira Ainthu Kottai Nadaalvaan, who had previously been under Kulasekaran's own administration. Additionally, he removed the severed heads of the Sri Lankan army leaders, which had been displayed at the gates of Madurai, under the Chola king's orders.

The letters and gifts that Parakrama Bahu had sent to Kulasekaran's army commanders were intercepted by Chola commanders, which alerted them to the Sri Lankan king's schemes.

Rajadhirajan then instructed Annan Pallavarayan to act. Their objective was to dethrone Kulasekaran and enthrone Veerapandiyan, the son of Parakrama Pandiyan, as the rightful king. Pallavarayan immediately led a large army, defeated Kulasekaran, and installed Veerapandiyan on the throne. As a reward for his valour, Pallavarayan received a gift of ten veli of tax-free land in Pazhaiyanur.

Thus, during Rajadhirajan's reign, the Cholas fought two wars against the Sri Lankan king, both related to conflicts in the Pandya kingdom.

1. First War: Led by the Chola commander Pallavarayan; this war ended in a victory for the Cholas, where they suppressed the Sri Lankan forces.
2. Second War: The Chola elder statesman, Annan Pallavarayan, successfully defeated the Sri Lankan king's forces again.

In both wars, the Sri Lankan king lost both his infantry and navy. Following these victories, Rajadhirajan earned the titles 'The Lord Who Conquered Madurai and Sri Lanka.' The phrase 'conquering Sri Lanka' here refers to the Chola strategy of weakening the Sri Lankan king by utilising forces led by Sivallaban. These wars likely occurred between 1169 CE and 1177 CE

Empire

Based on inscriptions from regional chieftains found in places like Nellur, Kalathi, Nandalur, and Gangapadi, Rajadhirajan can be recognised as a paramount emperor. It can be said that during his reign, the Chola empire remained in the same state of power and influence as it was during Rajaraja Chola's era.

Chieftains

1. Among the many notable regional chieftains, Nambi Pallavarayan, also known as Thiruchitrambalam Udaiyan Peruman of Karigai Kulathur, stands out. He was deeply devoted to Rajaraja, earning the emperor's trust and affection. Nambi Pallavarayan was also considered a close confidant and a steadfast ally of Rajadhirajan.
2. Next to him, the chieftain who held the same position and served diligently was Vedavanam Udaiyan Ammaiyappan, known as Annan Pallavarayan. These two leaders were instrumental in securing victories against Sri Lanka. Without their leadership and contributions, the Chola empire could have fractured into multiple smaller kingdoms. Annan Pallavarayan, in particular, made significant donations to Shiva temples in places like Thiruvarur and Thiruvalangadu. His ancestral home was Pazhaiyanur.
3. In both the South and North Arcot regions, Sambuvarayars and Kadavarayars were known for their strength and authority. An individual named Sengeni Ammaiappan Sambuvarayan is mentioned in inscriptions as having allocated revenues from these areas for the upkeep of the Thiruppulivanam Sivan Temple.
4. A person named Kandar Sooriyan is recorded as 'the one who conquered the Pandya Nadu.' He is credited with constructing a temple tower along the banks of the Thiruvakkarai River and naming it after himself. Additionally, he donated lands in Sitraramur as temple endowment.
5. Another notable figure, Sengeni Ammaiyappan Seeyan Pallavandan, utilised land revenues and other taxes to renovate or build temples in Munnur.
6. Just as there were many Sambuvarayars, there were also numerous Malaiyaman chieftains. Among them, one was Arulala Peruman,

known as Rajaraja Malaiyaman. He was the son of Kannappan Malaiyaman and is noted for having donated lamps to the Tirisulam Temple.

7. There were several Sedhirayars and Kovalarayars, who issued grants to temples in places such as Keelur and Athi (Keralanthaka Nallur).
8. Rajadhiraja Malaiyarayan, also known as Thiruvarangam Udaiyan, made numerous donations to the temple in Thiruppasur.
9. Another figure, Kolon Tirukkodungundram Udaiyan, also referred to as Ponnamaravathi Nishadarasan, is mentioned.
10. Pothappi Cholan, also known as Gangai Kondan, gained great renown for composing the *Kunamalai* and dedicating himself to Lord Shiva.
11. A chieftain who ruled Nellore is also mentioned.
12. Another was Rajaraja Vangara Mutharaiyan, who donated five *veli*s (a measure of land) to a temple in Thittakudi.

Many among these were in office even during the reign of Rajaraja. Among these chieftains, it was customary for two or more of them who were in close proximity to form mutual agreements and alliances. They pledged to assist and support each other in times of need. Several would come together and enter into a pact of alliance. These agreements were made without the approval of the emperor. Consequently, if necessary, these chieftains could potentially challenge or manipulate the emperor's authority.

Crown Prince

Rajadhiraja was the son of Neriyudai Perumal, who was the grandson of Vikrama Chola Deva. The one referred to as Sangamarasan in the *ulavu* (a record or document) is none other than Neriyudai Perumal. The one referred to as Nallaman in the ulavu is Edirili Perumal, who was Rajadhiraja. The second son,

Kumaramahitharan, was known as Kumara Kulothungan, later referred to as Kulothunga III. The third son was Sankara Rasan, also called Sankara Chola. These three were sons of the same father, with Kulothunga III serving as the crown prince.

SIX

Kulothunga III (1178–1218 CE)

Youthful Years

If it is true that Rajadhiraja was the elder brother of Kulothunga III, then the latter would have been only a year younger than him. Therefore, when Rajadhiraja ascended the throne, Kulothunga III would only have been three years old. He grew up in the company of his elder brother and acquired political experience early on. It must be assumed that his elder brother reigned for seventeen years and died at the age of twenty. Kulothunga III ascended the throne at the age of 18 in 1178 CE.

As he received the crown during his prime youth, and since he had already been exposed to politics alongside his elder brother, he was well-versed in political order. Moreover, having grown up under the care of the royal queens from a young age, he had a solid understanding of the country's political landscape, the history of the dynasty, and the governance system. Thus, it was only natural that even in his youth he was acquainted with great poets like Ottakoothar.

Date of Birth

The birthday of this emperor is celebrated in the Tamil month of Thai, on the day of the Hasta nakshatra. We know this from an order he issued, which states:

> From the sixth year of his reign onward, a festival named 'Rajakkal Nayan Thirunal' shall be celebrated as a sacred occasion (Theertham) on the Hasta Nakshatra day in the month of Thai, in honour of Lord Arugadeva at the Tirunarungondai Perumpalli, under his own name.

Thus, it becomes evident that the emperor had declared his birthday to be celebrated on this specific day, which aligns with what we read earlier about Rajaraja celebrating his birthday in the Chola-conquered Chera country.

Physical Appearance

He is described as having the hue of dark rain clouds, with a complexion like the *karuviram* blossom and the radiant *onbuvai* flower (both vibrant red flowers). In form and features, he resembled Madana, the god of love. In strength and stature, he was like Bhima—powerful and commanding. His beauty, manliness, and presence were such that all who saw him could not help but admire him. Such was Kulothunga Chola, as praised by a poet *(Asiriyar)* in *Kulothunga Kovai* (A poetic work honouring Kulothungan).

Inscriptions

Many inscriptions from his time remain. The most common phrase found in these inscriptions is *Puyal Vayththu Valam Peruga* (As the storm gathers, prosperity grows). Other frequent phrases in his inscriptions include: *Malar Mannum Pozhil Ezhum* (The garden where flowers bloom), *Poovmevi Maruviya* (The land that is fertile and abundant), and *Poovmevi Valar* (The land blossoms with growth). While some of these inscriptions are also attributed to Rajaraja II and Kulothunga II, they can be distinguished by references to military campaigns and other notable events mentioned in the texts.

State of the Nation

When Kulothunga III ascended the throne, the great Chola empire was well-administered by capable ministers. However, the central political system of the empire began to deteriorate. The main reason for this was that the local rulers, military leaders, and high officials began to assert their own autonomy within their respective regions, disregarding the central political structure. This situation first arose after the reign of Kulothunga I and gained strength during the rule of Rajadhiraja II. Outside the empire, the king of Eezham (Sri Lanka) entered into the politics of the Pandya kingdom, creating confusion and fluctuating successes and failures. In Telugu regions, small kings began to act independently. The absence of inscriptions from Rajaraja II and Rajadhiraja in the northern regions of Nellore can be attributed to these developments. In the north, the Chalukya empire swallowed the territories of the Kakatiya dynasty, growing in strength. Since the Western Chalukyas declined, the Hoysalas rose in strength in the Mysore region, gaining political influence. Aware of these situations, Kulothunga III made efforts to restore peace in the Chola empire and strengthen its power.

Military Operations

The Chola armies were highly skilled. They had been well-trained from the time of Rajendra Chola I, with well-established battle tactics. During the time of Kulothunga III, the elephant corps of the Chola army was particularly outstanding. In 1178 CE, a Chinese historian described the Chola elephant corps as follows:

> There is a large army of 60,000 elephants in the Chola kingdom. Each elephant is about two or three meters tall. On the battlefield, many warriors ride these elephants, carrying weapons such as spears, bows, and arrows. They are experts in long-range archery. Elephants that win battles are given special titles and a high-quality battle armour is draped over them to indicate their distinction. Every day, the royal elephant corps is assembled before the king.

Pandya Country Campaign

Among this king's military exploits recorded in inscriptions, his southern campaigns are most prominent. The inscriptions mention that he: captured Madurai, seized the Pandya crown, took control of the island of Eezham (Sri Lanka), captured Karur, captured Kanchipuram (Kachi), and performed both the Virabhisheka (heroic coronation) and Vijayabhisheka (victory coronation) in Madurai. Therefore, let us examine each of these events in detail.

The Capture of Madurai

Kulasekara Pandya, who had earlier been defeated by Pallavarayan (a general), passed away. At that time, Madurai was under the rule of Veerapandya. Vikrama Pandya, the son of Kulasekaran, sought refuge with Kulothunga III.

Why did Kulothunga, who succeeded Rajadhiraja II (under whom Kulasekara had been driven out), now accept Kulasekara's son? There could be several reasons: Veerapandya may have allied himself with the king of Lanka against the Cholas, or he may have acted contrary to Chola interests in some other way, or perhaps Veerapandya was deemed unfit to rule the Pandya kingdom.

Whatever the reason, the conflict that followed saw the Sinhala forces—who had come to support Veerapandya—suffer heavy losses, with many killed and the survivors fleeing by sea back to Lanka. Thus, the first phase of the war ended in a Chola victory.

Kulothunga captured both Madurai and the Pandya crown, erected a victory pillar, and later returned the kingdom to Vikrama Pandya as an act of favour.

The Seizure of the Crown

After his defeat, Veerapandya fled to the Chera kingdom. Gaining support from the Chera king, he attempted to reclaim his lost territories. He gathered his scattered army and, with the Cheran's forces, marched into the Pandya kingdom. Upon learning this, Kulothunga III mobilised his large army and met the enemy in Nettur. A fierce battle ensued between the two forces. What was the outcome? Veerapandya was defeated, and his soldiers fled in all directions. His crown was taken by the Cholas. Veerapandya's queen, Kopperundevi, was taken prisoner. Kulothunga had him placed under the custody of his royal household guard (*velam*).

Humiliated and unable to bear the disgrace, Veerapandya fled once again to the Chera kingdom. The Cheran, realising his mistake in aiding Veerapandya, came to Kulothunga III's court and sought refuge. The magnanimous Kulothunga received both of them with royal honours and treated them with dignity. He granted Veerapandya a part of the Pandya kingdom as a domain. Veerapandya bestowed upon his son the honorary title

Parithi Kulapathi (Sun of the Chola lineage—a title associated with Kulothunga), and presented him before the Chola king. Pleased by this gesture, Kulothunga conferred many distinctions upon the boy.

The events described above are part of what is known as the Second Pandya War. Since the crown of the Pandya king was seized in this battle, Madurai came to be referred to as *Muditthalai Konda Cholapuram* (Chola City of the Seized Crown). Both of these Pandya campaigns took place within the first two years of Kulothunga's reign. This is known from one of his second-year inscriptions (found at Thiruvakkarai). These same deeds have been praised and glorified in the *Kulothunga Kovai*, a poetic work composed in his honour.

War in Vela Nadu

After the previous battles, a new conflict arose when Veerakeralan, the ruler of Vela Nadu, opposed Kulothunga III and declared war on him. In this battle, Veerakeralan was defeated and lost his fingers. With no other option, he sought refuge with the Chola king. The gracious Kulothunga III welcomed him, offering him food and shelter, and even granted him back his kingdom, much to his happiness.

Conquest of Eezham (Sri Lanka)

Parakrama Bahu I, who had been the king of Lanka since the time of Rajadhiraja, had long sought—unsuccessfully—to diminish Chola influence. During the reign of Kulothunga III as well, he continued to hold power in Lanka. As he had done previously, he attempted to disrupt the prosperity of Madurai. To counter this, Kulothunga III sent a military expedition to Ceylon in 1188 or 1189 CE. The army managed to drive out the Sinhalese forces, forcing them to retreat. As a result, the Ceylonese king had no choice but to acknowledge Kulothunga III as the supreme ruler, as evidenced by the Thirumanikkuzhi inscription, which states that the Ceylonese king placed his crown under Kulothunga's control.

Conquest of Karur

At one point, Karur had been the capital of the Chera kingdom, and had also served as the capital of the Kongu region. The Chera kings, who held Karur as their capital, were vassals of the Cholas and governed the region in allegiance to them. During the reign of Kulothunga III, one of the local rulers, who was dissatisfied with Chola rule, rebelled and sought to reclaim his autonomy. In response, Kulothunga III sent an army to suppress the rebellion. A fierce battle ensued, and the rebel king was defeated. After his defeat, he sought refuge with Kulothunga III. Consequently, Karur came under Chola control.

Kulothunga III entered the city in triumph, where he was hailed as *Chola Keralan*, signifying his victory. From then on, he became known by this title and the Kongu region came to be called the *Chola Kerala Mandalam* (Chola-Kerala region). Despite his military success, Kulothunga III showed great magnanimity, granting the local ruler the right to govern his land under Chola supremacy, bringing peace to the region. Since he was crowned in Karur, the city came to be known as *Mudivazhangu Cholapuram* (meaning 'the Chola city that bestowed the crown' or 'the Chola city where the crown was conferred). As these events, particularly the Kongu campaign, are recorded in the inscriptions dating to the sixteenth regnal year of Kulothunga III, it is likely that the battle took place around 1194 CE.

Conquest of Kanchi

Since the inscriptions mention that 'Karur and Kanchi were graciously taken' it can be reasonably inferred that after the victory in Karur, the conquest of Kanchi followed. However, the exact details of this conquest are not entirely clear. A Telugu Choda named Nallachitthan Devan, who ruled Maharasapadi Elayiram, claimed that he had previously ruled from Kanchi. Therefore, it is likely that, while Kulothunga III was engaged in his southern campaigns, Nallachitthan suddenly attacked and took Kanchi. Kulothunga may then have swiftly turned north and retaken the city around 1196 CE, subduing the local ruler, Nallachitthan, in this process. We can make this assumption because for the rest of Kulothunga's reign, Nallachitthan appears only as a subordinate feudatory king loyal to the Chola empire.

Third Pandya War

According to an inscription from the twenty-sixth year of his reign, Kulothunga III conducted both a Veerabhishekam (Heroic Consecration) and Vijayabhishekam (Victory Consecration) at Madurai shortly before 1202 CE. The details of these events are elaborated in the Kudumiyanmalai inscription.

Jatavarman Kulasekara Pandya, son of Vikrama Pandya (who had been favoured by Kulothunga), came to rule the Pandya region from around 1190 CE. Within a few years, Kulasekara Pandya grew arrogant and rebelled against the Cholas, refusing to submit to their rule. He engaged in actions that directly opposed Kulothunga III. His official records reveal a tone of defiance and pride. The treacherous acts of Kulasekara came to the attention of the Chola king. Realising that the Pandya country—into which the Cholas had poured great effort to maintain peace—was being ruined under Kulasekara's rule, Kulothunga grew furious. He decided it was only right to oust Kulasekara and bring the Pandya land back under Chola political control.

He immediately launched a military expedition against the Pandya country with a massive army. Fierce battles occurred at Mattiyur and Kalikkottai. The army of Kulasekara Pandya was defeated. He hid in the forests to escape. Soon, the Chola forces captured Madurai, destroying structures like the coronation hall and other royal buildings. These areas were ploughed with the help of donkeys, and crops were sown, symbolically desecrating and devastating the area. Thus, Madurai was left devastated.

Kulothunga Chola's anger was now appeased. In Madurai, he assumed the title *Chola Pandya*, wore the *Veeramamudi* (crown of valour), and erected a victory pillar. Since he had conquered both the Pandyas and the Cheras, he earned the prestigious title *Tribhuvana Veeran* (Hero of the Three Worlds). Following this victory, the Pandya region was named *Chola Pandya Mandalam* as it came under direct Chola administration. Madurai became known as *Mudithalai Konda Cholapuram* (The Chola city where the crown was seized). The *Aththani Mandapam* (a pavilion in Madurai) came to be called *Chera Pandiyar Thambiran* (Lord of the Cheras and Pandyas).

After these great victories, Kulothunga Chola conducted both the Vijayabhishekam and Veerabhishekam as indicated by the inscriptions at Pudukkottai.

His major victory is also attested in an inscription from his twenty-eighth regnal year (1207 CE), where he is referred to as *Tribhuvana Veeradevan* (Brave Lord of the Three Worlds).

Northern Campaigns

Kulothunga is described as 'the one who waged war against the seven Kalingas, Kollapuram, and Urankai (Orangal) (referenced in lines 163 and 166 of the Pudukkottai Inscriptions).

Similarly, in later times, a king named Veerapandyan captured Chola country (Sonaadu) and performed both the Vijayabhishekam and Veerabhishekam rituals at Thillai (Chidambaram). During Sundarapandyan's reign, it is said that everything Kulothunga had once done, he did again in Sonaadu. This is mentioned in Kulothunga's *Kovai* (a poetic chronicle). Two inscriptions from Pudukkottai also refer to this. However, no inscription of Kulothunga has been found at those locations.

Moreover, Ganapati, the Kakatiya emperor, ascended the throne in 1199 CE, subdued the Western Chalukyas, and ruled the greater region of Perunadu (the large northern region). During that period, no epigraphic evidence from the northern country suggests that Kulothunga had campaigned there or achieved victories. Therefore, it is best to consider these claims as poetic exaggerations.

It is widely accepted by scholars that Kambar Peruman (the famous Tamil poet) was a court poet of this Kulothunga. However, historical records show that Kambar, having become disaffected with the Chola king, went and stayed with Prataparudra I of the Kakatiya dynasty (r. 1162–1197), who had made Orangal (Warangal) his capital and ruled Perunadu. Thus, it seems reasonable to believe that Kambar left the Chola court and joined the Kakatiya king, who was actually an enemy of the Cholas.

If this is accurate, then it suggests that there was rivalry or hostility between the Chola king and Prataparudra, at least in terms of imperial competition. If this enmity did exist, then the northern campaigns of Kulothunga mentioned in the Pudukkottai inscriptions cannot be dismissed outright as untrue.

The combined testimony of both the *Kovai* (poem) and the inscriptions indicates that these northern campaigns may have had a basis in fact. This matter, therefore, deserves further historical investigation.

The Great Chola Country

The inscriptions of Kulothunga III are found as far north as Nellore and Kadappa regions and as far south as Tirunelveli. To the west, they appear in regions like Hemavati, Avani, and Edurur in the Mysore area, as well as in the Kongu region. From this we can understand that his rule extended from Kadappa in the north to Kanyakumari in the south, and from Mysore in the west to the Bay of Bengal in the east. Among the various administrative regions under his control, the most prominent was Chola Mandalam itself. It was divided into nine *valanadus* (prosperous regions) and seventy-nine *nadus* (smaller provinces). Because of its size and significance, Chola Mandalam was also called *Periyanadu* (the Great Country).

Royal (Capital) Cities

During the reigns of the Chola kings who descended from Vijayalaya Chola, cities such as Ayiraththali, Thanjavur, Gangaikonda Cholapuram, and Rajarajapuram served as royal capitals (*Ko Nagarams*) suitable for the residence of kings. Ayiraththali was also known by names like Nandipuram, Pazhayarai, and Mudikonda Cholapuram. Towards the end of Kulothunga III's reign, or at the beginning of Rajaraja III's reign, this city was destroyed by the Pandya ruler Jatavarman Sundara Pandyan, who then conducted the Veera Abhishekam and Vijaya Abhishekam (similar to what Kulothunga Chola had done in Madurai). This suggests that Ayiraththali was the capital city of Kulothunga III. During the later Chola period, Nagapattinam became a significant port city.

Political Structure

The long reign of Kulothunga III was marked by integrity and an efficient administrative structure. There were several distinguished officials in his court, such as Kalappalarayar, Tondaiman, Nulambadhi Rajar, Vizhupparaiyar, Nandiyarajar, Vairadhi Rajar, Vanadhi Rajar, Kadavarayar, Kongarayar, Sittarasar, Vizhinyatharaiyar who played significant roles in various aspects of governance. These officials were responsible for overseeing government operations, managing regional matters, and supervising the activities of smaller towns and villages. Thus, it is evident that the central administration functioned efficiently during this Chola king's reign.

A noteworthy event during the thirty-eighth year of his reign was the land survey conducted in Thanjavur, which reflects the systematic nature of his governance.

Officials like Rajanarayana Muvendha Velan, Meenavan Muvendha Velan, Neriyudai Chola Muvendha Velan, who held the position of confidential ministers, played crucial roles in assisting the king with state affairs, providing him with vital information and aiding in decision-making processes.

Due to the presence of skilled and highly capable political leaders, the imperial structure during his rule remained strong and stable.

Malaiyaman Kings

During Kuloṭhuṅga III's reign, there were many minor chieftains or *sittarasar* who contributed to the governance of the empire. Among these were the Malaiyamans, known as Chetiyarayars. They hailed from the mountainous regions, and their rulers claimed to be descendants of the Chetiyarayar lineage. This group of rulers, also referred to as Malaiyamans, governed the region with Kovalur as their capital and ruled over lands like Thirukovalur, Kiliyur, and Adayur. These rulers were known for their military expertise and contributed to the empire's political stability.

During the period of Kulothunga III, one of the notable rulers from this lineage was Malaiyaman Periya Udayanan Rajaraja Chetiyarayar. Another was Malaiyaman Narasimha Varman Karikala Chola of Adayur Nadu. The former carried the honorary title Senai Meekaman (Commander-in-Chief), indicating his role as a prominent military leader of the Chola army. The latter, during the reign of Rajadhiraja II, participated in the Pandya country wars alongside Peruman Nambi Pallavarayar and defeated the Eezham (Sri Lankan) army.

Thus, under the leadership of Kulothunga III, the Chola Empire not only expanded its territory but also strengthened its internal administration with capable officers and smaller regional rulers who supported the imperial authority. The military campaigns, particularly against the Pandyas, and the efficient governance structure contributed to the lasting stability and prosperity of the empire.

Sambuvarayar

They were descendants of the ancient Pallava dynasty; they belonged to the Sengeni clan and served as officials in the Chola administration for the North and South Arcot regions. Over time, they became minor rulers and took responsibility for governing various regions.

One among them, who lived during the early reign of Kulothunga III was Sengeni Ammaiyappan–Pandi Nadu Kondan–Kandan Suryan Rajaraja Sambuvarayan. The honorific *Pandi Nadu Kondan* (Conqueror of Pandi Nadu) suggests that he served as a military commander in one of the Pandya campaigns led either by Kulothunga III or Rajadhiraja III and emerged victorious. He organised temple affairs in the Brahmadesam (in South Arcot district), built a hall in a town called Ennayiram, and issued two grants to the Achirapakkam temple.

Other notable Sambuvarayars from Kulothunga's time and after include: Sengeni Mindan Athimallan Sambuvarayan, Sengeni Ammaiyappan Kannudai Peruman Vikrama Chola, Veera Chola Athimallan, Kulothunga Chola Sambuvarayan, Aalap Pirandhan Edirili Chola Sambuvarayan

Among them, Kulothunga Chola Sambuvarayan built a palace at the Seymangalam Thoonandar temple and donated twelve *veli* of land as an offering to the temple.

Athimallan contributed to the maintenance of Shiva temples in places like Thiruvothur, Thiruvallam, Achirapakkam, and others.

Kadavarayar

Like the Sengeni lineage, they were also descendants of the Pallava dynasty. They often claimed to be descendants of the ancient Pallavas. They were minor rulers of the Thirumunaippadi and Sendamangalam regions. They were great supporters of the Chola Empire. Among them, during the reign of Kulothunga, were figures like Aalap Pirandhaan Veerasekaran and Valnilai Kandan Rajaraja Kadavarayar.

During the reign of the next Chola king, the Chola Empire faced turmoil due to the actions of Kopperunjingan, who was a descendant of this lineage. He was the son of Azhagiya Pallavan.

Vaanagovaraiyar

They were descendants of the Mahabali lineage. They were also referred to as *Mavalirayars* and *Bana Arasar*. They were minor rulers who ruled the Banar territories from the Sangam Chola period to the later Chola period.

They also existed during the Pallava period. This lineage ruled the Magadai region in the central part of Tamil Nadu. Their capital was Arai, also known as Aarakazhur (located in the Salem district).

During the reign of Kulothunga Chola III, two rulers from this lineage were prominent. One of them was Egavasakan Kulothunga Chola Vaanagovaraiyan. His inscriptions have been found in the districts of Salem, Tiruchirappalli, and Thanjavur.

Another leader was Ponparappinaan Vaanagovaraiyan. Songs about him are found in temple inscriptions in places like Thiruvannamalai. These songs appear to have been composed by eminent Tamil poets. Hence, it is evident that this minor ruler encouraged and appreciated skilled Tamil poets. He earned the title *Ponparappinaan* because he gilded the Thiruvannamalai temple with gold. A traditional song reveals that he participated in a war in the Pandya region and, following the orders of the Chola king, installed a Banar as king of the Pandya territory. This act is mentioned in the Chola king's inscriptions. Therefore, this information appears to be partially true. The inscriptions about him primarily emphasise his conquest of Madurai.

Adhiyamans

This lineage had been prominent since the Sangam era. They ruled a part of Kongu Nadu with Thagadur as their capital. They held titles such as *Adhiendrar* and *Tagadadhirayar*. During the reign of Kulothunga III, one of the Adhiyamans who ruled Thagadur was Adhiyaman Rajaraja Devan. He donated Malaiyanur, located on the northern bank of the Pennai River in Thagadur Nadu, as an endowment to the Arunachaleswarar temple in Thiruvannamalai. His son was Vidugatha Azhagiya Peruman, and others of the same lineage were Kulothunga Chola Thagadadirayar, and Samantha Adhiyaman. Among these, Vidugatha Azhagiya Peruman stated in inscriptions that he was from the lineage of the Sangam-era king, Adhiyaman Neduman Anji. He entered into a mutual alliance with Malaiyan, namely the previously mentioned 'Karikala Chola, ruler of Adayur Nadu', and with Athimallan, a member of the Sengeni clan. This alliance emphasised cooperation with the Chola emperor, signifying their cordial relationship with Kulothunga. According to an inscription at Thirumalai, he restored the Yaksha and Yakshini sculptures placed on the Thirumalai hills by one of his ancestors named Ezhini.

Ganga Kings

This lineage comprised minor rulers of Gangapadi. They ruled Gangapadi from the Sangam era. During the Pallava period, they frequently engaged in battles with the Kadambas with the support of the Pallavas. In the later Chola era, they lived as subordinate rulers under the Cholas. Their capital was Kolar, also called Kuvalalapuram. Among those who ruled Gangapadi under the Cholas were Prithivi Gangan Alagiya Chola of Bangala Nadu, Uttama Chola Gangan, and another ruler, Maraparanan Siyagangan. He ruled for thirty-three years; his wife's name was Ariya Pillai. His inscriptions are entirely in Tamil. He made grants exclusively to Tamil Nadu temples and supported Tamil poets. It was he who had the *Nannool* composed by the sage Bhavanandi. This Ganga king neither promoted Kannada nor Tulu but rather developed Tamil, bore Tamil names and issued endowments only to Tamil temples. His Tamil-centric contributions and grants to Tamil Nadu temples are commendable. If one says that his attachment to Tamil arose from his connection with Kulothunga III, a patron of rare arts, would that be an exaggeration?

Other than Siyagangan, another person belonging to that lineage is Prithivi Gangan Alagiya Chola. He was the lord of the Bangala region. He made several endowments to the temple in Thiruvannamalai. Another figure, Selva Gangan, also known as Uttama Chola Sungan, had a wife who established a statue of Thirunavukkarasar in Agathiyamalai in the North Arcot region.

Telugu Chodas

These rulers governed the northern parts of North Arcot and South Arcot, as well as the districts of Chittoor, Nellore, Kadappa, and others, dividing them into smaller regions. They identified themselves as descendants of Karikalan. Ruling from Pottappi as their capital, they were known as the 'Pottappi Chodas'. Another group, the Choda Sittarasars, ruled from Nellore, which served as their capital. This lineage was responsible for making significant endowments to temples in places like Thirukalathi. Notable figures from this lineage during Kulothungan's reign include Maduranthaka Pottappi Chola, Nallasittarasan, and Chodan Thirukalathi Devan.

These rulers were notable minor kings. They held positions not only as chieftains, but also as ministers, army commanders, treasurers, regional protectors, and tax collectors. Each of them had their own distinct troops that were made available to the emperor when needed. These minor kings governed various small villages and large towns and because they performed several charitable acts, they have been mentioned in inscriptions.

Agreement of the Minor Kings

These leaders often gathered and made agreements pledging loyalty to the emperor. Sometimes two or three individuals would form agreements among themselves. In the twenty-seventh regnal year of Kulothungan (1025 CE), ten minor kings came together and made an agreement opposing the emperor.

> All of us, having agreed among ourselves, hereby declare as per this inscription, that we shall at no time fail in royal duties and shall continue to serve as ordained by Sethirayar. In doing so, the ruler of Magadhai Nadu, Vanakovarayan, and Kulothunga Chola's Vanakovarayan, should not engage in any act of alienation or detachment, nor should they initiate any severance of relationship or agreements. Likewise, if these rulers and their supporters exhibit any reluctance to stand firm or show allegiance, it shall be reported at the feet of the deity without fail.
>
> If any one of us deviates and undertakes actions contrary to royal duties, Sethirayar's responsibilities, or our commitments, the deity and we shall administer justice upon that individual. If any among us betrays Vanakovarayan or Raja Kadavarayan, their actions shall be directly confronted with force, including deploying troops and cavalry.
>
> Should such measures be disregarded, we shall 'lift the sandals' of the Paraiyars (meaning 'serve' the Paraiyars) who guard the Vanakovarayars.

In this agreement, it is evident that Vanakovarayan and Kadavarayan acted contrary to the empire.

Similarly, there are agreements made by two or three minor rulers together, one of which was concluded during the fifteenth year of Kulothunga's reign. The details of this are as follows:

> Malaiyan... to the rulers of Adayur Nadu and Vikrama Chola Sambuvarayar, I, Rajaraja Adhiyaman, known as Vidukadazhagiya Peruman, swear as recorded in this inscription that I shall never betray them, and they too shall never betray me. Those who are my enemies shall be their enemies, and their enemies shall be mine. Their feud shall be my feud, and my feud shall be theirs. No alliances, friendships, or exchanges shall be made with the Yadavars, the Chalukyas, or the children of Kulothunga Chola Sambuvarayar without mutual consent... Thus, I, Vidukadazhagiya Peruman, have agreed to this. If I were to violate this agreement, may I suffer the humiliation of carrying the sandals of my enemy Sariyalvan and eating food in his assembly hall.

Such agreements were made without the emperor's knowledge. As a result, over time, several factions arose among the minor rulers. These factions gained strength in later years and caused the very stability of the empire to crumble. These factions did not exist during the times from Rajaraja I to the early years of Kulothunga I. During that period, the minor rulers were subdued and stood under the control of the empire, while the central government continued to function responsibly.

Artistic Growth

The inscriptions of Kulothunga III from the first twenty-four years of his reign indicate his military activities. The later inscriptions do not mention war, and therefore, the following sixteen years can be considered a period of peace.

During this period, many scholars in his court promoted the

development of Tamil! Some of the prominent scholars of his time were (1) *Kulothunga Kovai*'s Asiriyar (author), (2) Veerantha Pallavarayar, (3) *Sankara Chola Ula* Asiriyar, (4) Kambar, (5) Gunaveera Panditar, (6) Arulnilai Visagan of Arumpakkam, (7) Thiruvarangath Thamudanar, and (8) Bhavanandi Munivar, among others.

The author (*Asiriyar*) of *Kulothunga Kovai* praises Kulothunga Chola as, the one who knows all the arts, as 'the ocean of arts', and as 'the patron of many hundreds of poets'. Through such accolades, it is evident that he excelled in matters of learning and held scholars in high esteem.

The poet praises him as 'the divine poetic ornament of Tamil scholars', 'Kulothunga Chola who wears the epic garland of bards', 'prince who embraces and nurtures flourishing Tamil,' and 'the King who vanquished and scattered all the mighty rulers of the vast earth.' From such praises, is it not evident that he was a man of great learning, one who recognised the merit of poets and rewarded them accordingly? It was because he was such a great patron of letters that the supremely learned Kambar gained the honour of being part of his court and with it, worldwide fame.

As long as the Ramayana exists, as long as Kambar's name endures, so too will the name of Kulothunga remain.

Veerantha Pallavarayar

He was a court poet of Kulothunga. At his request, the king issued an order permitting Pararasa Vannavan, titled *Sakala-vinoda Nrittapperarayan* (the great lord of delightful dance), to conduct *Nattuva Nilai* (classical dance instruction) at the Shiva temple in Thirukkadaiyur. This shows the high regard the king had for this scholar.

The Grammar Hall (Ilakkanam Mandapam)

This was known as the *Vyakarana Daana Vyakyana Mandapam* (Hall for the exposition of the gift of grammar) in Sanskrit. It was located next to the temple in Thiruvottriyur. Here many students received training in Sanskrit grammar. There, many students also underwent grammar training in the Tamil language. This hall was built by a Sittarasar official who ruled Nellore. To support this educational institution, Kulothunga granted the village of Kavanur. The king ordered that this village be made tax-free (*iraiyili*). In this way, Kulothunga significantly advanced the cause of education throughout his vast empire; he honoured and supported Tamil scholars and promoted the spread of Tamil learning in the land. He made arrangements in temples for the recitation of the Tiruppadigams (sacred Tamil hymns) and for the instruction of Sanskrit to students.

Religious Status

Kulothunga III was a great devotee of Shiva. The *Kulothunga Kovai* praises him with titles such as 'beloved of *Kamari*,' 'he who never forgets the one who rides the white bull,' and 'he who adores *Nagabharanan* (the one adorned with serpents)'. A temple inscription from his twenty-fourth regnal year mentions that the deity Veedhividanga Peruman of Thiruvarur addressed him as *nam tozhan* (our companion) and expressed this in a directive to the temple's beneficiaries. This indicates how deeply connected Kulothunga was to Lord Shiva.

Spiritual Guru

Just as Rajaraja Chola and others had spiritual gurus, Kulothunga also had one. His guru was Iswara Sivan, a great Saiva saint. He was a native of Lot, a descendant of the Sandilya gotra, and the son of Kanda Shambhu. He was the one who consecrated the Shiva temple located in a place called Tribhuvanam.

Swami Devar

He was the head of a Saiva monastery. According to an inscription of a vassal king, Swami Devar was responsible for defeating the Sri Lankan armies through the greatness of his asceticism. Kulothunga granted tax exemption (*iraiyili*) to the Shiva temple at Achuthamangalam, which had been consecrated by him. Swami Devar also reformed the religious regulations that had been prescribed by this Chola king at Thirukkadaiyur. The king accepted these changes with great appreciation, which highlights the immense respect he had for Swami Devar.

Other Monasteries

The Gomadam of the Kalamukhas, known as the Mavirathigals monastery, was located at Thiruvanaikka. The Chaturanana Pandita Madam was in Thiruvotriyur, while the Varanasi Bhiksha Madam was located in Panttanai Nallur. The Kolla Madam of Varanasi Lakshadhyayi Raval was at Tiruppasur. All these monasteries served as Saiva Acharya Peedams during Kulothunga's reign.

The King's Contributions to Shaivite Temples

Kulothunga carried out numerous temple works. Noteworthy among them are: (1) In the twenty-sixth year of his reign, he granted ten *veli*s of land, as tax-free temple endowment to the Pidariyars and the seven women's quarters at Uttiramerur. (2) During the same period, he made two donations of sacred jewellery and ceremonial staff to the Shiva temple at Thiruvotriyur. (3) He established a street and festival in his name for the Lord of Madurai, Aalavaay Perumaan. He renovated the temple with the gold obtained from the southern regions, offering many devadanas and took great joy in doing so. (4) He completed the temple of Kambahareeswarar, also known as 'Tripuvaneswarar' in Tripuvanam. This temple stands as a significant monument of his reign. The temple's walls are adorned with exquisite sculptures and paintings. The sculptural depictions of the Ramayana are worthy of admiration. (5) He built the mukha mandapa of Nataraja at Chidambaram, the Amman gopura, and the temple's inner enclosure. He also established a western street named 'The Street of the Lord Who Received the Crown' (Mudithalai Konda Perumal Thiruveethi). (6) The Sabha Mandapam and the grand tower at Thiruvarur were both completed under his supervision. He also renovated the Ekambareswarar temple in Kanchi.

Vaishnavite Temple Contributions

Like his predecessors, Kulothunga was broad-minded in religious matters. He united three small villages at Velur under the name 'Kulothunga Chola Nallur' and donated them as a *devadana* to the temple of Lord Vishnu. He also renamed the temple as 'Kulothunga Chola Vinnagaram'. Many Vaishnava temple works undertaken by the Malaiyaman chieftains at Thirukovalur were done with his approval. Similarly, others also contributed to temple works during his reign.

Jain Temple Contributions

During his reign, Kadavetti Kulothunga Chola of Mandiyankizhar was a high-ranking official. He was a devotee of Jainism. Upon his request, Kulothunga granted 20 *veli* of land as donation to a Jain temple. He also conferred the *acariyappattam* (teacher's title) upon the Jain teacher Chandragiri Devar at Kottaiyur and donated 20 veli of land at Ambai. This great benefactor did not stop there; he also provided 10 veli of land income to the Jain monastery at Thirunarungondai to meet its needs and for the use of the Jain *Pitarars* (heads of religious establishments). A royal order was issued from Thiruvanai stating:

'Whatever the Jain Pitarars say regarding this land shall be done; the land shall remain under their authority.'

He also instituted a festival named after himself 'Rajaakkal Nayyan Thirunaal,' to be celebrated annually on the same day as the temple's Vaigasi Thirunal (auspicious day in the Tamil month of Vaigasi) and he assigned land specifically for this festival.

In short, it can be said that all religious institutions flourished during his reign. Temples were efficiently managed, festivals were celebrated in the right spirit, temple supervision was carried out properly, and criminals were punished promptly.

The King's Titles

He was called Parakesari Kulothunga Chola Devan. He also held the title of Tribhuvana Chakravarti. In addition, he was known as Veerarajendran, Kumar Kulothungan, Mudivalangu Chola (Chola who bore the crown), Tribhuvana Veeradevan, Mudithalai Konda Peruman (the crowned lord), Ulagudaiya Nayanar (Lord of the world), Ulagudai Peruman (Sovereign of the world), Ulaguyya Vantha Nayanar (The Lord who came to redeem the world), Rasaakkal Thambiran, Rasaakkal Nayan, Thani Nayagan (Sole ruler), and Tyaga Vinodhan (Delight of renunciation). These titles are found in his numerous stone inscriptions.

In addition, he also had the prestigious title of 'Konerinmai Kondaan.' One of his inscriptions refers to him as, 'Konerinmai Konda Veerarajendran Tribhuvana Veeradevan'.

Tyaga Vinodhan

Among these names, the one he cherished the most was Tyaga Vinodhan. This title was given to him by the people of his time. The inscriptions refer to him as 'Tyaga Vinodha Pattan,' 'Tyaga Vinodha Moovenda Velan,' and 'Tyaga Vinodhan'. This name was also given to towns. There was even a monastery named 'Tyaga Vinodhan Thirumadam'.

Just as Rajaraja was known as 'Tyaga Megam' and Vikrama Chola was referred to as 'Tyaga Samudram', this Chola king was called 'Tyaga Vinodhan'. This remarkable and unique title—unlike any held by previous Cholas—was specially associated with him. It was given to him by the great poet Kamban, who delighted in calling him 'the hero of the Chenninadu, Thyaga Maha Vinodhan' in his Ramayana! This great poet also referred to him as 'Amalan'. The term 'Amalan', like 'Akalangan', means 'one who is without guilt' or 'the faultless one'.

Royal Family

The birth name of his consort is unknown. She was referred to as *Bhuvanamuzhuthudhaiyal* (She who possessed the whole world). According to the traditions of the Chola dynasty, she had the privilege of sitting on the throne beside the king during ceremonial occasions. Another wife was referred to as *Ilaiya Nampirattiyar*. Since the king's inscription mentions *Nampirattiyar* (our consort), the younger *(Ilaiya)* of our consorts, it appears that the king had two wives. There is no information available about whether they had children. An elder woman in the royal family was Ammanga Devi, who is referred to in inscriptions as *Periya Naachiyaar Ammangai Azhwar,* the daughter of Sri Kulothunga Chola Devar, who exempted toll taxes. Her name appears in inscriptions from the fifth year of Kulothunga's reign, when she was likely around eighty years old. She was fortunate to have witnessed the reigns of six kings in her lifetime—Kulothunga I, II, Vikrama Chola, Rajaraja II, Rajadhiraja II, and Kulothunga III.

Noble Qualities

From the wars waged and the victories gained by Parakesari Kulothunga III, it is evident that he was a great and valiant warrior. He received with honour those who sought his refuge—such as the Pandya, Chera, Venad, and Karur kings—and reinstated them as rulers in their respective kingdoms, demonstrating that he was gracious to those who sought his protection. That he defeated hostile rulers and destroyed their cities reveals that he was like *Yama* (god of death) to his enemies. His friendship with great scholars like Kambar reveals that he was also a great patron of literature. He was known as a Tamil poet who respected and promoted poets.

His contributions to Saiva religious works confirm that he was a devout Shaivite. However, his involvement in other religious works demonstrates his broad-minded religious outlook.

When he conquered Madurai, it is said that he supported Brahmins well-versed in the Vedas by granting them an *agraharam* (landed settlement). Also, since he granted tax exemptions to the *Vyakarana* (grammar) school at Thiruvotriyur, we can understand the esteem he held for Sanskrit and for Sanskrit scholars. Thus it can be said that his generosity was exceptional.

He was one:

> Kulothungan, who showers gold upon classical Tamil,
> Kulothunga Chola, who gave gold so generously that it was like seven clouds pouring down at once.

Such praises found in the *Kulothungan Kovai* confirm his generous nature.

Kambar too praises his benevolence using poetic imagery:

> He whose arms are famed, Kulothungan the blemishless, whose glory spreads across the world—his palace was like the home of poets, overflowing with heaps of golden coins, garlands scented with sandal, and rows of radiant flower arrangements—all beyond measure.

❋❋❋

SEVEN

Rajaraja III (1216–1246 CE)

Inscriptions

Rajaraja III's relationship with Kulothunga III is unknown. As per convention, a prince or successor king would refer to his predecessor as *Periyadevar*; Rajaraja too referred to Kulothunga in this same manner. However, even from this, the connection between them cannot be determined. Rajaraja III ascended the throne when Kulothunga was still alive. Hence, inscriptions were issued in Kulothunga's name as well. The inscriptions of this third Rajaraja begin with the phrase *Seermannu Irunanju Thisai* and end with *Seermannu Malarmagal.* Historical details are scarce in these inscriptions; qualities and virtues of the king are exaggerated and presented in a literary fashion. However, one can somewhat piece together his history using his other inscriptions, those of smaller rulers, and inscriptions of the Hoysalas and Pandyas, along with a few literary references.

Political Context

This king ascended the throne in 1216 CE. From the outset, his reign was plagued by political troubles. In the south, the Pandyas, as a powerful military force, were biding their time to establish their dominance and seek revenge on the Cholas. In the west, the Hoysalas had established their empire; during this period, Hoysala Vira Ballala II was reigning. To the north, the Telugu Chodas had seized the northern part of the Chola Empire and were waiting for an opportunity to assert supremacy. To their north, the Kakatiya dynasty had grown strong. Meanwhile, in the region previously occupied by the Western Chalukyas, the new Sevuna dynasty had risen to prominence. Within the Chola territory, the Kadavarayars of Kudalur, who ruled the central region, were covertly strengthening their military power, aiming to annex the Chola country and restore the old Pallava Empire. Among them, Kopperunjingan, who ruled over Kudalur and Sendamangalam, held the leadership.

The First Pandyan Military Campaign

Sadayavarman Kulasekara Pandyan, who had ruled the Pandya kingdom with the support of Kulothungan, passed away in 1216 CE. Immediately, his brother Maravarman Sundara Pandyan ascended the throne. He ruled from 1216 CE to 1238 CE. Upon ascending the throne, he resolved to exact revenge on the Cholas, intending to redress every grievance caused by them in his vast territory. He desired to settle scores with Kulothungan while the latter was still alive for the numerous atrocities he had inflicted on his land.

Therefore, this valiant king led an invasion against the Chola empire, deploying the Seven Divisions of the Pandya army and auxiliary forces that were distinctive to his kingdom.

At that time, Kulothungan III, being advanced in age, had stepped away from governance, and Rajaraja III had just begun his reign.

Rajaraja III lacked authority and leadership; he was entirely devoid of the noble qualities befitting a king and had no understanding of political strategy.

'As the king is, so are the people'—thus, the very same soldiers who had served during the time of Kulothungan III, now became as if powerless and ineffective. As a result, the Chola land became an easy target for invasion.

Sundara Pandyan, who launched the invasion, easily conquered the Chola kingdom. Uraiyur and Thanjavur were reduced to ashes. Many mansions, temples, halls, and pavilions were destroyed. The Chola king fled and went into hiding. The women and children of the Chola land suffered greatly. In the places that the Pandyan king devastated, he yoked donkeys to the ploughs and sowed white mustard seeds.

He seized the golden crown and handed it to minstrels. He reached Ayiraththali at Adagapuri and performed a Veerabhishekam ceremony at the Abhishekam Mandapam of the Chola king.

Thereafter, he went to Thillai (Chidambaram) and rejoiced upon beholding Lord Nataraja. Later, he proceeded to Pon Amaravati and stayed there.

At that time, Rajaraja, who had fled and gone into hiding, came there along with his wife and children and stood before the Pandya king, pleading for his kingdom to be restored.

The Pandyan king, moved by compassion, granted the Chola kingdom back and was content. For this reason, he is referred to in inscriptions as 'Sundara Pandyan, the one who magnanimously restored the Chola land'.

There are no references to this Pandyan invasion in Rajaraja's inscriptions. However, the Pandya's *Meipugazh* (official chronicle) glorifies this event in exquisite Tamil prose, making it a pleasure to read.

Hoysala Assistance

From this inscriptional evidence, it is clear that the Pandya avenged his grievances, and Rajarajan regained his kingdom and ruled it. However, the inscriptions of the Hoysala king convey another narrative. The Hoysala king, Ballala II, describes himself as the 'Restorer of the Chola kingdom' and the 'Lion to the Pandya elephant'. Additionally, his son Narasimha is referred to as the 'Protector of the Chola dynasty'. These claims are found in inscriptions predating 1218 CE. Another inscription states that 'Narasimha, who protected the Chola king hidden amidst enemies, earned the titles *Chola Sthapanan* (Restorer of the Chola dynasty) and *Pandiyan Kandanan* (Conqueror of the Pandya)'. A Kannada text called *Sambu* similarly asserts that 'Rajarajan was protected by Ballala'.

Conclusion

Considering these claims alongside the *Pandya Meipugazh*, it appears that Sundara Pandya's campaign caused chaos in the Chola kingdom, leading to Rajarajan fleeing and hiding. Recognising that Sundara Pandyan had exacted his revenge, the Hoysala king Ballala may have sent his son Narasimha to the Chola kingdom. Narasimha likely arrived with his army, defeated the Pandya, or the Pandya himself may have made peace upon Narasimha's arrival and returned the Chola kingdom to Rajarajan. This interpretation seems plausible.

Internal Turmoil

Some inscriptions indicate that following the Pandya's initial campaign, the Chola kingdom experienced disturbances in various regions. A temple treasury and idols were moved to secure locations; records related to two small villages were destroyed.

Such actions might have caused distress to public administration and common people. Rivalries between minor rulers continued to exacerbate the situation. For instance, a battle took place in 1228 CE between Kadavarayar who ruled Urattur and Veera Narasinga Yadava Rayar. Kadavarayar also fought against the Hoysala prince Narasimha.

He later captured Kanchipuram from his predecessor. This event likely occurred either during or after the Pandya's initial campaign. By 1230 CE, Narasimha was controlling Kanchipuram, where his armies were stationed. Don't these events clearly highlight the weakened state of the Chola king, the disruption in governance, and the influence of the Hoysalas?

Pandiyan's Second Campaign

Pandiyan's Campaign

Around 1234 CE, Rajaraja came under Sundara Pandyan's ire. The Chola king failed to pay tribute to the Pandyan, and when questioned, he marched with a massive army against the Pandyan territory. The initial Chola vanguard suffered a massive defeat; warriors were slain, and elephants were killed. The main Chola forces were also vanquished. Many villages in Chola Nadu were burned, and mustard seeds were sown (as an act of desecration). Several women, including Chola Mahadevi, were taken captive. When Sundara Pandiyan entered the fortified Chola capital, he ordered people to welcome him with auspicious water and ceremonial offerings. He conducted a victory consecration in the palace there.

Kopperunjingan

Rajaraja, defeated by the Pandiyan, fled his kingdom with his entourage, heading toward Hoysala territory. But Kopperunjingan, a feudatory chieftain of Rajaraja, and a member of the Kadava lineage, had concealed both Lankan warriors and his own forces in the forests; he waylaid the king and fought against him. Eventually, he captured the emperor and imprisoned him at Sendamangalam. He then ordered his troops to destroy Vishnu temples in Chola Nadu.

Hoysala Narasimha

Hearing about the suffering in Chola Nadu, Narasimha departed from his capital, Dwarasamudra, with a large army. On his way, he defeated the king of Nadunadu, which was part of the Magadha region, in battle and reached the banks of the Kaveri River. There, he divided his army into two, keeping one half under his command and entrusting the other to his commanders, Appannan and Samudra Koppaiyan, with instructions to rescue the Chola king.

The King's Release

Narasimha's commanders raided villages such as Enneri and Kalliyur in Kopperunjingan's territory. They looted Thozhuthagaiyur, which belonged to his leader, who was called Cholar Kon. They killed the chiefs who opposed Rajaraja and an Eezham prince who had allied with Kopperunjingan. Later, they worshipped Lord Koothaperuman at Thillai (Chidambaram). They continued their campaign, destroying towns such as Tondaiman Nallur, Thiruvathigai, and Thiruvakkarai, and reached Sendamangalam. There, they set fire to crops, captured women, and looted the inhabitants. Witnessing the suffering of his people, Kopperunjingan sent word to Narasimha, offering to release the Chola king. Following Narasimha's orders, the commanders welcomed the freed Rajaraja with joy and returned him to Chola Nadu.

Pandyan's Defeat

As soon as his chief commander left to rescue the king, Narasimhan attacked the Pandyan with his army. The battle at Mahendra Mangalam was intense. Sundara Pandyan faced defeat in the battle. Narasimhan advanced as far as Rameswaram and then returned. The Hoysala inscriptions claim that the Pandyan agreed to pay tribute to Narasimhan. The Pandyan's *Meipugazh* (official chronicle) mentions events only up to his Vijaya Abhishekam. Since the Pandyan inscriptions neither mention the rescue of Rajarajan nor his reclamation of Chola Nadu, and also considering that Chola Nadu did not become part of the Pandyan territory, it becomes evident that Sundara Pandyan was defeated by Narasimhan.

Conclusion

Due to the intervention of Hoysala Narasimhan, Rajarajan regained the throne for the second time. Sundara Pandyan, humbled by his defeat, remained subdued. However, the influence of the Hoysalas deeply entrenched itself in both the Chola and Pandya territories. Hoysala officials and commanders established their presence in various locations across both kingdoms. In Kanchipuram, the Hoysala army was stationed on a permanent basis.

Deterioration of Administration

Treason against the State

Either due to involvement in the above-mentioned disturbances or from engaging in anti-royal activities during the remaining years of his reign, many individuals were accused, investigated, and punished in various locations. Their lands were confiscated and auctioned. Such confiscations occurred in regions like Sirkazhi, Valivalam, and Thiruvenkadu. For instance, in a place called Kovil Thirumalam, 5 veli and 4 ma of land worth 15,000 coins were seized.

Disobedience

Government orders were defied in several regions. For example, in the Sivapuram temple of Thanjai Fort, two Sivabrahmins handed over the goddess's ornaments—entrusted to their care—to a concubine; they misappropriated the temple funds placed in their charge; they refused to pay taxes and behaved inappropriately in many other ways. They not only defied royal commands but also assaulted and harassed government officials who came to collect taxes. Along with Kannada soldiers (Hoysala soldiers who looted Chola villages during their rescue mission?), they extorted 50,000 coins from the people and oppressed them. These Brahmins were investigated and duly punished by the *Maheswaras* (temple officials) and village assemblies.

Hoysala Influence

The Kadavarayas were subordinate to Rajaraja but they also posed as their most bitter enemies, particularly the notable Kopperunjingan. They dominated regions from Mayuram to Kanchi, encompassing many smaller territories. Kanchipuram itself was under their control. Later, Kulothunga III reclaimed Kanchi from the Telugu Chodas, but after his death, it again fell to the Kadavars. Eventually, Narasimhan of the Hoysalas captured it, necessitating a permanent Hoysala army there.

Narasimhan's influence led to Hoysalas spreading from Kanchi to Tirunelveli. An inscription states that Narasimhadeva took some sacred idols from the temple at Thiruvaduthurai in Virudhachalam region. Military leaders like Bhoothadeya Nayagan and Mahapradhani Ammannan were stationed in

Kanchipuram. They imposed various conditions on temples like Athithigiri and others. Another commander, Vallayan, issued conditions for the Thirumazhapadi temple. One of Narasimhan's queens Somaladevi's entourage issued conditions for the Thirukokarnam temple. Thus, the Hoysala commanders and officials gained significant influence in the Pandyan kingdom and became politically involved.

Chola Empire

The inscriptions of Rajaraja (dated upto his thirtieth regnal year) can be found in various regions such as Sithur, Nellore, and Kadappa. Hence, it can be inferred that the Chola Empire extended as far north as Kadappa. Inscriptions belonging to him can also be found in Salem. Therefore, it seems that the Kongu Nadu was also part of the great empire. However, under his rule, the Pandya kingdom became independent. Therefore, it is clear that the vast territories under the reign of Kulothunga III were no longer under Chola control during Rajaraja II's time.

Minor Kings

The feudatory rulers who were in power during Kulothunga's reign, continued during Rajaraja's time also. Among them, a few were notable. The chief among them was Kopperunjingan. Initially, he was the ruler of the lands surrounding Thiru Needur. Later, he expanded his domain to include towns like Sendamangalam, Koodalur, Virudhachalam, and Thiruvennai Nallur. He was from the ancient Pallava lineage, a valiant man, an excellent warrior, a political strategist, and a skilful ruler. There are numerous inscriptions about him. He fought wars with the Hoysalas and the Kakathiyars. While claiming allegiance to the Chola empire in his inscriptions, he effectively maintained autonomy.

He began recording his regnal years from 1243 CE and ruled autonomously for thirty-six years, until 1279 CE, governing a large portion of the kingdom. He fought with Sadaya Varman Sundara Pandyan in the south. This great warrior performed many temple renovations from Draksharaman in the north to Thanjavur in the south. He was a great devotee of Shiva. He deserves to be ranked among the prominent warriors of the southern region.

Next in importance are the Telugu Cholas, who ruled over regions such as Chittoor, Nellore, and Kadappa. Notable among them are Chalukya Narayanan, also known as Manuma Sittarasan and Maduranthaka Pottappi Chola Erra Sittarasan. They made many contributions to the temples of Kanchi city.

One Malamadevarasan was a minor king who ruled the Chittoor region. Among the Telugu rulers, Kanda Gopalan, also known as First Thikkan, a major emperor, is often mentioned in many inscriptions.

Inscriptions also refer to feudatories of lineages like the Vanar, Vaithumbar, Gangar, Yadavarayar, Sambuvarayar, and Chetiyarayar as part of the tradition. Thus, like the lingering aroma from a vessel that once held asafoetida, in the weakened Chola empire under Rajaraja, the minor chieftains—out of reverence for the Cholas' former glory and also out of fear of the Hoysalas—continued to refer to themselves as feudatories of the Cholas.

Royal Family

During Rajaraja's reign, the most notable palace was the Ayiraththali Palace (Palace of a Thousand Pillars). The royal palaces in Thanjavur and Uraiyur were destroyed by Sundara Pandya, and Ayiraththali was also partially damaged. Rajaraja had two wives. One of them was Kopperundevi, the daughter of Vaanakovaraiyan. The younger wife was known as *Buvanam Muzhuthudaiyal* (She who possesses the whole world).

Rajaraja ruled for thirty years. After his reign, in 1246 CE, Rajendra III ascended the throne. The inscriptions of Rajaraja begin with *Seermannu Irunaanju Thisai* (Glory spreading in all four directions) and *Seermannu Malarmagal* (He who is favoured by the glorious goddess).

EIGHT

Rajendra III (CE 1246–1279)

Introduction

Rajendra III ascended the Chola throne in 1246 CE. However, the exact familial relationship between him and Rajaraja III is not clearly known. Rajendra's reign seems to have begun during Rajaraja's lifetime itself. It can be assumed that Rajendra governed alongside Rajaraja during the latter's final years.

During Rajaraja's final period, his inscriptions are found only in regions like North Arcot and Nellore districts, while Rajendra's inscriptions from the same period are seen across the entirety of the Chola Nadu. This suggests that Rajendra III was well-received by the public and enjoyed considerable influence over the smaller rulers. His inscriptions bear similarities to the openings of his predecessors' inscriptions, though further classification is required to understand the events.

Hostility of the Hoysalas

During this period, Veera Someswara, the son of Hoysala Narasimha Deva, ruled the Hoysala kingdom. His father had protected and reinstated Rajaraja III twice as king. However, for reasons unknown, Veera Someswara displayed hostility toward Rajendra and aligned with the Pandya ruler. He referred to himself as *Pandya Kulakkapalan* (Protector of the Pandya Clan). Interestingly, in their inscriptions, both Rajendra III and Maravarman Sundara Pandya II (who ruled the Pandya kingdom after Sundara Pandya from 1238 to 1253 CE), refer to Someswara as their *maman* (maternal uncle). The exact nature of this relationship remains unclear.

Despite the unclear kinship, it is evident that Someswara supported the Pandya rulers and opposed Rajendra III. Some inscriptions reveal that Someswara sent his commanders to invade the Chola Nadu. In CE 1241, a commander named Singana Dandanayaka led an army into Chola Nadu. According to an inscription from Thirumarai Kadu, during this time, a temple that had been closed was reopened and consecrated with a kumbabishekam at the cost of 50,000 coins. Another commander of Someswara, named Ravideva, reportedly captured the Kaan Nadu region, according to an inscription from Pudukottai.

Pandya–Hoysala Relations

Maravarman Sundara Pandya II, who ascended the throne in CE 1238, was a weak ruler. In 1249 CE, he named a small village in Tirunelveli district after his uncle Vira Someswara, as per the latter's wish. In that same year, a military commander named Varakkanna Dandanayaka came from Tirunelveli.

At that time, the region surrounding Thirumaiyyam in present-day Pudukkottai was known as 'Kaan Nadu' and belonged to the Pandya kingdom. A conflict between Shaivites and Vaishnavites had caused unrest there. Peace was restored by Appannan, a Dandanayaka (commander) under Someswara.

The Pandya king's brother-in-law was a Hoysala prince named

Vikrama Choladeva. He held considerable influence within the Pandya administration.

Chola-Telugu Relationship

Since Veera Someshwaran started supporting the Pandyas, Rajendra Chola III made an alliance with the Telugu Chodas, who were enemies of the Hoysalas. The Telugu Chodas, who ruled Nellore, were known for their aggression. Their rule stretched from Nellore to Chengalpattu. They had been vassals under the Chola Empire for a long time. At that time, Kandagopaladeva, also known as Thikkan, was the reigning Chola ruler. He had defeated Sambuvarayar, Sethiyarayar, and Kadavarayar, making them accept the Chola Empire. Through this victory, he curbed the intrigues of Kopperunjingan. He governed a large part of the Tondai Mandalam region while remaining subordinate to the Chola Empire. Thus, just as the Hoysalas helped the Pandyas, the Telugu Chodas helped the Cholas.

Chola Pandya War

During Rajaraja's reign, Sundara Pandyan had twice attacked the Chola country ravaging and humiliating it. In retaliation, Rajendra Chola, after forming an alliance with the Telugu Chodas, launched an attack on Pandya land, defeating the weak second Sundara Pandyan. He captured his crown and handed it over to Rajaraja, then looted the Pandya kingdom. However, this victory lasted only three years. Before long, Veera Someshwaran attacked the Cholas and defeated them, while Kopperunjingan also attacked the Cholas. Both were repelled by the Chola ally Kandagopalan.

Each of these rulers claimed victory in their inscriptions. The author Kethana, in his *Dasakumara Charitam*, states that the Pandya paid tribute to Kandagopalan. Kopperunjingan referred to himself as the *sutradhara* (architect) of the restoration of the Pandya mandala. Tikkana, in the preface to his Ramayana, asserts that Kopperunjingan first defeated Rajendra III in battle; then accepted him when he came seeking refuge and offered him protection. He also defeated Someswara in battle and, upon Rajendra's surrender, restored him to the throne—thus earning the title *Chola Sthapana Acharya* (one who re-established the Chola king). A Hoysala inscription from 1240 CE mentions that 'Someswaran attacked Kandagopalan'. These events lead us to conclude that Someswaran's intervention brought benefits to the Pandya kingdom. However, if Kandagopalan had not helped the Cholas, the Chola country would likely have fallen prey to both the Pandyas and Kopperunjingan.

Sri Lankan War

There is an inscription that states, 'Just as Rama defeated the land filled with fierce rakshasas in Lanka, Rajendra Chola, this Rama, defeated the northern part of Lanka filled with fierce rakshasas'. Therefore, it is evident that Rajendra Chola must have defeated the *Veera Rakshasas* (valiant rakshasas). Who were they? The Sambuvarayars of North Arcot region referred to themselves as *Veera Rakshasas* and ruled over the area. During their reign, the great Mahabalipuram, also known as *Maha Ilangai*, must have been part of their kingdom. Rajendra Chola must have defeated them in battle. His ally, Kandagopalan, also defeated the Sambuvarayars, and other neighbouring enemies, taking control of Kanchi, as mentioned by Tikkanar in his work. This clearly indicates that the Sambuvarayars were subdued by both Rajendra Chola and Kandagopalan.

Kanchinagar

In this city, inscriptions from the reign of Rajaraja Chola have been found up to 1245 CE. There are no inscriptions from the period of Rajendra Chola. During Rajaraja Chola's reign, the city was under the supervision of Narasimha Deva of the Hoysalas. What happened afterwards? An inscription dating 1249 CE from the Kakatiya king Ganapathi has been found. Inscriptions from Kandagopalan dating a few years later have also been discovered. Therefore, history indicates that the city of Kanchi was under the Hoysala Narasimha Deva during Rajaraja Chola's period. After 1245 CE, it came under the rule of the Kakatiya king or a Telugu ruler, possibly under the Kakatiya supervision. Eventually, in 1257 CE, it passed into the hands of Sadaya Varman Sundara Pandyan, who had ascended the throne that year as indicated by historical records.

Hoysala Alliance

Sadaya Varman Sundara Pandyan became the Pandya king in 1251 CE. He was a great warrior who established the Pandya Empire during his reign. He did not have much respect for the Hoysala king Veera Someswaran. Offended by Sundara Pandyan's power and disregard, Veera Someswaran formed an alliance with Rajendra Chola, whom he had previously considered an adversary. Through this alliance, he hoped to secure the friendship of both the Cholas and his own enemy, the Telugu Cholas. If successful, he could defeat Sadaya Varman.

As a result, many Hoysala political officers came to Chola Nadu, stayed there, participated in Chola politics, and handled temple-related matters. The friendship between the two nations continued even after Someswaran's death. Two inscriptions issued in the tenth and fifteenth regnal years of Ramanathan, the Hoysala ruler of southern Karnataka in 1295 CE, are found in Thiruchottruttur.

Pandya Empire

Around 1256-57 CE, Sadaya Varman Sundara Pandiyan led a large army and invaded the Chola country. He conquered Chola lands and made Rajendra a subordinate vassal under him. He also defeated and chased away Veera Someswaran who had come to aid Rajendra. Again, in 1264 CE, Someswaran rose in revolt. The battle occurred at a place called Kannanoor, where Someswaran was killed.

Later, this Pandyan rejected the offer sent by Kopperunjingan, a Pallava descendant, and instead laid siege to his capital, Sendamangalam. He captured the city and its treasures and after handing them back to Kopperunjingan, made him a vassal under his control and headed northward, conquering regions like Maghadha Nadu which belonged to the Vanars and Kongu Nadu. He killed Kandagopalan in battle and performed the *Veerapandiyan Abhishekam* at Nellore, proclaiming his supremacy. He made Kanchipuram the capital of the northern part of his empire.

Thus, with the sudden rise of this valiant Pandya king, the remaining part of the Chola Empire was destroyed, and Rajendra was reduced to the status of a minor chieftain. After this downfall, the Chola dynasty never rose again and faded into history.

Extent of the Kingdom

Many inscriptions of Rajendra are found in Chola country. One inscription from his thirteenth regnal year has been found at Nandalur in Kadappa district and another from his fourteenth year at Tripurantakam in Kurnool district. After 1267 CE, no inscriptions of Rajendra are found beyond the Chola country. This indicates that initially, his empire extended up to Kadappa and Kurnool, whereas in the later part it was confined to the Chola country alone.

The End of Rajendra

His rule lasted until 1279 CE. He ruled for thirty-three years from Gangaikonda Cholapuram. His family deity was Thillai Natarajar. It is known that he had a wife named Cholakulamahadeviar. An inscription at Thirukannapuram reveals that he had a son named Semappillai. With the decline of his rule, the number of subordinate kings also dwindled. Only two names, Cholagangan and Kalappalan are mentioned as vassal kings during his time.

After Rajendra, there is no evidence to suggest that any Chola king ruled over Chola Nadu. Therefore, it is appropriate to conclude that with Rajendra, the Chola dynasty's independent rule and the great empire established by Aditya came to an end.

The Decline of the Chola Empire

It is known that even under the Pandya Empire and in the northern regions, some individuals who claimed descent from the Chola lineage continued as minor chieftains and political administrators until the fifteenth century. Just as the Pandya kingdom lost its autonomy during Paranthaka's reign and merged with the Chola Empire, in 1280 CE, Chola Nadu became integrated into the Pandya Empire established by Sadaya Varman Sundara Pandyan. This serves as a fitting example of 'history repeating itself'.

About the Author

M Rajamanikkam (1907-1967)

Dr M Rajamanikkam, Professor of Tamil, authored more than twenty-five significant books on the history of ancient Tamil Nadu. He is one of the 180 Tamil scholars and writers featured in the Hall of Fame at the Anna Centenary Library in Chennai, recognised by the Government of Tamil Nadu for his contributions to the Tamil language and its literature.

About the Translators

Translated from the Tamil original by Peer Mohamed Azees, Srivarshini V and M Kavya

Peer Mohamed Azees started his writing career with the Tamil edition of *India Today*, contributing to the literary section of the magazine as a sub-editor and translator. He is currently a literary agent and translator.

Srivarshini V worked as a Professor of English at a Chennai college and is now a full-time translator.